MW00436117

The Connected Species

The Connected Species

How the Evolution of the Human Brain Can Save the World

Mark A. Williams, PhD

ROWMAN & LITTLEFIELD
Lanham • Boulder • New York • London

Published by Rowman & Littlefield
An imprint of The Rowman & Littlefield Publishing Group, Inc.
4501 Forbes Boulevard, Suite 200, Lanham, Maryland 20706
www.rowman.com

86-90 Paul Street, London EC2A 4NE

British Library Cataloguing in Publication Information Available

Library of Congress Cataloging-in-Publication Data

Names: Williams, Mark A. (Neuroscientist), author.
Title: The connected species : how the evolution of the human brain can
  save the world / Mark A. Williams.
Description: Lanham : Rowman & Littlefield, [2023] | Includes
  bibliographical references and index.
Identifiers: LCCN 2022061678 (print) | LCCN 2022061679 (ebook) | ISBN
  9781538179000 (cloth) | ISBN 9781538179017 (ebook)
Subjects: LCSH: Social participation. | Belonging (Social psychology) |
  Brain—Evolution.
Classification: LCC HM771 .W55 2023 (print) | LCC HM771 (ebook) | DDC
  302/.14—dc23/eng/20230110
LC record available at https://lccn.loc.gov/2022061678
LC ebook record available at https://lccn.loc.gov/2022061679

To my two wonderfully connected kids,
Arianna and Casey.

You inspire me to be a better person.

Contents

Acknowledgments   ix

Introduction   xiii

Part I: Humans as a Connected Species

1   A Very Short History of Us   3
2   Why We Think without Knowing   15
3   Identifying People   25
4   A Puppet on a String   35

Part II: How Does Connection Work?

5   We Are Pack Animals   47
6   Connected to Learn   59
7   Home-Cooked Meal for the Soul   67

Part III: The Negative Consequences of Our Drive to Connect

8   Racism, Sexism, and Other -Isms   77
9   Viral Viruses   89
10 A Crowded Room   99
11 Modern Technology Thrives on Connection   109

Part IV: How Can We Fix It?

12   Common Humanity Perspective   125
13   Get Real   137
14   Connected Development   151
15   The Future for the Connected Species   157

Notes   167
Bibliography   183
Index   197
About the Author   209

Acknowledgments

$\mathcal{N}$one of us do anything without the support of the people around us and those far away. So I would first like to acknowledge the role of everyone, the entire connected species, in supporting and enabling my work and life over the years.

Of course, there are those people who have made a direct and significant contribution to this piece of work. First, and most importantly, I would like to thank my significant other, Anina Rich, who is not only my life partner and the mother of my wonderful children but also someone I have collaborated with for many years. She is my sounding board for all of my crazy ideas, the first person to read and comment on anything I write, and my most influential critic. She read and commented on numerous versions of this book and continually supported and encouraged me when I faltered. Thank you so much.

I would also like to thank Jenny Ginsberg, who, after retiring from teaching, undertook a master's degree examining Denmark's connected and supportive community and how it rallied behind the Jewish community during World War II. Look out for Jenny's book, which I am sure she will write in upcoming years! Even though she recently commenced a PhD, Jenny read, commented, recommended readings, sent numerous emails, and continues to support this work. You are an inspiration.

And to Sam Ginsberg OAM, who is the epitome of a connected person. He has worked with street kids in Afghanistan during the war, with street kids in India who were left at train stations, with homeless kids in Papua New Guinea after the tsunami, and with deaf and blind kids in Australia, in addition to working on so many other incredibly important projects. Sam read, commented on, and spent long periods chatting with me about this book. Thank you so much for your insights and continual support.

Thank you to Anita O'Hart for taking time out of your busy schedule as an environmental lawyer and a mother to read an early version of this work and then to spend time walking and talking with me, discussing so many different aspects and angles of the book. Thank you for your constructive and insightful feedback, which helped to shape the final manuscript.

To Gunter Swoboda, thank you for reading the book and inviting me to cowrite our upcoming book, *The Great Man Con*. I greatly value the provocative and insightful discussions we have had.

I greatly appreciated the early read by my father-in-law, Bob Rich, whose extensive writing and editing experience was extremely helpful. More broadly, I want to thank others in my extended mentoring and support network, Gayle Avery, Harald Bergsteiner, and Mark Hodgson, who have inspired me to pursue alternative career goals.

During my career in science, so many collaborators have contributed to different aspects of this work both directly and indirectly. I would really like to thank them all individually, but that would take too long! Instead I'll just highlight a few people who had a significant impact on my career and my worldview. I would like to especially thank my postdoctoral supervisors, Nancy Kanwisher and Jason Mattingley, who supported and guided me when I was first starting out on my journey as a scientist and continue to mentor and inspire me. And to Max Coltheart, who founded the Macquarie Centre for Cognitive Science at Macquarie University. He envisaged a university department that had no boundaries, where people from diverse backgrounds and disciplines would come together and collaborate on important questions. Thank you, Max, for hiring and mentoring me. I was lucky to have worked in this supportive cross-disciplinary department for more than a decade. Sadly, that very successful experiment has not survived the university restructure, but the legacy will live on. It was a privilege to work alongside neuroscientists, psychologists, linguists, computer scientists, physicists, physiotherapists, anthropologists, and cognitive scientists—thank you all.

I would also like to thank Suzanne Staszak-Silva, Joanna Wattenberg, Mary Wheelehan, and the entire crew at Rowman & Littlefield for taking a chance with this book and for all your support throughout the editing and publishing processes. I am very grateful.

And finally, thank you to all the people I have chatted with about the themes in this book—my friends and family (repeatedly!) and the numerous teachers, principals, parents, children and young people, CEOs, company directors, and leaders. Thank you for sharing your stories and experiences. You have all played a role in consolidating my ideas and reinforcing the importance of working on these topics.

If you would like to keep up to date on what I am working on, check out https://www.drmarkwilliams.com.

Introduction

$\mathcal{S}$ociety is facing many crises, including racism, sexism, marginalization, and extremism. We seem to be splitting at the seams, and people are looking for answers. Come join me on a journey to explore how the evolution of the human brain drives us to connect. This process has spurred us on to great innovations while also forcing a wedge between groups and inciting people to commit horrendous acts.

Together, we will examine how human beings evolved from being "just another primate" to the most dominant species ever observed on earth. We investigate the idea that it was our ability to socialize and connect that catapulted our species to phenomenal heights of innovation, through collaboration and specialization. This drive has fine-tuned our unconscious perception of faces, facial expressions, body language, and touch. Our primitive drive to connect changes how we perceive the world and the people around us—not figuratively but *literally*. We see, hear, empathize with, and understand others differently depending on whether they are a member of our in-group or not. This unconscious drive to connect can draw us together but, sadly, can also drive a wedge between us. Multiple factors, including overcrowding, new technologies, and the media, are exacerbating this issue. To move forward we need to become more aware of the strong influence our unconscious brain has on our behavior and how these processes may be negatively affecting us. With awareness and understanding of how our brains drive our group mentality, we can mend bridges and improve societies for everyone.

Who am I, and why did I write this book? I'm a cognitive neuroscientist—which is a fancy way of saying I study the brain and cognition—with more than twenty-five years' experience in research and teaching. I have worked in both Australia and the United States and have presented my work all over the world. I have friends and colleagues on just about every continent and from every walk of life. Why am I telling you this? Well, like for many of us, my childhood was very different.

I grew up in a small country town in Australia in the 1970s and 1980s; there was high unemployment, and the town was very white. I remember there was a Greek family that ran the fish-and-chip shop, and an Asian family arrived and set up a Chinese restaurant. Although both shops were popular, I don't remember seeing either family outside the restaurants. This is perhaps not surprising given that the White Australia policy, which restricted immigration to European settlers, existed in some form or another until 1973. The town was not at all welcoming of perceived outsiders.

As an example, in my first year of high school, a family arrived from Canada. There was a boy my age—let's call him John. I can vividly remember eating lunch with a couple of friends when John came running past followed closely by a group of boys. He headed for a classroom door, but sadly it was locked, and he was cornered in the alcove. I can still see his glasses flying and hear his screams for help. No one came. He was white, but he had an accent, and therefore he was different. He was an outsider. Our fathers knew each other through work, and so he tried to befriend me. I wasn't friends with the kids who were bullying him, but I still told him to leave me alone in no uncertain terms. His father told my father, and I was punished. But I didn't feel able to stick up for him or to be his friend, even though I knew I'd get further punishment from my father. The family left the town not long after.

What I did was morally wrong. I stood by and watched as another person was tormented. I should have been ashamed, and I was, but at the time I didn't feel as though I had a choice. I needed to be part of the in-group, and he was seen as an outsider. It is one of my greatest regrets. But I knew what happened to outsiders, and I did not want to be one.

Why is discrimination in some form or another rife in all societies? Why do we need antidiscrimination laws to stop this behavior? Discrimination is innate. It occurs because of our need to connect. Yes, one of our greatest attributes, connection, is the reason for one of our most dreadful traits, discrimination. This drive to connect can help to explain many of the issues we see in our society today, including racism, sexism, fanaticism, extremism, and nationalism. Understanding our implicit drive and the way the brain has evolved to support connection can help us to eliminate the insidious need to segregate, isolate, and discriminate.

Connection is not all bad though. We didn't become the alpha or "top dog" here on earth because of our physical prowess. We became the alpha because we work together, collaborate, communicate, and pass on knowledge. And we do this through connection. If we look back in our evolutionary history, there are many arguments about what happened when and what had the biggest impact. Tool creation and use, control of fire, complex language, and group hunting methods are all important aspects of our evolution. And all of these important adaptations would have benefited from, and even been driven by, connection.

Let's take tool use, for example. Having people in a group that you can trust and work with would have been vital to developing new and better tools. We are not the only species that uses tools, but we are the only species that has developed tool use to the extent that we can fly around the world and live literally anywhere. What is the difference? When other animals use tools, they do it for themselves. Individual chimpanzees, for example, will find a twig and remove the extra bits and pieces so they can fit it neatly into a termite hole to extract the termites. But they won't create the same tool for other chimpanzees. In contrast, we have toolmakers who make tools and then offer them to other people. You can imagine even hundreds of thousands of years ago, clans or tribes would have had a few people who were good at toolmaking. They would have spent long hours making tools and refining their skills. They would also have had hunters who would use those tools to hunt. The group wouldn't want to risk the lives of the toolmakers in hunting. So, they would end up with specialized jobs and a strong need for a group working together based on trust—a drive for human connection.

This specialization is what has propelled us to become the super species. I am currently typing on a laptop in a café. I could not have built the laptop I am typing on. I could not have built any of the parts that make up the laptop. I rely on other people's expertise to produce the bits and pieces that make up the laptop and put it together. I also didn't construct the table, or the chair, or the cup, or the café building, or the electricity—I could go on for pages. Think about all the things you use every day. All the people who are involved in creating those things. All the services you rely on. How many of those things could you make or do yourself? Now think about the generations of people that have gone before us, who would have specialized and collaborated to enable the innovations that we take for granted today. None of this would have happened without our ability to socialize. Our ability to connect.

The huge technological advances we've made came about because we are the connected species. To make these advances, we needed people to specialize, and you cannot specialize if you don't have others to support you. Imagine if Leonardo da Vinci was unable to sit around and ponder the human form, or the stars, or machines like helicopters. Imagine if he needed to gather his own food to survive on his own. Or if Marie Curie did not have the time to discover radium or invent the first X-ray machine because she needed to go hunting. Or if Bill Gates was unable to invent the personal computer because he was busy building a shelter to live in. The only reason we know these names is because they had the time and freedom to specialize—because their needs could be met by other people. They could purchase food, shelter, books, and everything else they required because others specialized in those areas. If there weren't other people producing all the things they needed, then they would need to learn how to do those tasks themselves. This would take most of their time, and they wouldn't have the time to make great discoveries. We all specialize because we live in large groups that are interconnected and support each other. This enables each and every one of us to focus on a particular area and become experts at it. And then that propels innovation. But it is only possible with connection.

Our brains are made up of billions of neurons, and each neuron is connected to thousands of other neurons. In fact, there are about one hundred trillion connections in every person's brain. What an incredible array of connections within such a small space! And all of those neurons, all of those connections, work seamlessly together to enable us to sleep, drink, walk, think, cry, laugh, talk, hear, and so much more. These neurons are grouped into specialized areas that can be mapped across the brain.[1] If any of these groups is damaged or disrupted, it can cause catastrophic issues across the brain. And just like our brains, we, as a species, rely on an intricate web of connections that can be mapped across the entire world. We also group into specialized areas for different reasons, and damage to any of these groups can result in issues throughout our species.

A significant proportion of the human brain is dedicated to maintaining connection with others. Socializing is a very complicated process that requires the ability to identify and remember others, to understand what they're feeling, read their body language, deduce their intent, and understand their emotions. The majority of the brain is involved in these processes, including multiple areas dedicated just to the perception and memory of faces. There are also brain regions allocated to perceiving other people's facial expressions and understanding their intent. And still other areas are involved in detecting where other people are looking and their body language. Our ability to connect relies on a lot of very exclusive neural real estate.

At this point, I should confess that faces and facial expressions have long been a passion of mine. In my PhD work, more than two decades ago, I discovered that we orient to faces even before we are aware that they are there.[2] There is a mechanism in our brain that *forces* our attention toward faces. At the time, this discovery required well-established models of attention to be revisited. It was surprising because the other things that we automatically orient to are very low-level salient features like color and movement.[3] Faces, though, are complex and require high-level processing. It turns out, faces are so important to us that we have evolved a special mechanism to ensure that we automatically notice them.

And yet, it probably should not have been surprising that faces are prioritized, given that for at least eight million years (and probably much, much longer), humans have lived in groups and worked collaboratively to facilitate survival. These groups were originally just family members, like many mammals we observe in the wild today. At some stage, though, we started connecting more widely, enabling trade and specialization. This allowed us to become the only species to occupy every continent of the world. We are also the only species that allows members to choose what they specialize in and how they will contribute to the group. Other species specialize—such as bees, who have a queen, workers, protectors, and so on. But they do not choose which role they will devote their time to. They are assigned a role. They also can't decide to create a new job for themselves. We are the only species to enable choice of specialization—and this choice is because of our special connections.

Our need to connect and our ability to choose how we specialize results in the creation of groups. The very definition of a group, though, means that some people don't fit in. For every in-group, there is an out-group. Of course, most of the time this is fine. I was a founding member of the Australian Cognitive Neuroscience Society, and although you may not be a member, it probably doesn't worry you too much. I also support a particular Aussie Rules football team (Go Cats!) and have done so for many years. I identify with that group, and my children now support the same team. I love to watch them play; I'm disappointed when they lose, and I celebrate the wins. I make cracks and jibes at people who support other teams, but I don't discriminate against them or physically attack them. Of course, this is not always the case. In Europe, football team fanaticism is so strong that supporters must be kept physically separated at games with high, barbed-wire fences. There have been riots and even deaths. Even in sport, some groups engender important, positive social connection; others breed fanaticism. We need to be ever aware that for every in-group there is always an out-group who may feel isolated.

Why am I telling you this? Because this evolutionary drive to connect has shaped our brains and our behavior over millions of years. This instinct has become so strong that without others we will literally die. Solitary confinement is an extreme punishment because it is completely against our nature. It causes stress, anxiety, depression, and psychosis, and can result in death. Even loneliness causes both mental and physical illness. Look at the impact that Covid-19 lockdowns had on our mental health. Our evolutionary drive to connect means that we need people around us or we suffer greatly.

After decades of research, we now have a better understanding of group mentality. We are driven to create groups, and we automatically associate with them. This happens at many levels, including local groups, such as friendship groups, work groups, social groups, and school and college groups. It can happen at a national level, such as political affiliations, regional associations, and national sporting teams. Or it can happen at more global levels, such as religion, nationality, sex, ethnicity, and race. Some of these groups are flexible, and some are static. For example, I can change the sporting team I support (not that I ever would!), but I can't change my race. We are all members of groups, and the impact they have on our world is greater than we may realize.

One of the amazing aspects of connection and our group mentality is that we see the world differently depending on our group membership.

I don't mean that we just contemplate a concept or idea differently. People hear, see, and feel differently depending on their group membership. Yes, we literally hear what someone says differently if they are a member of our group compared to an outsider. For example, if you are a member of the Make America Great Again movement, you will perceive and subsequently remember a speech by Donald Trump differently from someone who is not a supporter. Of course, this is a major issue if we are trying to get members of another group to listen to us. They are unlikely to hear what we think they are hearing. So how do we start repairing some of the major divisions in our society?

We need to keep several aspects of groups in mind when trying to move forward and reconcile differences. First, membership is not always static; it can change based on a person's experiences and expectations. Second, not all members are equal—some are more dedicated or entrenched than others, and some have a lot more power within the group than others. Third, we are all members of many groups that have different impacts on us at different times. Fourth, the defining qualities or objectives of a group are determined both by the group's members and by those who are not members. And fifth, groups change, and members may leave or join as the group evolves. All of these aspects of groups need to be considered when we attempt to connect to or disrupt a group that may be causing issues in society.

Most importantly, we need to understand why and how we create groups. Our social world is infinitely complex, and our brains automatically categorize to simplify that world. Our face-perception and memory abilities highlight and reinforce our connections to members of our group and automatically detect outsiders. Our body language, speech, accent, clothing, and habits identify our group membership and result in differential treatment. And our primitive "fight-or-flight" response is intricately linked to these innate processes. We are hardwired to create and maintain groups.

In the first few chapters, we start with the evolution of the human brain's specialization for connection. We explore the fascinating way we automatically process how people and groups are feeling and thinking. In the second section, we move on to how connection works in practice and why it is important for learning, innovating, and maintaining health and well-being. The third section discusses the negative consequences of our drive for connection and how it can explain racism, sexism, nationalism, and many of the other major issues in society today. We will also discuss its role in Covid-19 and previous pandemics and why similar global events are inevitable. No discussion of connection and our social selves could be complete without touching on social media and the internet. We cover how multinational technology companies are taking full advantage of our need to connect and the negative impact this is having on our health and well-being. In the final section, I hope to bring a positive perspective to this discussion by examining how we can use our drive for connection to expand our in-group to include our extended multicultural societies for the good of our planet. There are many positive aspects of our drive to connect. By understanding human connection, we can use it effectively to work together toward a less divided, more sustainable future.

Part I

HUMANS AS A CONNECTED SPECIES

"Humans are social beings, and we are happier, and better, when connected to others."

—Paul Bloom[1]

1

A Very Short History of Us

*L*et's go back to the beginning. Actually, the beginning is still quite controversial, so let's go back to when we first stood on two feet. According to the Smithsonian, our ancestors started walking upright around six million to seven million years ago.[1] This ability to walk on two legs freed our hands for doing other things. Ever watched a dog or cat try to move something around with its mouth? It's not easy! Having the ability to carry things while moving would have made a huge difference to our opportunities, and our brains got larger in response.

Around 2.6 million years ago, our ancestors started making tools, and about one million years ago, they started making fire. These things we can be reasonably certain about from fossil records. The evolution of spoken language is much harder to determine. Professor Quentin Atkinson from the University of Auckland analyzed the phonemes present in 504 languages and estimated them to have originated between 80,000 and 160,000 years ago.[2] Though not quite as sophisticated as the language we possess today, it was spoken language nonetheless—although some might argue that modern language is regressing quite quickly—LOL!

Reading and writing came much later. In fact, the majority of humans have had the opportunity to learn to read and write only in the last hundred years or so. An eyeblink in the history of our evolution.

This isn't to say that our ancestors were not able to communicate before 160,000 years ago. Quite the opposite, in fact. They would have relied on gestures, facial expressions, body language, and simple vocalizations. Based on fossil evidence and nonhuman primate studies, we believe that these forms of communication could have evolved more than twelve million years ago (possibly more than fifty-five million years ago), which is why these functions reside in the more primitive and subconscious parts of our brains. Our modern reliance on spoken and written language is astounding when you consider how recently it has occurred. And yet, abilities that we have had for millions of years are often unknown and ignored, despite their influence showing up in all aspects of our behavior and society. But more about that later.

When did our ancient ancestors become so driven by connection? And I don't mean our supposed "connection" through technology! I mean the inherent, deep-seated drive to connect with other humans—to live in groups collaboratively. It was this change that required the development of strong social abilities. Based on the fact that we are social mammals, it was probably well before we even started to stand up six million to seven million years ago. We don't have any direct evidence that we lived in groups back then, but clues come from our closest relative, the chimpanzee, with whom we share about 99 percent of our genetic material. These primates also live in groups and show many of the same behavioral traits as humans, including in-group/out-group mentality, collaboration, across-group conflicts, and the need for close connections. Blair Hedges and his colleagues estimate the genetic line between chimpanzees and humans split around five million to seven million years ago,[3] so I think it is a safe bet to assume that our abilities underpinning connection and group living evolved at least eight million years ago.

Okay, so, we have been living in groups for a very long time. This means that all the traits and abilities that we need to live in groups have been refining and embedding themselves in our brains for at least this period of time. It's all in there, influencing our behavior, and yet we are often completely unaware of the processes and factors that allow us to interact with other people. Why? Because the brain has an extremely limited capacity for conscious thought. So, while you are reading this book, you are probably not aware of other things going on around you (except, because I suggested that you weren't, you will now attend to your surroundings, so now you probably are aware!). Anyway, because we can only be conscious (or aware) of limited things, the brain must do a lot of things *automatically*. These automatic processes include life-supporting functions like breathing, keeping our heart beating, and so on, but also all the processes that underpin your ability to move, see, hear, feel—all at once. More recent abilities like language and reading, though, require 100 percent of our conscious thought processes. Why is this important? Because many of the abilities that we evolved and refined to enable us to live and thrive as connected beings are now automatic and unconscious—we are not aware of them, but they are there, influencing our behavior.

Let's look at an example of how we know these processes that enable living in groups evolved a long time ago and are deeply embedded in our brains, automatically influencing our behavior. My early research focused on how we automatically perceive faces and facial expressions. These abilities are vital for connecting with others and living cooperatively in groups—and would have been even more important before we developed spoken language. Reflecting this importance, both face and facial expression perception have areas of the brain dedicated to them—areas that are in "primitive" brain regions.

In one of my early studies, we discovered that the *amygdala*, a region deep in the brain known from animal and human studies to be involved in fear, responds to facial expressions even when people are not consciously aware of a face being present.[4] After several studies on the role of the amygdala in facial expression perception, we concluded that it must receive information about faces and expressions via a secondary subcortical pathway that doesn't even go to the conscious parts of our brain. This extensive processing had to be going on at the same time as (actually even faster than) the known cortical and more conscious processing. This was a controversial claim at the time but is now quite well accepted. Why am I telling you about this? Well, this finding means our ability to quickly process faces and facial expressions and the brain network that underpins it are very old indeed—and highly automated. Traits and abilities that use these primitive parts of our brain evolved a long time ago. They include things like breathing, swallowing, detection of movement, and detection of pain. These primitive abilities are part of all mammalian (and reptilian) brains and support things that are essential for our survival; for humans, this includes facial expression perception.

Another way to examine when a trait or ability evolved is to explore if it occurs in other species and, if so, when we separated from those other species in the *phylogenic tree*. The phylogenic tree is basically a diagram depicting all the known species and how closely related they are from an evolutionary point of view. Of course, a trait or ability could co–occur in two different species without there being a common ances-tor. For example, both fish and dolphins have fins and live in the ocean, but these aspects of fish and dolphins are thought to have evolved sepa-rately. However, if the species is reasonably closely related and the ability evolved in most species on that section of the phylogenic tree, then it is a pretty good bet that it evolved in them all *before* they separated.

Most primates, including lemurs, live and cooperate within groups—and yet, that part of the tree diverged around fifty-five million years ago.[5] Could it be that these abilities evolved so long ago? Unfor-tunately, we will never know exactly when our brains developed the extraordinary drive to socialize and live in groups, but we can assume, based on this type of data, that it was well before we started walking upright. As language didn't evolve until very recently, our abilities would have focused on face recognition, facial expression perception, body language and physical gesturing, and rudimentary vocalizations. These abilities were essential for early hominids to work and live together productively—as they were for all primates. It was thus these abilities that enabled our ancestors to have more food, better protection, and better childcare, leading primates (both human and nonhuman) to develop complex social structures to support improved survival.

You might now be thinking, "Hang on, how does this fit with the whole 'survival of the fittest' idea we hear so much about?" If Charles Darwin was correct and evolution occurs because only the fittest and strongest survive, how would helping each other work to improve our survival? This was one of the big questions Darwin tackled in *The Descent of Man*, in which he argued that cooperation could evolve through natural selection if it conveyed reproductive improvement of the family.[6] Natural selection is about passing on one's genes (although genes were not recognized in Darwin's time), and family members share genes. So, if those with similar genetic material (i.e., families) help each other to survive, then they help to pass on those genes associated with that family. This theory is evident throughout the animal kingdom: whenever groups are working cooperatively, they are usually genetically similar, a family.

Living in groups, even of family members, requires the ability to recognize and remember individuals. We need to know who is a mem-ber of our group and also keep track of who is working for the better-ment of the group. If we are going to help others, we want to ensure that they are also working to help us. This is probably why we scorn laziness and why we are all so ready to accuse others of not contributing enough. And we humans have an amazing memory capacity compared to other mammals.[7] But to remember who is lazy and who is contributing relies on being able to recognize individuals within the family. And so, we return to the primary automatic primitive mechanism we started with: our phenomenal ability to recognize and categorize each other using faces.

I still remember John's face and those of all his tormenters vividly. I think if I ran into them tomorrow, even after the many years of aging, I would recognize them immediately. This is because of the regions of our brain dedicated to face recognition, combined with areas devoted to memory, which allow us to remember vast numbers of faces over many, many years.[8] This is crucial for us to succeed in groups—we need to remember those who have helped us and those who have not. Haven't we all held a grudge against someone from high school who did us wrong? This power of recollection is an ancient ability that enables us to work cooperatively, but it can also literally change our perception of people. We will talk more about face perception and how amazing it is in chapter 3, but there is just one more study I want to tell you about now.

We all recognize six basic facial expressions: happy, sad, fearful, angry, disgusted, and surprised. These are recognized across cultures and are often called the primary facial expressions.[9] We recognize them automatically and extremely quickly. Now this confused me, because my intuition was that when I see someone I really dislike who is smiling (think, for example, of a smiling Adolf Hitler), my perception seems to be one of anger, not happiness. So we decided to explore how information we know about people influences our perception of their facial expressions.[10] We had participants memorize photographs and corresponding vignettes that described fictional people. They were either very nice people or evil people (the fictional characters, not the participants!). When we later scanned the participants' brains while showing them the previously learned faces—we found that their brains responded differently to an "evil" person smiling than to a "good" person smiling. The participants' brain and behavioral responses were consistent with an automatic response as if the smiling face of an "evil" person were an *angry* face. The negative information participants knew about this person literally changed the way they saw them. This influence of what we know on how we see people's facial expressions would have been essential millions of years ago. Knowing who was trustworthy and who was dangerous was very important—a matter of life or death, in fact. Now skip forward to today. Think about the barrage of stuff we read about people we don't even know. How is this affecting us? What we showed in this study is that mud not only sticks but literally changes the way we see someone.

Where are we, then, in our very brief history of us? We'd been living in relatively small groups surviving through cooperation without any meaningful language. To enable this to happen, we evolved the ability to recognize faces so we knew who was part of our small group and who wasn't. We evolved a good memory for faces so that we could remember who was doing what and when, so we would be happy to help those who helped us. We evolved an ability to recognize facial expressions because we needed to understand what other people were thinking or how they were feeling without language.[11] We evolved an ability to recognize body language to help with understanding others' thoughts and emotions, especially from a distance when hunting or traveling. We also evolved the ability to understand gestures like pointing and different noises and grunts.[12] All of these abilities would have evolved very early—which is why we now do these things automatically and often without any awareness at all.

As we've covered, these abilities would have enabled our ancient ancestors to work together, providing them with more food, better protection, and better childcare, which in turn improved reproductive success. These groups would have been made up of family members like what we see today with other primates, elephants, wolves, lions, hyenas, dolphins, and orcas. The reproductive success could be explained by Darwin's theory of evolution. And this would have continued for millions of years, in fact, most of our evolutionary history. But then something changed: we started cooperating in larger groups that were not limited to family members,[13] and this, I believe, is what makes us different from other similar species.

To understand this step change, let's return to the shift we started with—when we started walking on two legs. This happened because the forests that covered the earth started to give way to savannah areas. It is suspected that as the forests decreased, our ancestors wanted to traverse the grasslands, and this is more efficient on two legs.[14] We also could take extra stuff with us when we moved from one place to another.[15] At this point, though, although we probably did interact with other groups when we came across them, we remained in small family groups.

During the last ice age, which came next, we almost became extinct. The evidence suggests that we got down to only a few hundred thousand hominids—potentially even fewer at some stages.[16] Our numbers were so low that we would have been classified as an endangered species! It is funny to think that we were so close to no longer existing, and yet today we are overpopulating the world. What happened next? We migrated, moving out of the small pocket in Africa, slowly moving across the world. And we started making tools.

Toolmaking was a great leap forward because it allowed us to make better shelter and clothes and to hunt more efficiently. And it signaled the start of cooperation *across* groups. Making good tools takes time and skill. To begin with, everyone probably made their own tools, and they may have copied techniques they saw others use. But to get good takes lots of practice. We can easily imagine a time when an individual started focusing on making tools while others used those tools to hunt and make other things. Then an exchange or understanding would have happened: one individual would not have needed to hunt because they supplied such great tools. This would then allow the toolmaker to focus on making tools, and the tools would get better and better. But before this could occur, division of labor would have had to be common.

The reason family groups stuck together originally would have been to help with child rearing. Child rearing for humans is much more demanding than for other animals as we are born completely vulnerable. Human babies are born unable to move around at all; it takes months before they can crawl, let alone walk. Compare this to a giraffe, which can walk within moments of being born. Child rearing is time-consuming and effortful for humans, and so it would have required cooperation and a division of labor.[17] Now the ironic thing here is child rearing for humans is demanding because we have large skulls to accommodate our large brains. And we have these large brains because we evolved the ability to socialize, which takes a lot of brain power. It is a bit of a chicken-or-egg scenario: Did we evolve a larger brain and then start cooperating to raise young, or did we start cooperating to raise young, which resulted in needing a larger brain to enable further cooperation? Alas, we will never know. This does mean it would not have been such a big leap to have a second division of labor based on the skill of toolmaking.

And now I'm going to speculate. I think toolmaking resulted not just in division of labor within family groups but also in trade across groups. You can imagine one family group that became experts at toolmaking. Perhaps they found new and innovative ways to make tools or a supply of excellent rocks. Another family group that had traveled some distance had some nice pelts from another area, and they decided to trade. We know that our face-perception abilities were such that these people could recognize and remember faces. They could remember who these individuals were and if they were hostile or friendly. Next time they came across each other or perhaps sought each other out, they could recognize each other and continue the collaboration. Perhaps they then started traveling together or in close proximity so that they could trade more often.

Could this be possible? Could prehistoric hominids have started engaging in such transactions? Well, there is certainly evidence that they had the brainpower to do it. We know monkeys can and do trade for goods and services. For example, Professor Laurie Santos and her colleagues from Yale University have shown that capuchin monkeys can be trained to use money to exchange for rewards.[18] Not only were they able to use the money (actually tokens), but they could even be taught the value of different tokens. Even more astounding is that Professor Jean-Baptiste Leca from the University of Lethbridge has shown that wild macaques at a temple in Bali have learned the value of different objects.[19] They steal from tourists and will only give back objects if the value of the reward is great enough. They will also exchange the goods for tokens that have value, which they can then exchange for food. This suggests they understand the value of the tokens and the value of the food—they will only exchange if the price is fair! Given we separated from monkeys millions of years ago, and our brains have evolved considerably since then, it is no great stretch to imagine our primitive selves engaging in such exchanges.

So now we have the situation where humans are very social within family groups, and we have started cooperating with other small family groups to aid in the innovative process of developing better tools. Perhaps we even exchange people! Family groups work well to improve reproductive success, but after one generation either the male or female siblings need to leave the group. Otherwise, inbreeding occurs, which negatively affects the gene pool. This is why marrying close relatives is seen as taboo and we have laws against it. Different animal groups deal with this issue in different ways. Lions, for example, usually have a dominant male that mates with all the females. The male offspring, once they get close to breeding age, are moved out of the group. These rejected males usually form male groups of their own and roam until they are old enough and strong enough to challenge a dominant male from another group. For our ancient relatives, perhaps the small groups that we started exchanging goods with were also groups to exchange people with. This would allow gene pools to continually improve and develop new bonds across groups.

We are extremely good at detecting relatives using our superior face-detection abilities.[20] And we tend to have a positive neural response to those who look like ourselves in those ancient subcortical areas of our brain.[21] By having groups that exchanged and crossbred, our links would become stronger and more beneficial for survival. Of course, the other side of that equation is that these same regions of the brain respond in a negative way to those that don't look like us, but we will talk about that in chapter 3. Overall, we cannot be sure which came first, but suffice it to say the exchange of goods and the exchange of people helped our survival and promoted the expansion of connections between cooperative groups.

Next came our ability to control fire. Fire was another game changer.[22] It allowed us to keep warm, see better at night, cook our food, scare off animals, and make better tools. Fire would have been another asset to exchange and would have enabled the creation of a warm and safe place to connect both within a group but also across groups. Imagine if your group was one of the first to learn how to create and capture fire. The bargaining power and awe that this new technology would have garnered would have been immense. At this time, there were several species of hominids, including Neanderthals. Neanderthals were stronger than our ancestors, and it is thought that they also lived in cooperative groups, made tools, used fire, and wove cloth. But who gave whom fire, or was it acquired by both groups independently? We will never know, but we do know from genetic analysis that our ancestors bred with Neanderthals.[23] Perhaps they did so in exchange for this or another ability? Or perhaps it was just that romantic atmosphere created by sitting around a campfire. We are all drawn to fire, especially sitting around one and exchanging stories or just watching as it burns. It brings warmth and safety that would have been critical to those living a million years ago. It also brings us together, and that, again, is probably something that is reflected in the million years of evolution that were spent sitting around fires with those we trust.

Then sometime between 80,000 and 160,000 years ago, we evolved spoken language. Remember that reading and writing came much later,[24] but this is when the ability to speak relatively fluently and communicate via a relatively sophisticated language evolved. This massive leap forward came about due to our connection, because we lived in groups and needed to communicate. We needed language when we started engaging with other groups and working cooperatively, probably exchanging or bartering resources. We needed language when we started allocating roles to different members of the group so that they could develop, hone, and innovate different techniques and abilities.

It always surprises me how heavily we now rely on our language ability, considering how recent a development it is in evolutionary history. Language is very taxing, requires a lot of our limited capacity, and is draining. Language, whether spoken or written, requires attention and explicit cognitive control; it is massively effortful—and yet it has become integral to our survival.

And while we rely heavily on language, which is effortful and a recent addition to our repertoire, we ignore the many social abilities that we relied on for millions of years. We, as the connected species, have a large brain that is dedicated to socializing and can do these things automatically. Just as you can walk without thinking about it, you also detect faces, distinguish whether they are happy or sad, ascertain if you know them and if they are from your in-group or a potential out-group, determine if they are hostile or friendly, and so on. Just like breathing, our ancient abilities to recognize people and their moods are completely automatic. It is important for us to reconnect with these ancient abilities and understand how they impact our lives today. Without awareness and understanding, we are driven toward separation, segregation, conflict, extremism, and mistrust. Embracing and controlling these abilities will help us to restore faith in our species and to, once again, thrive.

As a card-carrying cognitive neuroscientist, I firmly believe that understanding our brain and how it works will help us understand our behaviors and how to control them. Since I started studying the human brain some twenty-five years ago, the advances and huge leaps we have made are mind-boggling. Much of this work has come about due to the development of fantastic new technologies that allow us to peek inside the skull of a human that is still living. And it is amazing how much of our brain is dedicated to connecting with others. We will start to look at this next.

In summary:

- Group living and socializing served as the catalyst for many of the great advances that we have made.
- For millions of years, we have lived in groups and evolved a myriad of important abilities to enable us to socialize.
- Language and literacy are very new abilities that require conscious thought.
- It is our ability to collaborate and specialize that sets us apart from other species and has resulted in our vast number of innovations.

TIP OF THE CHAPTER

Look through your photos and reflect on how you respond to each face you see. How does it make you feel? Now reflect on how you are connected to the person in each photo. Is he or she a friend, a relative, a work colleague, or a stranger? Reflecting on our automatic responses can help us during future social interactions.

• 2 •

Why We Think without Knowing

$\mathcal{I}$ just picked up my coffee cup and went to take a sip, but it was already empty. I drank a whole cup of coffee without knowing it. What did you do today without thinking? Have you ever thought about how many things you do on autopilot?

It's not just the mundane stuff that we do automatically. I often work with schools on improving both learning and well-being. Whenever I'm running a workshop at a school, I like to arrive early to set up. It gives me a chance to get a feel for the environment. And I don't mean the physical environment; I mean the community vibe—the connections between the staff and the students. Just walking onto a school ground and observing the interaction of the staff and students from a distance can tell me so much about how connected the school is. And this is often done unconsciously by my brain.

I remember one school in particular. It was a lovely-looking school. It had recently been rebuilt, and the grounds were immaculate. When I arrived at the administration building, the staff were polite and professional, and the principal was welcoming. But I got a feeling that something was not quite right. There was something my brain was telling me that wasn't obvious from the overt signs. And my brain was right. The workshop was hard. There was quite a division among the staff, and getting interaction and collaboration was nearly impossible. Why, you might ask? On reflection and some honest conversations with members of the executive team, I found the answer. The new build had improved the aesthetics of the school, but the increased size resulted in more students and more staff. This had caused a rift, and the connection across the school was lost. This was not a great situation for anyone concerned, and it took a lot of work to get things back on track.

What's the point of this story? Well, our brain processes so much information, especially about how people are feeling, outside of our conscious control. It usually seems as though we are aware of what our brain is doing. But as the coffee and school examples highlight, it does a huge amount without our conscious control.

Why does our brain process information outside of our awareness? There are two main reasons. First, the world is very complicated, and nothing is more complicated than our social lives. When you sit down at a meeting or a dinner party, you are processing not only what is being said but how people are reacting, how you feel about it, and how you might respond to it, while making sure that you are not missing out on other conversations that might be occurring around the table. But then we also have a second issue to contend with: what we can consciously be aware of at any moment in time is extremely limited. As a result, most of what our brains do, they do without our awareness. And it is this unconscious information processing that we need to know about because it affects the way we respond and interact with people.

The activities that occur automatically and without awareness are usually called implicit processes. And the activities that we are consciously aware of are called explicit processes. But the implicit processes far outweigh the explicit processes. If I ask you to think of your favorite movie star, you consciously start thinking of the many people you have seen on the big screen. As you think of different individuals, you probably have emotional responses when you remember different roles they performed or gossip you have read about them, until you finally come up with one favorite (or maybe a few if, like me, you can never choose). This is an explicit decision. And to do this, you activate your working memory. But it was impacted by the implicit emotional responses you had while visualizing the actors.

Explicit decisions rely on our working memory. Working memory has been called many things, and there are still discussions on how it works. For example, do we have separate systems for vision versus sound? There is consensus, though, that our working memory is involved in conscious thinking, and it is limited. Very limited indeed!

What do I mean by limited? Well, if I ask you to remember groups of letters like those in Example 1, you will use your working memory to do it. And you should find it difficult to remember all these letters. Professor George Miller, from Harvard University, first coined the concept of the magical number seven.[1] Miller argued that working memory in adults is limited to seven items. The idea is that we have around seven slots in working memory that we can use to hold and manipulate information. We can use all seven slots to hold around seven things in working memory, but that leaves no space for anything else.

Example 1:
XMA
RVE
LHE
ROX

Working memory is also where we manipulate, calculate, and contemplate things in our thought processes. Imagine if I asked you to remember my phone number and at the same time asked you to divide 288 by 12. I'm sure you could do either of these things separately, but I doubt you could do them both at the same time (without writing them down). The phone number would take up all your working memory slots, and there would be none left for the calculation. Or you would be able to do the calculation, which would take up all the slots, but you would not remember the phone number. We need slots available to remember items and empty slots to manipulate, calculate, and contemplate.

Now, it is important to understand the difference between working memory and long-term memory. As just discussed, working memory is the process that we are aware of when we are thinking. Long-term memory, as the name implies, is where memories are stored for a long time. These are all the memories from our past. As for working memory, there are discussions and debate over the different types of long-term memory and how many we have, but suffice it to say here that we have a long-term memory that stores information.

Now, without looking back, can you remember the letters from Example 1? Probably not. If you now look at Example 2, you will find it much easier to hold all these letters in working memory. Why? Because you have a long-term memory trace for both "Marvel" and "Hero," so they only take up one slot each. Importantly, information, knowledge, and processes that are in our long-term memory can be accessed and manipulated without taking up as many slots. The number of parts has not changed, but now you can chunk the information more efficiently because I have highlighted the words—and those words are in your long-term memory. So this magic number seven is the limit to what we can both hold and manipulate in our working memory but not our long-term memory.

Example 2:

X

MARVEL

HERO

X

The big difference between working and long-term memory is that we are explicitly aware of the information in working memory, but we are not able to directly access the information in our long-term memory. We access long-term memory by bringing the information into working memory. For example, right now you are not aware of all the actors you have ever seen. They are stored in your long-term memory outside your consciousness. However, if I asked you to list all the actors, you would use your working memory to retrieve them one by one and reel them off. Your working memory can access your long-term memory and bring those memories to awareness. But remember it has a limit of seven items or chunks. Each actor would be an item. Try and hold all the actors you know in your explicit awareness. You might try to visualize a large group of them. But you still would only be aware of a few actors at any one time.

This is why our long-term memory and our brains' ability to do lots of things implicitly is so important. For example, imagine not being able to do anything else when driving a car. You can't think about that important meeting you must attend; you can't chat to your kids in the backseat; you can't listen to the radio—you can't do anything but concentrate on driving. All seven of your working memory slots are taken up by the difficult task of driving the car. Well, as we know, when we first learn to drive a car, that is exactly the case. All our attention and working memory are focused on the processes and procedures needed to drive a car. But after much practice (with a very stressed driving instructor!), all those processes and procedures are transferred to long-term memory and fine-tuned. Our brains can then do it on autopilot, and we can use our working memory for other things. And you might be surprised about how much our brain does and decides on autopilot without our conscious control.

Cognitive behavioral therapy talks about this with the metaphor of riding an elephant.[2] Our working memory or consciousness is the person on top of the elephant, and our unconscious or automatic processes are the elephant. If the person on top is a good elephant trainer, he or she can direct the elephant where to go. However, most of the time the rider is just sitting there, and the elephant is doing its thing. The elephant can step over things and walk around without input from the rider. And the rider just gives simple instructions most of the time but doesn't control every movement.

Now think of yourself. When you decide to get up and get a drink of water, for example, you don't consciously organize or consider the host of steps involved. Imagine if we had to consider every single muscle that needed to be contracted or relaxed just to stand up and walk. It would be tiresome and very slow—as patients recovering from a brain injury affecting the motor system know. The autopilot parts of our brain do it for us automatically, freeing up our conscious mind for more important jobs. It is the older parts of our brain that underpin these automatic processes that allow us to move, hear, see, and use many of our social skills. More recently evolved abilities like talking, reading, and writing are far less automated. So, most of the time, what you are perceiving, feeling, or thinking is based on a very crude and fast analysis that happens completely without your awareness.

Let's circle back to the dinner party. You are talking to someone who is sitting beside you. Modern verbal language is a new ability that is very complex and demanding, so listening to and interpreting what the other person is saying and then formulating a reply takes up all the slots in your working memory. But at the same time your brain is also implicitly processing the other person's facial expression, body language, and eye gaze. It is also keeping an eye on the people around you and their feelings and intentions based on the same information. You also process information like the prosody of the conversations in the room to examine how people are feeling. All this extra information, which helps us connect with the people at the party, is occurring automatically.

Why is it so important to understand the limits of what we are aware of and what our brains do automatically? Because the world we see is not a veridical representation of the world outside. Our brains don't have access to the outside world. They are encased in very hard skulls and only receive input via our senses. This is not like a camera or a microphone where the recording is simply a direct reflection of the external source. Take sound, for example. When someone is speaking to you, their voice box vibrates to create a movement of air. That movement creates a wave that travels through the atmosphere and then bounces off your eardrum, causing it to move. That movement shifts three tiny bones, which move a small membrane, which moves the cochlea, which results in tiny hair cells being pushed up against a membrane. Depending on which hair cells are activated, specific chains of neurons in the brain fire, and your brain, based on information in your long-term memory, creates a sound that you "hear."[3] Two things are important here. First, the sound is not what was "out there" but what your brain creates. Second, the sound we experience (hear) is determined not just by the input but also by what is held in long-term memory. It is similar for all our senses and everything that we perceive. Plenty of illusions on the internet show this (see https://en.wikipedia.org/wiki/Optical_illusion). Or perhaps you have watched a magician with fascination as your awareness is manipulated. Both are simply using the fact that in our long-term memory we have a vast store of knowledge, experience, and rules that our brains use to determine what "reality" it is going to show us. Illusions and magicians manipulate these rules to trick your brain into creating a perception that is not real.

For example, if you look at Figure 2.1, the two trees may appear to be different shades of gray when, in fact, they are identical. The reason you see them differently is that it looks as though one tree is in the shade. Your brain knows that things in the shade are dimmer than things in the light. Even though the frequency of light reflected off both trees is the same, and initial activity in the brain is the same, your brain makes the tree in the shade look brighter. Based on knowledge about the world stored in your long-term memory, your brain alters what you see. Our experience changes our perception. Now that you know that both trees are the same, can you change your perception? No, you can't, because it is automatic and outside of your conscious control. So what other aspects of our perception are not as they appear?

Figure 2.1.   Light contrast illusion created by placing one object in the dark and the other in the light. Even though both trees are identical, one looks darker because it is in the light, and the other looks lighter because it is in the shade.

Remember that our brains don't have direct access to anything outside our skulls and instead receive information via sensors that are activated when we interact with the world. But the information received is incomplete (and the world outside is extremely complicated), which means our brains make a whole lot of assumptions. These tend to be based on our prior experience about what is "most likely" there—sometimes these assumptions are correct, and sometimes they're just plain wrong. I know this sounds weird, but it is true. And nothing is more complicated than our social lives.

Let's head back to the dinner party and the conversation we were having with one of the guests. If this person is someone you like, then you will automatically interpret what they are saying and how they are saying it in a positive way. If this is someone you dislike, though, your perception of the conversation will be quite different. This is especially so in a noisy environment like a large dinner party where it is difficult to hear clearly what is said. Our brain must use more prior information to interpret what it is hearing, and this is based on our previous experience with the speaker. It is automatic and beyond our control.

Our interpretation of our dinner conversation's meaning is influenced not only by our previous experience with that person (and therefore our expectations) but also by our unconscious categorization of them. Our stereotyping of others is a short-hand "heuristic" to save our limited capacity from having to think too much—and it results in widespread implicit bias.

How can things like implicit bias, stereotypes, and racism be caused by the limited amount of information that we can be aware of at any moment in time? Essentially, our brains simplify the world and group things within it. Complicated things that are grouped can then be held and manipulated in working memory more easily. Remember, we only have about seven slots. We categorize and group constantly to allow our brains to process the complex world. In science, this happens all the time in the way we classify animals and plants or the models we create. We also see this in our language and throughout daily life. We have categories of things like tools, restaurants, motor vehicles, and places. And we do it to people—millennials, baby boomers, techies, nerds, men, women, Asians, Christians, and so forth. We group because it is easier than remembering all the items or individuals. We will talk about this much more in chapter 5, but the important thing here is to recognize that because of the limited capacity of our brains, we group things to simplify our very complex world—and this includes people.

We will talk more about implicit bias later in the book, but it is important here to acknowledge that it has evolved to enable us to connect within our groups and to not only survive but thrive. Implicit biases are thought to be determined or learned by experience or influence from others. They are associations between particular qualities or behaviors and different social categories such as race, gender, or sex. They are another example of how we group things in our world to simplify it. For example, consider the idea that women can multitask or that the French are fashionable. Of course, there are also many negative biases as well that I'm sure you are aware of, which I won't mention here. We all have many, many stereotypes that we automatically associate with different groups. Implicit bias provides a way to save our brains' limited resources, our working memory, and allows us to think without "thinking."

Our implicit biases are then reinforced by the fact that we humans like to be right and to maintain the status quo. Our brains are constantly looking to confirm what we think or believe.[4] We notice what confirms or supports our bias. It is very difficult for us to notice information that does not support our biases—even if we strive to do so. We have all seen the parent at a soccer match who complains to the coach that their child should always be starting on the field. They can list a whole bunch of amazing game-winning passes the child made, while we are thinking the child is probably average at best. Or, alternatively, there is the parent who is always screaming at their child every time he or she makes a minor mistake. They never seem to notice when the child does something well. These are examples of confirmation bias, and we are all susceptible to it. It is why so many people are convinced that their arthritis is worse when it is going to rain. It rains, and they think, "Ah yes, my arthritis was playing up last night." They don't notice when it doesn't rain but their arthritis was painful. Similarly, a parent who thinks that their child is exceptional at soccer notices all the amazing things they do and doesn't notice the mistakes. We are constantly automatically confirming all our implicit biases.

Confirmation bias occurs in every aspect of our lives. It is why professional sports players often continue to get contracts well after their "best before" date. Daniel Kahneman and Amos Tversky studied the fact that we have so much difficulty not falling afoul of our confirmation bias.[5] And confirmation bias reinforces our implicit biases or stereotypes. We are told that a certain race is more aggressive than others. We see confirmation of this in movies, advertisements, TV programs, and the news. We are then far more likely to notice when a person of this particular race is aggressive as opposed to kind. This reinforces the implicit bias that this race is aggressive, and the cycle continues. How many stereotypes are in our heads? How many do we not even realize we have? How does this impact our perception of people from that race, sex, religion, or nationality? If we are driven by many implicit processes and confirming biases, no wonder there are so many issues in our multicultural societies. How do we move past our past?

Just like the different perception of the two trees, our implicit and subsequent confirmation bias cannot easily be altered. We need to be aware that what our brains do outside our awareness is altering the way we see the world. We need to reflect on how we are feeling and the assumptions we are making. And we need to be willing to acknowledge that our feelings, behaviors, perceptions, and memories are affected by processes outside of our control or awareness. We are the elephant trainer sitting on top of a huge elephant. If we are a good trainer, we can direct the elephant where to go and what to do, but we need to be vigilant, and we need to be consistent.

In the next chapter, we delve into the implicit processes that underpin our ability to perceive faces.

In summary:

- Most of what our brains do, they do without our awareness.
- Working memory is the conscious process of our brain, but it is limited to only seven slots.
- We don't have conscious access to our long-term memory, where we store the rules and regulations we have learned.
- Due to the limited capacity of conscious thought, we group things to make the complicated world simpler.
- Unconscious bias is a way to simplify the world, and confirmation bias reinforces these beliefs, making it difficult to overcome our biases.

TIP OF THE CHAPTER

Next time you encounter someone you don't like, stop and consider why you don't like them. Is it because their face reminds you of someone else? Is it because their body movements make you feel awkward? Does the way they are speaking get up your nose? Is it their clothes, hairstyle, or glasses? Or perhaps something else? Reflecting on our automatic responses is an important step forward.

· 3 ·

Identifying People

$\mathcal{I}$n the last chapter we talked about how limited our conscious brain capacity is and how most of what our brain does is automatic. Let's now look at a specific social skill we evolved to enable us to live in social groups: face perception. We will discuss why and how our brain evolved this automatic skill and the consequence of this ability in our large multicultural societies.

Just the other day I was standing on a street corner waiting for a friend I was meeting for coffee (yes, I do love coffee). While I was waiting, a woman got out of her car and smiled at me. I politely smiled back. She then walked straight toward me and asked, "What are you doing here, Jason?" Before I could correct her, her smile turned off; she looked down at the ground and exclaimed, "Sorry, I thought you were someone else," as she walked briskly away. It was a sunny day, so I was wearing sunglasses and a hat, which might explain her mistake. Then again, there are lots of older bald blokes around our area. Her reaction, after she realized her mistake, is understandable, given that we are usually very good at recognizing people we know, and approaching a stranger is quite the social faux pas.

To live in social groups, we need to be able to recognize individuals. As the example highlights, it is embarrassing when we misidentify someone. I mean, can you imagine trying to socialize without knowing who is who? It just wouldn't work, right? Now, whatever we primarily use to identify individuals needs to be accessible, to remain static across time, and to vary across individuals. It won't work if we need to get really close to perceive it, if it changes regularly, or if lots of people are identical in it. A person's face is perfect. The face is usually visible when someone approaches or is greeting you (not many people walk around backward!). And although people change their hairstyles, put on makeup and glasses, and get wrinkles as they age, the structure of the face changes very little over a lifetime. And the structure of an individual's face, like a fingerprint, is unique to that individual. The face is the perfect body part to use to recognize individuals. In fact, did you know that even cows recognize each other by their faces?[1]

The importance of this face-recognition system can be seen in people with "face blindness." Face blindness, scientifically known as prosopagnosia, is a disorder that can develop early in life, or it can be acquired after a brain injury.[2] I studied individuals with prosopagnosia for many years, and the impact it had on them was profound. I remember one individual in particular.[3] She was a postgraduate psychology student attending one of my courses. She had above-average IQ and achieved outstanding marks in her undergraduate studies. During school and undergraduate university, she relied on routine to know who her teachers and lecturers were (they stood at the front of the class) and who her fellow students were (they sat in the seats). She had a group of close friends whom she recognized based on where they usually sat in class and other cues like their glasses, hairstyles, and bags. However, she was really struggling in her postgraduate program because she was required to attend placements at different hospitals and clinics. She had to interact with many different people and couldn't remember who was who from one moment to the next. It was extremely difficult for her, and unfortunately she ended up dropping out. Can you imagine if your face-recognition system didn't function? How difficult would it be just to hold down a job? People with prosopagnosia really highlight the importance of our face-perception ability for the connected species.

How does our face-perception system automatically identify and categorize faces? Essentially, it is a relatively simple template-matching process. The issue for our recognition system is that although each face is unique, they are all quite similar: we usually have two eyes, a nose, and a mouth. So how do you discern thousands of these faces? Professor David Leopold and his colleagues have shown that our brain stores a template of an average face.[4] To identify a specific face, we then automatically and unconsciously calculate the difference or deviation from this average template. Each face deviates from our face template in specific ways, allowing us to identify individuals. It also allows us to identify members of a family because their deviations are more similar than those of members of different families. This system gives us a very nice, neat, and fast means of identification and classification.

What is important to appreciate is that our face template is an average of all the faces we have seen. And faces that we see a lot have a bigger impact on the template. This allows us to tune our face-detection and -recognition system for faces we see regularly, who belong to our in-group. Millions of years ago, members of our in-group would have been family members. By definition, these people would have been from the same race. Even today, the people we look at and see the most are usually members of our family and therefore usually members of our race.

Have you ever had difficulty recognizing people of another race? The phenomenon is called the "cross-race effect" or the "other-race bias." It was first studied in 1914 by Professor Gustave Feingold, who found that people have a harder time recognizing faces from races other than their own.[5] This is now a well-studied phenomenon and has been replicated across many different races. It is usually demonstrated by either showing two faces and asking participants to identify if they are the same person or not, or showing a series of faces and asking participants to remember the faces for later recall. In each case, it has been shown that there is a difference in performance depending on whether the faces are from the participants' own race or a different race.

When the cross-race effect was first studied, we didn't understand how our brains were able to recognize faces of our own race with such incredible accuracy but not those of other races. The discovery that we have a face template that is an average of the faces that we are exposed to provides a very eloquent explanation for the poor performance across races. Our face template is biased toward our own race because that is the type of face that we see most often during development. This then makes it harder for us to recognize, remember, or discern faces from other races.

This cross-race effect has serious implications throughout our societies today, especially in our justice systems and for military forces occupying foreign countries. We are poorer at identifying whether two photos are of the same person or different people if they are from another race. And our memory for members of other races is worse than for people of our own race. Now imagine if you were on trial for a crime that you did not commit, but all the eyewitnesses were people of another race? This is an issue that is often not discussed or recognized within the law or the military, but it is really important. And the more multicultural our communities become, the more of an issue this cross-race effect will be for particular individuals and groups.

Did I already mention that I'm a little obsessed with face perception? We discussed in the introduction that during my PhD studies, I found that our brains perceive faces automatically and extremely quickly. I used a method called priming, which has a long history in perception research. The basic method is to present a "prime" object to a participant very briefly (between one-half and one-thirtieth of a second) and then to present a second object (the "target") for longer. We can then see if the participant reacts differently to the second object based on what the first object was. For example, the two objects could be either words or nonwords (e.g., CAN or CZN). The participant is asked to say if the target letter string is a word or nonword. If the first and second letter strings are both words, then participants are faster than if the prime and target are a word and nonword (or vice versa). How briefly the first object can be presented and still impact the response to the second object tells us how quickly that prime object is processed by the brain. Words take around half a second to be processed, while very low-level stimuli like movement or color are processed much quicker. How quickly do you think faces are processed?

In one study I presented faces to participants for such a brief time that they were completely unaware of it (a thirtieth of a second). I then presented a second face and looked at whether the first face had an impact on the process of perceiving the second face. I found that the prime face, despite being completely "unseen," was processed to the level of identification—that is, not just to the level of "there was something there" or even "it was a face rather than another object," but to the level of *whose* face it was.[6] This was fascinating because the common belief at the time was that only crude or basic features, such as colors and movement, could be processed this quickly.[7]

I also showed that faces catch our attention when they are in a large, complex scene.[8] I did this by adopting another common method called visual search. Have you ever looked at a *Where's Wally?* or *Where's Waldo?* book? It is tough to find the little fellow in those crowded scenes. In a visual search task, we do basically the same thing—present subjects with a crowded scene in which they must search for an item. The basic premise is that when we see a large array of items or objects, we are only aware of the items we attend to. We need to move our attention from one object to another in a slow and conscious manner—unless the object captures our attention, like if it is a unique color or shape. For example, if Waldo was red and everything else in the picture was gray, you would find him easily. Your attention would be captured by the color red, and he would be obvious. The theory is that low-level aspects of a scene such as color or movement capture our attention and complex objects don't. My research showed that despite being complex, faces also capture our attention in these displays.

We now know that several different aspects of a face seem to capture our attention, providing yet another piece of evidence that faces are processed in a special way by the brain. So, we can remember and recognize a huge number of people based on a face template-matching system. This template is the average of all the faces we have seen and is biased toward those that we see a lot. This means that faces that are distinctly different from our individual template (often other races) are not recognized as well. And we implicitly process faces extremely quickly, and they capture our attention. Perhaps this all seems obvious to you. It probably fits with your experience. What these results tell us, though, is important: they suggest that we have evolved specialized areas of the brain specifically for perceiving, recognizing, and identifying faces. Faces are complicated objects that should require high-level conscious analysis. But they don't. So how do our brains manage to achieve this?

Several areas of the brain are specifically dedicated to enable this fast, automatic face perception. I was lucky enough to work with Professor Nancy Kanwisher at the McGovern Institute for Brain Research at the Massachusetts Institute of Technology early in my research career. Nancy and her colleagues were the first to discover that humans have areas of the brain that are specifically dedicated to face perception, which they named the fusiform face area (FFA), because it is on the fusiform gyrus, and the occipital face area, because it is in the occipital lobe.[9] It has now been found that similar regions exist in nonhuman primates and even in many other mammal species, suggesting that these face-specific regions evolved very early in our evolutionary history. But this isn't the only evidence that face perception is an ancient skill.

More evidence of the age of these face-perception regions comes from the work of Professor Stanislas Dehaene and his colleagues from the Collège de France. They discovered another region of the brain on the fusiform gyrus but in the left hemisphere only. This area of the brain is involved in reading, and they called it the visual word form area (VWFA).[10] What can a word area of the brain tell us about face perception? Stanislas made an amazing discovery when he studied individuals from Brazil who were illiterate.[11] He found that they did not have a VWFA and that the face area of the brain, the FFA, was the same size in both hemispheres of the brain (the left FFA is usually much smaller). However, after these Brazilian participants were taught how to read, he found that the left FFA decreased significantly in size, and a VWFA had appeared in its place. The VWFA, an area involved in a relatively new ability (reading), had taken some of the FFA's brain real estate.

Not long after this discovery, Stanislas was visiting me in Sydney, and we discussed his finding in relation to his reuse theory of the brain (over coffee, of course!). This is the idea that the brain takes over old areas or functions when we need to develop new abilities. It is a bit like the High Line Park in New York City. Space is a major issue in New York, and so every inch is used. Anything that is no longer in use is repurposed, like the transformation of a disused section of railway line into an elevated park. Exclusive real estate is reused when no longer needed or needed for another purpose. The fact that the FFA in one hemisphere seemed to have been "taken over" by reading supports the idea that face perception is a much older ability than reading. The new ability has taken some of the FFA's brain space to enable reading.[12] This was further supported by the later discovery that the Brazilian participants' face-perception ability was *negatively affected* by learning how to read.[13] The FFA is a very ancient area of the brain, and part of this area has been recruited for this new ability, reading.

Have you ever had the experience of seeing a face, and then on second glance you realize it isn't actually a face? Check out Figure 3.1. We know that there isn't a face there, but we can't stop ourselves from seeing one—this is called pareidolia. Faces are such an important part of our lives, and so much part of our neural hardware, that we continuously monitor the world for them. And this means that we often see faces when there isn't actually a face present! We see this in art all the time. Giuseppe Arcimboldo, a famous Italian artist, made face portraits entirely

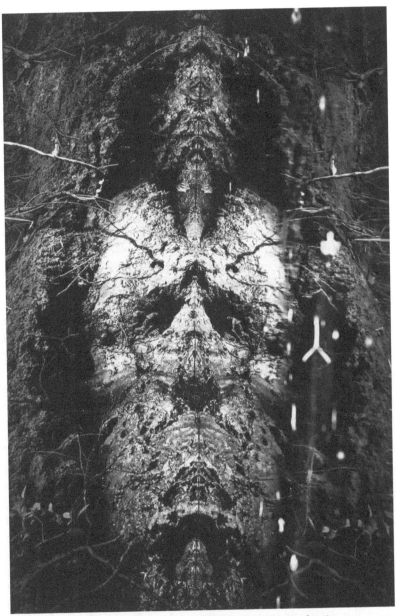

Figure 3.1. Photograph of a tree by Rob Rich. Do you see a face?
© Rob A Rich @ https://www.facebook.com/IllusionsoflightPhotography

of fruits and vegetables. A more modern trend is to make face portraits entirely of very small photographs of other pictures, often depicting aspects of the person's life. These are all examples of how our brains are continuously monitoring the environment and trying to detect faces to distinguish friends from foes.

Where are we then in our exploration of our face-perception ability? We, as the connected species, needed a way to identify who was friend and who was foe. A very, very long time ago, well before complex language, we evolved a clever face template mechanism that enabled us to recognize thousands of faces. This ability was fine-tuned to process faces extremely rapidly, without our awareness, and to direct our attention to potential faces outside our current focus. This system is so sensitive that it sees faces even when they are not present. However, this mechanism is also biased to recognize some people as "outsiders," or potential threats, based on their faces.

The strongest evidence that our face-perception mechanisms evolved from our ancient need to identify those from within our group as opposed to those from outside our group is from a series of visual search experiments conducted by Professor Daniel Levin of Vanderbilt University. He found that we find faces from other races faster in a visual search display than we find faces from our race.[14] For example, a white participant will find a black face faster than a white face. At the time, this effect was surprising. However, if we put the evolution of this system into the context of the connected species, it starts to make sense. We evolved our face-perception abilities to recognize members of our clan or family group. We needed a way to identify who was friendly and who was not, back when the world was dangerous and we were not the only hominids roaming around. We needed a quick way to know who was in our group. As we started interacting with different groups and exchanging goods and services, this would have become even more important. Survival depended on being extremely good at identifying members of our group—and groups at this time would have been from the same race. Today, the world is not so dangerous, and we have wonderful mixing of different racial groups. Unfortunately, our face-perception system has taken millions of years to hone an exceptional automatic process of identification and categorization based on template matching, so we still have this automatic reaction to those whose face is different from our face template.

The outcome is an automatic racial profiling system that we need to acknowledge and confront. We orient faster to people from a different race than our own race. It is unlikely that this automatic process evolved to detect other races, but that is the outcome. We are more likely to notice people of other races than people of our own race in a crowd. Given that we are driven to see faces and are poorer at recognizing people from other races, is it surprising that we have racial tensions in the multicultural societies that we live in today?

In summary:

- Faces allow us to automatically recognize individuals and members of our family.
- We are able to recognize large numbers of faces by using a template face that is the average of all the faces we see.
- We automatically attend to faces in our periphery, and we prioritize those that are not part of our in-group or are from different races.
- Our face-perception ability is very ancient and would have evolved to allow us to connect.

TIP OF THE CHAPTER

When you encounter someone from another race or ethnicity, be mindful of your automatic reactions and potential implicit biases. Stop for a moment and consider how you are feeling and how your body is reacting. Being aware of the potential for automatic racial profiling is an important step forward.

· 4 ·

A Puppet on a String

$\mathscr{I}$ recently headed down to Melbourne for my niece's engagement party. I hadn't been to Melbourne for nearly two years because of Covid restrictions, and I was excited to see my family and friends. I also hadn't done much face-to-face socializing for quite a while, so I was a little apprehensive. On the tram on my way to the party, I realized my palms were sweaty and my heart was racing. There were quite a few people packed into the small space of the tram, and no one seemed to be pleased with the situation. When I finally arrived at the party, I didn't see anyone I knew, and yet I immediately felt comfortable. Even before I found a few familiar faces, I was already feeling relaxed. It was crowded and there were a lot of strangers, but I knew I was safe and that this would be fun. And it was a great night.

Have you ever felt cautious or wary of someone you just met? Have you ever felt anxious when you were at a party or function with a large group of people? Have you ever entered a room of people and suddenly felt joy?

In the last chapter we talked about how we recognize people. But we don't just want to know if someone is friend or foe. Even a friend can be dangerous in some circumstances. And just because someone is a foe, that doesn't necessarily mean they are dangerous. We also need a way to identify how people are feeling. Are they happy, sad, angry, or fearful?

The abilities to detect facial expressions, body language, and eye gaze are also ancient, with dedicated brain regions. These abilities are automatic and often occur without our conscious perception or awareness. This makes sense from an evolutionary point of view. Before we

35

had language, we needed a way to know what others were thinking and feeling. Knowing that someone was either angry or happy when they were holding a club or spear would have been very beneficial. So we evolved a way to both detect and understand how others are feeling via their facial expressions and their body language and what or whom they are focusing on by following their eye gaze.

The evolution of facial expression perception was first discussed by Charles Darwin. In fact, he wrote an entire book on the subject in 1872 titled *The Expression of the Emotions in Man and Animals.*[1] He suggested that facial expressions are universal and that they are important for communication in both humans and other animals. Since then, there has been much work on this topic, most famously by Professors Paul Ekman and Wallace Friesen at the University of California, San Francisco.[2] They traveled to the highlands of Papua New Guinea to tribes that had limited contact with the outside world. The study was quite simple. They had photographs of white people, and they asked the locals to describe the facial expressions. They showed that there are six basic or universal facial expressions that we all recognize regardless of where we live or the culture we come from: happy, sad, afraid, angry, disgusted, and surprised. These six distinct facial expressions communicate information crucial for survival.

I think it's pretty easy to appreciate why these particular facial expressions evolved and are universal. For example, it is thought that disgust recognition evolved as an ability to help us avoid toxins. Before language, disgust would have been important to recognize when someone ate, saw, or smelled something that was likely to make us sick. This is why, when we see someone looking disgusted, we feel a little ill ourselves, so we don't eat the food. Similarly, the other basic facial expressions held positive evolutionary advantages in a time before language—and even now they are crucial in understanding other people.

Early in my career, I undertook a follow-up experiment to my PhD research. I was working with Professor Jason Mattingley at Melbourne University, and he asked me to set up an experiment that all of the first-year psychology students could complete as part of their course. I thought it would be interesting to look at attentional capture of all our basic facial expressions. And I assumed that even first-year university students could identify different emotions! I used the visual search paradigm, and we varied the number of faces that the students had to search to find a particular facial expression. We found a striking effect: out of all the facial expressions, angry faces capture attention the most.[3] This seemed to make a lot of sense—if someone is angry, you want to attend to them very quickly so that you can react appropriately if they are a threat.

How does this threat-detection system work? Seeing an angry face activates an area of our brains called the amygdala. The amygdala is involved in our fight-or-flight response—an acute stress response that prepares the body to react. Heart rate increases, blood is redirected away from our internal organs to our muscles, our pupils dilate, and so on. These responses are evolutionary adaptations to increase the chances of survival in threatening situations. So rapid identification of an angry face would initiate this important survival mechanism.

As part of the study, we also looked at whether there was a difference between finding male versus female faces. We discovered that angry male faces are automatically detected faster than any other combination. This was surprising at the time and caused quite a ruckus in the international media, including articles in the *New York Times* and the *Economist*.[4] In our scientific article, we hypothesized that angry male faces are prioritized because, from an evolutionary point of view, males were more likely to be physically aggressive and therefore more dangerous than females.[5] This, of course, is still the case, as shown by the percentage of males versus females convicted of violent crimes—or is this situation exacerbated by the automatic detection of angry males? In a crowd, it is more likely that our attention is drawn to, and therefore we "see," the angry male than the angry female. And males are more likely to be questioned about, arrested for, and convicted of violent crimes.

This implicit and automatic orientation to male angry faces is even more concerning when we consider the other-race effect. As mentioned in the previous chapter, we orient to the faces of people of other races faster than to those of our own race. Now combine this with the fact that we orient to angry male faces, and I think you can see why perhaps certain people get noticed more than others in potentially criminal or violent situations. Then consider the fact that we don't remember, nor are we able to identify, people of other races as well as we do members of our own. We will come back to this idea a little later.

Not long after we discovered that angry faces capture our attention, we investigated whether angry faces are also registered by the amygdala if the participant isn't actually "seeing" them consciously.[6] We did this by presenting participants with stimuli under conditions that induce *binocular rivalry*. If you present one image (in this case, a face) to one eye and another image (in this case, a house) to the other eye, your visual system can't resolve the conflict. Instead of seeing both images, you'll only see one of them, and after a while, you will see the other instead—the images "rival" each other. This occurs very early in the brain: the information from the unseen stimulus never gets past the very first stages of visual processing.[7] While scanning participants' brains, we looked at the activity in the amygdala relative to what the participant was reporting they saw. Even when participants were seeing the house and had no idea there was an angry face, the amygdala responded as though they had seen an angry face.

At the time, we made the controversial suggestion that facial expressions may have privileged access due to their evolutionary importance and that fast, implicit, automatic processing may occur via a subcortical route that bypasses the normal conscious route to perception.[8] Although provocative at the time (to say the least!), this is now well accepted. So, our amygdalas and our fight-or-flight responses become active automatically when we see angry faces that we aren't even aware of. Think about that for a minute. Your heart rate may increase, and your palms may become sweaty in response to a face you didn't even see. Is it any wonder people get anxious in crowded cities?

An initially puzzling finding in this study was that unseen *happy* faces also resulted in activation of the amygdala. Happy faces don't usually have that result, which makes sense because happy faces don't usually indicate a threatening situation. So why is the amygdala activated by happy faces when we aren't aware of them? This finding provoked us to think more about what the unconscious system might be capable of. It seemed that the prioritized processing would provide a crude indication of whether there was a face that differed from the average, rather than a detailed analysis. It is a system to indicate that we need to attend to something, and then we can use our clever, controlled, conscious capacity-limited system to decide whether it is a potential threat or not. In the experiment I described, the participants could not attend to the face because it was outside their conscious vision, so the amygdala continued to actively signal that there was something that needed to be attended to. Since this study, there have been numerous research groups that have shown similar effects. We now believe that an automatic crude analysis of faces is performed, and anything that deviates from neutral activates the amygdala and drives us to look at the face—which would then allow us to determine whether it represents a potential threat or not.

Now, it is important to think about this for a moment. Any face that is not neutral will initially activate the amygdala and our fight-or-flight response. To turn off this threat-detection system, we need to attend to the face and process it consciously. But what happens if we are busy chatting to a person in front of us and don't notice other faces in the room? Or if there are just too many faces to attend to all of them? Would this result in an overactive amygdala and essentially what would look and feel like a panic attack or social anxiety? Yes, pretty much so.

Early in my career, I was at a cognitive neuroscience conference in New York. There was a symposium held early in the morning—usually a death sentence for drawing a crowd, but this event was packed. Professor Giacomo Rizzolatti and his colleagues from the University of Parma were presenting their discovery of neurons in the brain of macaque monkeys that were active when a monkey performed an action, when a monkey observed the same action, and, most surprisingly, when the monkey heard or imagined an action.[9] The same neurons were active in all three situations. Why was this so amazing? Well, this demonstrated that the same set of neurons in the brain are activated when we see someone do something as when we do that action ourselves—they are now called mirror neurons. Specific areas of our frontal lobes have evolved to automatically mimic or copy what we see others doing. When someone else reaches out to grab a glass in front of us, we activate that motor response in our brain to understand what they are doing. And not only does the brain respond, but the muscles that would perform that action are slightly activated as well.[10]

The mirror neuron discovery sent a wave of excitement throughout the scientific community, especially in areas of communication and social neuroscience. For example, mirror neurons could explain how we understand others' facial expressions. The area of the brain involved in activating the same muscles in our face to make us smile are activated when we see someone else smile.[11] This then results in us experiencing the same emotion as the person we are viewing. So, in the case of someone smiling, we also feel positive, just like the other person.[12] Hence the well-known saying that a smile is contagious! This system allows us to automatically understand what others are feeling and therefore thinking.

This amazing system can explain why we feel positive about or enjoy the company of certain people—even, perhaps, people we have never met before. We are mimicking their emotional state. It can also explain why walking into a room full of people may make you feel completely comfortable (if they are happy) or very tense (if they aren't!). The emotional state of the people in the room affects your emotional state within moments—without your awareness. We are affected emotionally by those around us without a single word being said or any prior engagement with the people. Emotions are contagious (and better than catching the flu)!

This emotional contagion is even more intriguing because we don't just process individual faces implicitly; we are also able to gauge the average expression in a large group implicitly. Ever felt as though you could feel the mood of a large crowd? A part of this feeling may be the fact that we implicitly identify the average expression in large groups. Professor David Whitney and his colleagues from the University of California, Berkeley, demonstrated this by presenting pictures of many faces to participants too briefly for the images to be individuated.[13] Despite the brief presentation, participants could identify if the majority of faces were happy or angry. This is astounding when you consider the faces could not have been processed deeply or in a meaningful way. Yet participants could ascertain how the majority of the people felt!

If you think back to my tram ride heading to my niece's celebration, this automatic detection of the average emotion of a crowd is probably why I felt anxious. Melbourne had long periods of lockdown during the Covid pandemic, and many people were still feeling anxious in crowded places. Similarly, arriving at the engagement party, where everyone was there to enjoy the event, I automatically felt safe and secure. My mirror system detected the mood of the crowd and changed my mood accordingly. A little like a puppet on a string, we are controlled by the mood of the people around us.

Our implicit perception of facial expressions, abilities to infer emotions of crowds, and tendency to have our mood influenced by others might also explain why a negative or violent reaction in one part of a group can spread very quickly through a crowd. When people are involved in these experiences, they often don't know exactly how or when the mood changed or may only realize afterward that they became angry and aggressive. We implicitly detect the mood of a large group, which impacts our own mood or emotions. There are frequent examples of peaceful demonstrations or gatherings that without warning turn nasty. And often it is due to a small group inciting the aggression. Maybe these incidents can be explained by our implicit perception of facial expressions.

Our automatic face and facial expression processing systems and how they influence our attention are important to consider because we now live in very large groups, often surrounded by hundreds and sometimes thousands of individuals. Your amygdala automatically responds to any face that is not neutral so that you will attend to it.[14] And we can only attend to one face at a time. Now consider the fact that our amygdala sets off our fight-or-flight response. So what is happening to our amygdala when we are in large groups? Lots of activation cannot be reduced by attending to every relevant face! Overly frequent or inappropriate activation of the fight-or-flight response is implicated in a range of clinical conditions including most anxiety disorders.[15] Is it any surprise that we are seeing an increase in mental health issues in our communities?

Combining face and facial expression abilities with the implicit biases discussed in chapter 3 would have been beneficial a million years ago. We lived in small groups and needed to react quickly to survive. Automatically orienting to a group of Neanderthals in the forest and implicitly knowing that they were stronger and more aggressive than you would have potentially saved your life. You didn't need to think about it. Your amygdala set off your fight-or-flight response, and you reacted before even realizing why you were running. We now live in a very different environment with multicultural societies, and yet we are still puppets of this ancient system, resulting in major problems.

We have very little control over the impact of our automatic system unless we are aware of it and factor it into our decisions. Is it any surprise, then, that an African American person walking into a room full of white people may feel anxious? Not at all! Most of the white peoples' brains will have detected that a person from another group has entered the room, giving them signals that they need to be vigilant.

The amygdala then sets off the fight-or-flight response, which increases their awareness, speeds their heart rates, and pumps more blood to their skeletal muscles. This response is automatic just in case they need to respond. These people are probably not racist but just have millions of years of evolution kicking in. If they are not aware of the source of this reaction, they may feel stressed and anxious, without knowing why. Their body language and facial expressions may indicate fear or heightened alert. This system will direct their attention to the only African American person in the room. That single individual's auto response will be triggered by this attention, and he or she will also feel anxious. Now imagine if an African American person walks into a room full of armed white police officers! The officers' ancient unconscious processing leads them to be more inclined to detect the African American as a threat—and vice versa. I'm suggesting not that people cannot control their reactions but rather that, by understanding the evolutionary and neural bases that underpin our automatic responses in social situations, we can then consciously control our behavior. We will return to issues of racism later, but for now we need to get control of that elephant so we are not simply a puppet.

Let's move on from facial expressions for a moment and talk about another mechanism we use to identify intentions: body language. We can gain a huge amount of insight into how a person is feeling from his or her body language and movement.[16] Slouching forward and moving slowly often reflects sadness or possibly depression, sitting forward with tilted head can mean interest, crossing arms and sticking the chest out can indicate aggression, and a raised club could indicate it is time to run! We process these cues automatically, and they help us understand how well our interaction with the person is progressing. Do they like us or perhaps not? Are they interested in what we are saying or bored? Hopefully, you are sitting forward with a tilted head while reading this book!

Having a keen interest in human behavior and the opportunity to visit universities all over the world, I always find the social groups that wander around at different institutions interesting—especially because, although they vary, there are many similarities. Groups of people in their late teens to early twenties are hanging out together, dressed the same, acting the same, and speaking the same. Even near home at the beach or a café, it is interesting to observe a group of friends sitting together—they all behave similarly. Motivational speaker John Rohn said that we are the average of the five people we spend most time with.[17] Although we are not actually an average, we do tend to act like the people we are most closely connected to.

Have you ever noticed that when two people are sitting talking, they will often end up mimicking each other's sitting position? One person will cross their legs, and then the other person will also cross their legs. The mirror neuron system is believed to be involved in body language perception, understanding, and mimicry.[18] When we see a person slouch, the same motor neurons that would cause us to slouch activate, priming our muscles to perform the same movement. This helps us understand how they are feeling. The mirror neuron system is also involved in our automatic mimicry of other people. By mimicking another person, we show connection and understanding. The mirror neuron system helps us to automatically understand what a person is doing and how he or she is feeling, and that facilitates mimicry to increase connection.

Following and interpreting another person's eye gaze is also supported by the mirror neuron system.[19] Eye gaze is incredibly important during social interactions as it tells us what a person is talking about or whom they are talking to. We look at objects when we are trying to get someone else to look at them as well. And we usually look directly at someone when we are talking to them (although not necessarily the whole time). Babies track and follow eye gaze extremely early in their development, and it is believed to be essential for learning. When a caregiver looks at a particular object, for example, and says its name, babies learn that the object goes by that name. Or if a caregiver is looking at someone else and talking, the infant will readily understand that the caregiver is talking to that individual. Ever had an infant grab your face and direct it to them when wanting your attention? Babies know instinctively that if we are not looking at them, we are not attending to them.

In fact, the ability to use eye gaze and to understand its importance is a critical diagnostic tool in autism spectrum disorder (ASD).[20] Often one of the first indicators that a child has or is developing ASD is a lack of looking directly at the caregiver and an inability to understand that eye gaze is an indicator of attention. Many therapies for children with ASD center around teaching the use of eye gaze and what eye gaze means. Without this ability, it is extremely difficult to understand the meaning of other peoples' actions and intentions. And it is extremely difficult to connect.

Facial expression, body language, and eye gaze perception before language would have been hugely advantageous. This is highlighted by the fact that most (if not all) mammals use these cues in one form or another to communicate with each other. Those puppy dog eyes that your dog gives you are not simply cute; they are a signal of submission. And it is fascinating watching wolves, elephants, and other wild animals communicate via facial expressions, body language, and eye gaze. These abilities are automatic and implicit, and they are long established in our evolutionary history.

In summary:

- The mirror neuron system helps us understand the intentions of others and connect with others by mimicking their facial expressions and body language.
- Facial expression detection is an ancient prioritized system to enable fast detection of potential threats.
- We detect the average mood of a crowd implicitly, and this system is also involved in activating our fight-or-flight responses.
- Eye gaze detection is an important mechanism that enables us to understand who someone is communicating with or what they are talking about.

TIP OF THE CHAPTER

When you enter a room full of people, remember that your brain is trying to process all the faces and establish who is in a positive mood and who is not. This could set off your fight-or-flight response, sending your heart racing and making you feel anxious. Stop for a minute and look around the room. Give your brain time to process the situation and take a few deep breaths to calm yourself down.

Part II

HOW DOES CONNECTION WORK?

"The need for connection and community is primal, as fundamental as the need for air, water, and food."

—Dean Ornish[1]

• 5 •

We Are Pack Animals

In 1992, *The Oprah Winfrey Show,* with the help of Jane Elliot, a teacher and diversity expert, ran a social experiment. For the episode, the producers separated the audience based simply on their eye color: brown-eyed people and blue-eyed people. They then treated the two groups differently. They allowed the brown-eyed group to enter the studio and be seated first and gave them refreshments. The blue-eyed group was made to wait. Elliot explained to the audience that brown-eyed people were ranked higher on several psychological factors including intelligence and empathy. This was a complete ruse, and yet the groups quickly turned against each other. (You can view the episode on *The Oprah Winfrey Show* website.[1] It is fascinating to watch, and not just for the 1990s hairstyles!) The speed at which the two groups became hostile toward each other is quite disconcerting. People in the brown-eyed group quickly came up with examples of when they experienced blue-eyed people being rude and ignorant. In response, the blue-eyed people got irate and aggressive. This behavior then reinforced the brown-eyed group's opinion of the blue-eyed group. The episode is touted as a demonstration of racism, but it is about much more than that (not that racism isn't horrendous in itself). The episode demonstrated the general effect of in-group/out-group mentality at full throttle for the world to see (the trendy term is *tribalism*).

Have you ever not been invited to a party? Have you ever been refused entry to a club or institution? Have you ever missed out on a promotion because you were not part of the old boys' club? Have you ever been discriminated against because of your ethnicity, race, sex, sexual orientation, or religion? These are all results of this in-group versus out-group thinking.

Why do we group just about everything in our lives? In chapter 2, we talked about how the brain has a limited capacity for conscious thought, and the world is a complicated place. We cannot be aware of the enormous amounts of information coming in at any given moment. It is a bit like trying to drink from a fire hose. Way too much water too quickly, and you would literally blow your head off. Our attention filters the flow of information, and our long-term memory groups that information so that we can make sense of the world. And there really isn't anything more complicated than our social groups—our family groups, our friendship groups, our sporting groups, our work groups, our political groups, our ethnic groups, and our spiritual groups. We group things to simplify our complicated world and to make sense of it. This grouping, though, has major implications for the way we process information—the way we hear, see, feel, and empathize.

In the Oprah Winfrey case, it was reported that the ruse was stopped early because the situation started to get out of hand. There are many demonstrations of these types of experiments conducted by scientists under more controlled settings. Arguably the most extreme version was the Stanford Prison Experiment conducted in 1971 by Professor Philip Zimbardo of Stanford University.[2] (There's a 2015 film based on the experiment if you're interested.) He recruited a group of college students, randomly allocated them to either a prisoner group or a guard group, and gave them uniforms to highlight their roles. He turned the basement of a university building into a makeshift prison and recorded what happened. The experiment had to be canceled early due to the behavior of the guards toward the prisoners, which was bordering on sadistic. Again, completely arbitrary groupings resulted in significant in-group/out-group hostility.

What I find fascinating about both examples is that normal people placed into random groups became entrenched in group mentality. These were not people selected for their discriminatory tendencies or aggressive traits. They were people like you and me. And that is what makes these experiments so relevant today. Look around at some of the groups that have formed and the radicalization that is occurring across the world: the US Capitol riot of January 6, 2021; the riots that occurred in the name of the Black Lives Matter movement. But why is it that an average individual can so easily be convinced that people not within their group are the enemy?

We need to think back, not to just pre-Covid times, but way back before we had language. We talked already about how we aren't the fastest species, we aren't the strongest species, and we aren't the largest species. We needed a way to survive and pass on our genes in a very inhospitable environment. There is always safety in numbers. Having others to watch over young while one is out foraging or hunting, having spotters to look for potential danger, and sharing what food is available are positive aspects to living in groups. They give species like us an advantage. But our connected species has taken group living and social cooperation to a whole different level, and before language, this required some pretty sophisticated neural hardware to support it.

We needed a way of knowing who group members were, and this system needed to be adaptive and flexible. If I'm a member of the tool-making group, I need to recognize and remember who the other members are. Why? We would want to keep our skills and knowledge within our group to ensure that we remain important to the larger group. But I would also be a member of the larger group—the group I slept with, ate with, raised young with, and traveled with. I may at some stage be traded to another group to ensure genetic strength is maintained and inbreeding doesn't mess up our genetic health. I must be able to incorporate this new group into my group. And when my group met up with other groups in joint meetings or festivals, I would need to incorporate this even larger group into my group mentality. However, if a hostile group threatened my smaller group, I would need to respond quickly. So our group mentality system had to be flexible but also entrenched. Our group mentality has become so powerful that it literally changes the way we perceive the world.

Ever felt as though someone just won't listen to you? Have you ever had someone talking at you, but what they were saying just didn't make sense? Professor Pascal Molenberghs and his colleagues from the University of Melbourne have looked at whether we hear people from our in-group differently than we do people from our out-group.[3] Participants were assigned to different groups based on their political affiliations. The researchers then scanned participants' brains while they were listening to either positive or negative statements spoken by a member of their political in-group or out-group. The brain activity differed depending on group membership! Although the statements were the same, what the participants *heard* was different simply because of the speaker's group affiliation. No wonder members of one group don't understand the message of another—they literally hear what is being said differently.

We not only hear things differently but also speak a "different" language when we are part of a group. Language constantly evolves: the meanings of some words change, and new words appear, and different groups adopt their own languages. "Cool" used to mean cold, then it meant good, and now I'm not sure what it means, but my kids laugh when I use it. When I listen to my kids talk to each other, I am often confused by the terms they use. And when I first moved to the United States, I was surprised at the amount of Aussie slang I used that wasn't understood by my colleagues. I often had groups of intelligent post-graduate students at the Massachusetts Institute of Technology looking at me as though I were speaking gibberish! Each group adopts its own language as another way of cementing the connection within the group and highlighting the out-group.

Did you know that even emojis are interpreted differently depending on the group you belong to? Recently I was reading the *Wall Street Journal* and found out that Gen Z apparently uses and interprets emojis differently than millennials do. For example, the smile emoji, while seemingly innocent to people of my age, is seen as sarcastic or ironic to the younger generation. I remember my mother was very disappointed to find out that LOL meant "laugh out loud." She thought it meant "lots of love" and had been misinterpreting texts from her grandkids for years. I had a similar moment when I read the *Wall Street Journal* article "Sending Smiley Emojis? They Now Mean Different Things to Different People."[4] No more smiley faces from me.

Not only the words and symbols used but also a person's accent can change or evolve within different groups. When I was in my early twenties, I worked for a short period at a hotel in Melbourne. It was a hot spot for international tourists, and they used to come in bus loads from the airport. One day I remember a gentleman from Texas called me over and asked what language I was speaking. He and his wife had been listening to a conversation I was having with the desk clerk, and neither of them could understand what we were saying. I told him we were speaking English, which seemed to confuse him even more. But of course, even though we were speaking the same language, there is a huge difference between the US and Australian accents. This then makes it more difficult to understand what a person from a different country is saying as words are pronounced differently. Even within countries, there are striking differences in accents. The Boston and New York accents are strikingly different even though the cities are geographically fairly close. Even within cities there are differences—the cockney accent from South London compared to the BBC or Queen's English spoken in the traditionally wealthier areas. Accents indicate membership in different groups and alter peoples' perception. Did you know that there is a relationship between your accent, your perceived status, and your salary?[5] Like language, accents evolve within groups to indicate membership and belonging.

Group membership doesn't just influence how we speak and what we hear; we also *see* the faces of our in-group members differently than we do the faces of out-group members. I know it sounds crazy, but even when participants are randomly selected into groups, they later categorize the faces of people in the in-group as more attractive, more trustworthy, and more intelligent than members of the out-group. Even the brain responds differently.[6] And yet, this is simply based on viewing faces and knowing that the (randomly allocated) person is either in your group or another one! People literally see other people differently depending on whether they are or are not part of their in-group.

We also know that people empathize differently with members of their in-group than with members of an out-group. Professor Henri Tajfel and his colleagues from Bristol University asked participants to allocate money or winnings to other participants.[7] They could allocate the money any way they wanted. Participants consistently rewarded members of their in-group more than those of the out-group. Remember, these are randomly allocated groups, and who receives the money makes no difference to participants, yet they still preferred to give more money to their in-group! Our empathy and support are greater for those like ourselves—who are in our "group."

In previous chapters, we discussed how we detect greater potential threat from out-group members compared to in-group members. We orient to those who are perceived as out-group, and then we're more likely to attribute negative behavior or thoughts to them and to assume potential danger from them. We also see this in laboratory studies during game-playing experiments. Participants believe that members of their out-group are picking on them or out to get them, whereas members of their in-group are perceived as more helpful. This occurs even when the player strategies are controlled by a computer. There is no systematic or malicious intent, but despite this, the group membership creates the perception that the out-group members are behaving badly. Imagine how these things combine to create difficult and potentially explosive situations in real life.

The negative effect of our group mentality plays out constantly on the internet, especially on so-called social media platforms. Somebody posts a message, a picture, or a video that members of their in-group respond to positively. However, then people who aren't members of the in-group pick up on the post, and the vitriol is released. Members of the out-group may read the message or perceive the video quite differently. And the person who posted the content is then shocked by the response.

One recent glaring example of this in-group/out-group mentality occurred when a woman from South Africa posted a picture of a dead giraffe that her husband organized for her to shoot for Valentine's Day. She thought it was the sweetest thing her husband could have done, and many members of her in-group agreed. Then, according to a *Sun UK* news article, she was quickly slammed for her actions.[8] Now, I'm not going to get into the debate about hunting in game reserves and whether it has a role in conservation as this woman argued. Nor will I make a wisecrack about some of the Valentine's gifts I have given in the past. My point is that when she posted the piece, she was expecting her in-group to respond positively (and they did). What she did not expect was a negative response from those outside her group. And conversely, those in her out-group could not understand why someone would be excited to shoot a giraffe for Valentine's Day. (That toaster doesn't seem like a bad present now, does it?) The impact of our group membership on our interpretation of information is pervasive and needs to be widely understood.

Schadenfreude is a German word that means gaining pleasure or enjoyment from another person's misfortune. And as you might have guessed, schadenfreude also occurs when we believe the other person is in our out-group. In fact, in one study, Professor Mina Cikara and colleagues from Harvard University found that people enjoyed hearing that members of other groups had suffered even though it had no impact on them.[9] As the title of the article states, "Their pain gives us pleasure." These findings suggest that the violence that we see when opposing groups clash has a basis in our fundamental human processes—although, as we'll see later, that doesn't mean there is nothing we can do about it!

In most of the cases discussed, the groups in which participants were placed were random or meaningless, yet our primal need for group association still affected perception, behavior, and decisions. This drive is evident throughout our society, and we are strongly influenced by the nonrandom groups with which we identify. Spend any time in a school playground or at a sporting event, and you will quickly see this need to form groups. The shocking scenes during and after the 2020 US election reflect the extremes this group mentality can lead to. Our allegiance to a country or a god tends to place this "groupthink" on steroids. For most of the last eight million plus years, this group mentality was very beneficial, resulting in humans thriving and making amazing discoveries and innovations. Now, though, we live in safer environments than ever before, and our multicultural, multiracial, and multireligious societies highlight the urgent need for a change in how we relate to each other.

An extreme version of this in-group thinking is often observed when armies invade. The army is a group of its own with very strong in-group mentality. War crimes often occur during invasions or occupations. An example was highlighted in a report on the actions of the Australian Special Forces in Afghanistan.[10] The report blamed the murders of "prisoners, farmers and civilians" on an unchecked "warrior culture" among soldiers. These terrible incidents occur not only in the Australian Special Forces but often in war more generally and can be traced back to our primitive in-group/out-group mentality. The troops strongly identify with their in-group. Their perception of threat is increased, their empathy for the out-group is decreased, and their ability to listen is decreased. Times of stress and heightened danger are likely to increase this group mentality. Importantly, the out-group here includes not just enemy soldiers but anyone outside the military group, which is why these crimes often also affect civilians and innocent bystanders. This extreme version of in-group thinking that occurs when armies invade or occupy territories creates a tinderbox situation that takes very little to get out of control.

We also need to consider the impact of group mentality regarding local law enforcement. A recent study by Professor Frank Edwards and colleagues from Rutgers University found that in the United States, black men are 2.5 times more likely to be killed by police than white men are.[11] Similar disproportionate rates are evident in other countries, including the United Kingdom and Australia. It is a very complex issue and not one that can be easily solved. But issues around implicit bias among police officers and differences in perceived policing methods across different communities can and should be addressed. Police officers and law enforcement being perceived as part of the community is also important. Community policing involves embedding officers within the community and shows promise in areas with systemic issues.[12] However, creating a belief that law enforcement is part of the community is often difficult. Understanding group mentality and creating a situation where the community and the officers see themselves as members of the same group working toward a common goal is essential.

We need to increase our awareness of the groups within our communities and then expand those circles. We need to understand that this is an automatic primitive process that is no longer necessary in our safe society. We need to be aware of the impact on our perception and empathy for those not within our group and focus more on what we have in common than what divides us.

Is everyone susceptible to in-group mentality? Yes! We are all members of groups, and we are all affected by these relationships. However, some people seem to be more affected than others. Have you ever had the experience of chatting with a friend about a specific topic that you both agree on when, suddenly, the friend goes to an extreme level that shocks you?

In 2019, I was involved with a group of staff and students who were rallying against changes to the university structure. I organized a letter to the university executive that was signed by more than 50 percent of the university's professoriat, and we organized several rallies and information sessions. I was pretty embedded in this group. At one of these rallies, I was shocked when another member of the group yelled, "Let's smash the windows and drag the #$@*!% out here." This was someone I had known for years, and as far as I am aware, he had never done anything like that before. But membership in this particular group seemed to really drive his passion to a level beyond reason. I managed to talk him out of the idea—smashing windows is not a great look.

The reasons some people are more susceptible to this in-group mentality are as diverse as they are complicated. There are often specific attributes of an individual's personality that can drive their want or need for group membership. Individuals who are more trusting or less confident tend to put more weight or value on group membership. There are also external factors that contribute, including scarcity of resources or a sense that resources are unfairly distributed. Aspects of the group itself can impact an individual's feelings of belonging. Some groups will specifically target a person's vulnerabilities or sense of themselves. And an individual's current situation or mental state can also affect their willingness to get involved. The members of the group, particularly if they include trusted friends, can influence a person's involvement. And finally, a very charismatic or manipulative group leader may more readily indoctrinate members into the group. Let's look at each of these important drivers in more depth.

Individuals who are less confident or feel a need for support will often seek out groups to join. They feel more confident if surrounded by like-minded people and enjoy the support and commitment of the group mentality. They are also more likely to embed themselves in the group for safety. If the group is safe and healthy, then this could be a great opportunity for the individual. However, such people can be drawn to more extreme groups and are often then willing to go to extreme measures to demonstrate their allegiance. We often hear in the media that family and friends never suspected a certain individual could be violent. And yet, the person has attempted or achieved horrific acts in the name of a specific group or movement. In so doing, this individual is seeking the support of the group to increase his or her confidence and feel safe and needed.

Group membership can also occur in response to real or perceived scarcity of resources. A catch cry of the Nazi propaganda machine was that Jews were taking all the jobs and resources. Germany was in a severe recession with significant unemployment, extreme inflation, and much suffering. The Nazi machine created an out-group by blaming the Jews and others for the situation. The outcome was horrific. Those who perceive scarcity of resources are more likely to turn to a group, and the in-group mentality is often much stronger as a result.

The recent increase in right-wing male chauvinist groups is a good example of groups targeting a person's vulnerabilities or sense of self. With the second (or maybe third) wave of feminism and movements such as #MeToo, there are men who feel they are being discriminated against. Such men have grown up in a patriarchal society in which males (particularly white males) have had control. They see this changing, with women gaining more power, and they don't like it. It affects their sense of who they are as men and where they belong in relation to power and control. Groups like the Proud Boys and influencers like Jordan Peterson target these insecurities and give these men a group whose members think like them—people who want patriarchy strengthened and feminism squashed. They target the men's vulnerabilities and their sense of self-worth, feeding on the intrinsic need for group membership.

Donald Trump, whether you like him or not, is an example of an incredible influencer, whose charisma and bravado garners support. Trump's ability to attract members who think he relates to them is quite astounding when you consider his background. He is a privileged white male who was born into extreme wealth. He has never gone without, yet many of his most devoted followers are from poor or struggling areas of the United States. He surrounds himself with people like himself, and yet he can separate or isolate himself from those people at the same time. Look at his inner circle, and you see a group of men and women who are also extremely privileged. Yet his followers see him as a man of the people. Trump is a great example of an influencer who is extremely good at attracting group members and activating their in-group mentality.

But it is not only the influencers who control the group. We need to keep in mind that political and social groups are made up of individuals. Without the individual members, there is no group. This seems obvious, but often these groups are perceived as being static or permanent, when actually they evolve as more members join or as members leave. The leaders or influencers often evolve or change as well. For example, the feminism movement has shifted dramatically since its first inception in the 1890s into its current form. Society has changed, and the expectations and beliefs of both women and men in society and within the movement have changed. Some groups are formed to solve a problem or address an issue. Once the problem is solved, the group either disbands or evolves. Or, as the problem or issue changes, the group shifts to deal with it. We need to realize that the political and social groups that are around today will either evolve or fade away tomorrow.

I wonder what groups will form in the coming years. I don't think anyone could have expected the many antimask, antivax, pro–conspiracy theory groups that popped up during 2020 and 2021. How will these groups that emerged during the Covid pandemic evolve? Some will become more popular, some will have new influencers take the reins, and some will slowly fade away. As the climate continues to change, perhaps one or two of the conservation groups will grow in popularity. The British royal family is going through quite a transition now with the passing of the queen and Harry and Meghan's move to the United States. How will the Republican and Democratic parties evolve after quite a tumultuous period? Perhaps some obscure YouTube or Facebook influencer will create their own movement that shifts the political landscape completely. We will have to wait and see.

What we need to remember is that we are all constantly affected by in-group mentality. Most of the time this is not a major issue as the groups we belong to are mainly innocuous. The fact that I might be less likely to listen to a person who supports the Bulldogs because I support the Cats isn't going to impact either of our lives. The fact that an innocent person is pulled over and searched unnecessarily because they are not a member of the police officer's in-group, on the other hand, is an issue. The likelihood that an eyewitness incorrectly identifies an innocent out-group person as the perpetrator of a crime is an issue. The fact that a doctor treats a patient differently because they are not a member of their in-group is an issue. The fact that a civilian is killed while tending to his fields by a foreign soldier who is influenced by his in-group is an issue. We need to understand when in-group mentality is an issue and how we can be conscious and in charge of our decisions.

In summary:

- We group things in our very complex world, including people, to make sense of it.
- Our in-group mentality is so strong that we perceive the world differently because of it.
- Even when randomly allocated to groups, we hear, see, and empathize differently depending on another person's membership.
- We need to be aware of our groups and widen the circle whenever there is discrimination.

TIP OF THE CHAPTER

Reflection is an important first step to improving our relationships. Spend some time thinking about the many groups you are a member of and how these might impact your perception of other people. Who are the members of these groups, and who aren't? Do you treat out-group members differently?

· 6 ·

Connected to Learn

$\mathcal{O}$ur in-group mentality impacts every aspect of our lives, especially whom we listen to and therefore what we learn. In my younger days, I hated school, and I was one of those kids teachers struggled with. I connected with very few teachers. I was a truant during most of those years, and, to be honest, I didn't give school a chance. In fact, my high school principal told my parents that I would be dead or in prison by the time I was twenty-five. I was part of the bad kids' in-group. Ironically, it was at age twenty-five that I went back to school and fell in love with learning—due to a physics teacher who inspired me. We made a connection, and it changed my outlook completely. I hope you can remember teachers in your past who inspired you. Did you feel connected to them? Connection is the key to enabling students to learn. Without it, students just don't show up—either figuratively or (in my case) literally.

As we have discussed in previous chapters, spoken language has only been around for about 160,000 years. Yet we have been living in groups and cooperating for millions of years. It could be argued that it is in the last few hundred years or so that we've made our greatest innovations and discoveries—advances that allowed us to thrive in ways unimaginable in any other species. But it is the foundations that occurred during the earlier part of our evolution that enabled those great advances. Learning from each other through connection was arguably our greatest advance: learning and teaching enabled all our subsequent innovations.

Learning from other members of your species (or even from other species) is not unique to humans. Virtually all mammals learn from other members in one form or another. I am a huge fan of David Attenborough's documentaries, in which we often see animals learning—for example, the polar bear searching for a seal and her cubs following, watching intently and then copying her behavior; an infant chimpanzee mesmerized by his mother's use of a twig to pull termites out of a mound, then clumsily trying the same experiment without much success; lion cubs practicing their stalking and pouncing on each other, learning from what they have seen older lions do, playing the same actions with each other. There are many more examples of young animals learning in this way.

It's not just the cute factor (and amazing cinematography) in the Attenborough documentaries that draws us in. We anthropomorphize the animals—attributing human thoughts and emotional states to them. It seems as if the animals are teaching their offspring how to do specific tasks because of a humanlike bond. We do know that animals feel pain, and some animals grieve when they lose group members, but we don't have any evidence that animals set out to teach the way we humans teach.[1] Animal learning happens through the viewing of normal behavior, mimicry, instinct, and a lot of trial and error. Humans do all these things as well, but we also set out explicitly to teach. We even have groups of individuals who have specialized in teaching. (I call them neuroplasticians; you know them as teachers!) We can consider how we are going to teach; we can and should reflect on how it is working and how it can be improved. These techniques of teaching to optimize learning, our metacognition, are unique human characteristics.

Despite the differences between us and other animals, our learning and teaching are still based on a more primitive system that all mammals use. A big part of learning and understanding is driven by our *mirror neuron system*. Remember the finding that when you see someone perform a particular behavior, your brain activates the same motor plan as if you were also performing it? This allows you to understand what they are doing because your brain is mimicking their action—but without your physically doing it. It is this mirror neuron system that is vital for learning and teaching.

In chapter 4, we discussed these mirror neurons with regard to learning and understanding facial expressions. When you see someone smile, the mirror neurons activate as if you had smiled yourself. This results in a similar brain response, which is thought to be the way that you understand what they are doing and perhaps make inferences about why (e.g., smiling because they are happy).

Professor Michael Arbib from the University of California, San Diego, and others have argued that this mirror neuron system was instrumental in the evolution and development of language.[2] Babies fixate on our faces when we talk, watching our mouths move, which activates the same motor patterns in their brains. They then try to mimic the movements to create the same sounds. Speech pathologists use this in therapy, both for children learning to speak or for older patients after brain damage. The patient focuses on the therapist's mouth when they speak and then tries to repeat the words. And any decent coach of a young sports team will tell you that they demonstrate different actions when teaching; they don't just give verbal instructions. It simply wouldn't work. The mirror neuron system is an integral part of our learning process.

Mirror neurons support learning in other species as well. As seen in the amazing documentaries discussed above, many animals watch other members of their group to learn new skills and to understand others.[3] Wolves, for example, are spectacular pack hunters—they can communicate a great deal via body language and subtle movements to coordinate attacks. These behaviors are communicated and learned through the activity of the mirror system. This mirror system allows us and other mammals to communicate, understand, and learn the movements and behaviors of others—and it has evolved over millions of years.

In most mammals, the group is centered around a family to improve the survival rate of the genetic material. We talked about this earlier—from a Darwinian perspective, it is our genes that we want to pass on, so helping and protecting family members benefits this drive. Wolves have several generations within a pack. The older ones look after the pups, the healthy and fit hunt and protect the weaker members, and so on. And for millions of years, we would have survived similarly. From whom do we learn in this environment? We learn from others within our group whom we trust and have a strong connection with. Learning from our close family members improved our survival.

This need to have a connection with those we learn from continues today. Remember we don't hear, see, or relate to people in our out-group the same way we do people in our in-group. How, then, can we learn effectively from someone we don't relate to or listen to? In fact, we don't learn well from people we don't consider as part of our in-group;

we only learn from people with whom we have a connection. Professors Hadas Wiseman and Orya Tishby from Hebrew University showed that psychotherapy sessions only work if there is a strong relationship between the counselor and the client.[4] Without that strong connection, the client doesn't learn, and the therapy goes nowhere. Similarly, Professor Sandra Christenson from the University of Minnesota and her colleagues have shown that students who don't connect with their teachers don't learn as well as students who do make a connection.[5] And teachers who connect well with students, who create classrooms full of members of their in-group, have much better outcomes. This need for connection to the person teaching is as important today as it ever was in the past.

Think back to the teachers who had a positive impact on your learning. I'm willing to bet that they were the teachers that you felt some connection with. And you can probably remember something you learned from them. You probably even got good grades! Now think back to a teacher whom you disliked (for whatever reason). I'd predict that this class was a struggle and your marks were not as strong. This story is consistent in the schools I work in and the teachers I work with. Teachers will tell stories about students they just can't connect with and what a struggle it is to teach them. Principals highlight those amazing teachers who connect so well with their students and how well all their students do. We learn from those we connect with, and we need that connection to learn.

I have seen the positive effects of connection and learning so many times. I regularly go to low-socioeconomic-status schools with the Macquarie University Widening Participation Unit. For one such session we were visiting a primary school in a small country town. I watched one of the teachers as he greeted each of his students at the beginning of the school day. When the bell rang, he appeared at the door of the classroom, knelt so the children were at eye level, shook each child's hand in turn, and welcomed them to the class. Later, I noticed how polite and engaged the students in his class were during my presentation. And the school principal confirmed my suspicion that his class had the lowest rate of truancy and greatest grade improvements over the school year. Connection is so important.

The idea that we need to connect, to be part of the teacher's in-group to learn, is not new. Professor Alfred Adler, who founded the individual psychology discipline in the early part of the twentieth century, highlighted the importance of connection between the therapist and the client. Adler's work was expanded by Professor Rudolf Dreikurs, who suggested that children and students misbehave as a result of not belonging to the in-group.[6] His work emphasized the importance of connection with a child or student before trying to teach or discipline. Without connection there are often behavioral issues and a lack of learning. A teacher can only teach those whom they connect with and who are part of their in-group.

So why is connection to the person you are learning from so important? Let's return again to the ancient past. We needed to be sure that those we learned from were going to teach us the right stuff. We humans are amazingly good at learning. We can learn from just one or two trials. For example, when a baby is first learning the names of things and a loved one looks at a dog and says "dog," the baby automatically realizes that the loved one is referring to the thing he or she is looking at (no mean feat in itself). But the baby also hypothesizes that either that thing's name is "dog" or there is a whole category of those things that are "dogs." The next time a loved one looks at another dog and says "dog," the baby eliminates option one and learns the category of dog. It takes thousands of trials to teach a computer the same thing. It really is amazing!

Given we learn so quickly, we need to be sure that the people we learn from are trustworthy and are teaching us the correct things. It could be potentially dangerous if we learned from just anyone. Imagine how easily people could manipulate us if we could not discern who was a reliable source. So we need the teacher to be part of our in-group, to be connected. Then they are trusted and seen as a reliable source of information. I'm talking not just about schoolteachers but about anyone in our lives whom we are going to listen to and learn from. This includes mentors, parents, colleagues, partners, presidents, gurus, media personalities, influencers, Facebook friends, and anyone else in your life whom you interact with. If they are perceived as a member of your in-group, you will learn from them very easily.

Learning from those within our in-group has become an issue in modern societies where peer groups dominate. In the past, family groups, tribes, and clans were intergenerational. The younger ones were part of a group with older, wiser members, who taught them their culture, ethics, morals, and everything else that was seen as important. Since the Industrial Revolution, peer groups have become more important, and in schools, sporting groups, camps, and so on, children and teens are separated into age-defined cohorts. In fact, play groups and the like have become a necessity in many societies. But as Gordon Neufield and Gabor Maté explain in *Hold On to Your Kids*, children and teens who are strongly peer oriented see their friends as the most important source of truth.[7] Unfortunately, their peer group is immature, like themselves, and therefore what they learn is often not appropriate. A peer-oriented child will also reject those in the out-group, which could include all who are not peers. This makes learning the many important lessons from teachers, parents, and other more experienced members of society very difficult.

Learning from our online connections is unfortunately also a contributing factor to the modern radicalization of people. For example, people start with friends on Facebook they know and like. Other friends join the group and become part of the conversation. They are all part of the group and speak the same language. Slowly individuals post more on a topic that sparks interest and reactions among their friends, which gives them positive feedback to do more and more. This can quickly escalate into more and more extreme views. But more about that in a later chapter! Here we're going to stick with this idea that learning from those we trust, members of our in-group, has led to humans being the dominant species.

As discussed in chapter 1, at some stage in history, our groups got larger, and we started specializing. This seems to be the major difference between us and other mammals—family groups started associating with other family groups and cooperating. Of course, there are huge herds of mammals such as zebra and antelope, but these usually associate for protection, not for the exchange of goods, services, and knowledge. These herds are not cooperating or connecting in the same way as the connected species. This seems to have been a key shift in human evolution.

We can only speculate, but combining family groups probably started because it facilitated hunting. There is safety in numbers, and bigger prey could be hunted with a bigger group. Hunting as a group requires good communication and coordination between members, so this would have honed our ability to perceive faces and to read facial expressions, gestures, body language, and eye gaze. Remember, at this point, we did not yet have spoken language. This larger grouping would have also allowed specialization. Some individuals would have stayed at camp to look after the young, some would have led the hunt, some would have followed direction, and so on. These early allocations of responsibilities within larger groups to aid with hunting may have been the precursor of greater specialization.

The amazing thing about the connected species is that from these clans and this drive to connect, we have enabled ourselves to specialize and learn. When we started living in clans, we started relying on each other, trusting each other, and allowing people to specialize. We enabled people to become good at one thing and to trust that others would supply them with all the other things they needed to survive. This is an amazing shift, when you think about it. I couldn't survive very long on my own. Despite my children thinking Bear Grylls can survive anything, I think even he, with all his impressive survival techniques, would struggle if he had access to nothing at all. It is our connection and specialization that allows us to thrive.

It is a truism that we stand on the shoulders of those who came before us. We have built up knowledge through thousands of generations of connected people. We have become more and more specialized in our roles within our groups, and that has allowed us to innovate. The great advances might seem like massive leaps, but they actually reflect the efforts of hundreds of thousands of individuals working in unison, learning from previous generations, and being allowed to focus on a specific area. This is what has resulted in our continuous development as the connected species.

But, of course, this takes trust and connection, or else it all falls apart. If I train to be an engineer, and I dedicate my life to being the best engineer I can be, I trust that I will be rewarded for being an engineer. In exchange, I will get food, shelter, and all the other things I need but don't have the time to create myself. Now we use money as an intermediary step, but it still works the same. Everyone within the group needs to be supported and feel as though what they do is valued by the rest of the group. And the rest of the group needs to understand why that person is doing what they do and how it contributes.

Some things are valued more than others and, as a result, are rewarded more. This has probably always happened. One can imagine that the strongest or best hunter probably got first access to the food. Or someone gifted in making stone tools would have received more goods for his tools than someone who made poorer quality tools. Those who were better at their craft or more talented would also attract more students or people who wanted to learn from and work with them. They would then be able to choose the students with the most potential, which would result in more innovation and better outcomes. One can then see how being good and working hard at a skill could result in many benefits and make specializing very rewarding. And, of course, the expert would not only attract the best and brightest but would also be able to choose students with whom he or she connected better. Having a good connection results in better learning, reinforcing the process.

As the connected species, we have evolved amazingly interconnected societies that thrive through specialization. Our mirror neuron system helps us learn through understanding and mimicking the behavior of others, but we learn most effectively from others within our group. Our ability to collaborate and specialize has driven our innovation and creativity, enabling us to thrive like no other species. The need for connection to enhance learning is great, but connection is also integral to our health and well-being. We'll look at that next.

In summary:

- Group mentality affects every part of our lives, especially what we learn and from whom.
- We are extremely good learners, and therefore it is important for us to know whom we can trust to teach us and whom to avoid.
- We learn from many different groups and from many different people, but we must be a member of the in-group to learn.
- Our amazing ability to collaborate and specialize has driven our incredible innovation and creativity.

TIP OF THE CHAPTER

If you want someone to listen to you or, more importantly, learn from you, you need to connect with them first. They need to feel as though you are part of their group, someone they can trust. Share with them who you are and why they should trust you. Otherwise, you might as well be talking to a stone!

· 7 ·

Home-Cooked Meal for the Soul

I often work with school psychologists and counselors. During the lockdowns, when schools transitioned to online learning, those working in schools in health and well-being were overrun by students needing help. A private girls' school in my area had several suicide attempts within a couple of weeks of each other—devastating for all concerned. But I also heard about a school in a poorer neighborhood that didn't shift to online learning. Many of the students didn't have access to a computer, so it just wasn't feasible. Instead, they came up with an innovative plan. Instead of requiring students to spend hours each day on a screen, the teachers drove around to each student's house a few times each week and met with the students on their front lawns. They gave them hard copies of the work they wanted them to do and picked up the work they had completed. And they spent some time just talking. I heard this school community fared much better than those that went online. Why? Because we need face-to-face communication. We need to have the opportunity not only to talk to someone but to really connect with them. We need to see their facial expressions, see their body language, look them in the eye, smell their scent, feel their touch, and communicate directly with them as we have done for millions of years.

Connecting online, while necessary in some circumstances, is not the same as meeting face-to-face. I liken it to fast food compared to a home-cooked meal. We often crave fast food because of the fat and sugar hit we get when we eat it. But it doesn't really satisfy us. And it is not healthy long term—just like connecting online. A good home-cooked meal, made with fresh ingredients, is far more satisfying in the short term and much healthier in the long term. Socializing in person can be more difficult and time-consuming, just like cooking, but is so much more worthwhile. This was highlighted during the lockdowns that occurred due to Covid. Mental health issues increased dramatically, and we are continuing to see the results of everyone relying on online connection.

Have you ever felt lonely? Have you ever thought about *why* we feel lonely? Our need for connection is so entrenched that we suffer mentally and physically when we are lonely.

Solitary confinement, for example, is used as a brutal punishment because it restricts a person's ability to connect with others. We, as the connected species, need contact with other humans. Isolation can result in anxiety, stress, depression, panic attacks, hypersensitivity, hallucinations, paranoia, psychosis, and suicide. It is an awful situation to place someone in because it goes against all our basic instincts. And it doesn't have to be forced solitary confinement. Studies show that people who live alone are more likely to show signs of depression, anxiety, stress, and suicidal thoughts.[1] In many countries, the rate of people requiring support for mental illnesses doubled in 2020 and 2021, during and after the periods of lockdown. Restricting a person's access to others is damaging.

In fact, we know that loneliness causes physical as well as mental health issues.[2] You can literally die from loneliness. A recent report from the National Academies of Sciences, Engineering, and Medicine showed that elderly individuals who are isolated or feel lonely are more likely to acquire chronic diseases and die younger than those who have a group of close friends and relatives they feel connected to.[3]

A similar picture has been shown in monkeys. Lonely individuals feel constantly under threat, which activates the sympathetic nervous system.[4] Chronic activation of the sympathetic nervous system creates an inflammatory response in the body, which results in a decreased ability to fight off viral infections or other pathogens.[5] If the body is unable to fight off infection, then chronic illness and death are likely. Loneliness kills!

The flip side of this research on loneliness is that connecting with people, being part of a group, can improve our health and well-being in a myriad of ways. From a mental health perspective, this is probably no surprise. I'm sure you have friends who make you feel good when you are feeling down. These are people you feel close to, people you like grabbing a coffee (or something stronger) with and chatting about anything and everything. Just seeing them brightens your day. Well, this is because we need people. Groups keep us safe and help us thrive, so we evolved a whole bunch of brain and body responses that reinforce this drive to connect.

When we see a member of our group, someone we like, our brain releases a swarm of neurotransmitters—chemicals that allow our cells to communicate—including serotonin and oxytocin. Serotonin is the neurotransmitter that makes us feel good. It is released when you see a cute puppy, for example. And oxytocin is involved in bonding and connecting to people. (It's also involved in orgasms!) Both these chemicals help us relax and make us feel safe and secure. They eliminate stress and anxiety. You can see why just spending time with a friend or group member can help with mental health. If we feel bonded, safe, and secure, we can relax. And if we decrease our stress and anxiety, then we are less likely to feel anxious and overwhelmed. Just hanging out with someone we like is a huge bonus for our mental well-being.[6]

A great example of "hanging out" having a positive effect on mental health is the International Men's Shed Organization. It started in Australia in the 1990s in response to the growing number of men committing suicide. There is a macho mentality in many areas of Australia, especially in country towns, in which men are expected to be stoic. Chin up and get on with it. Have a beer if you've got a problem. Don't talk about your feelings. The Men's Shed gives men a healthy alternative in-group, which is particularly helpful in staving off loneliness for those without other groups. Community sheds are set up for men to meet up and work on different projects together. They usually have metal and woodworking equipment and other things that you would find in a good workshop. Men can join a Men's Shed to use the equipment, to go and do some so-called men's work. An important side product is that Men's Sheds provide the opportunity to connect with other men outside alcohol and sport. They have become extremely successful and are now running in seven countries around the world—a great way to battle the loneliness among this group. We all need a positive in-group.

Having a connection to others and spending time together reduces stress levels through the release of those all-important neurotransmitters, serotonin and oxytocin. Now, a small amount of stress in our lives is important. Why would we get out of bed in the morning if we didn't have any stress, such as the need to feed ourselves or get our kids off to school? Why would we go to work if we didn't have the stress of paying bills and earning a living? Without any stress, we would not do much at all, but things start to decline quickly with too much stress! There is a nice inverted-U-shaped function that shows the relationship between stress and performance or output—called the Yerkes-Dodson law—and once you are past the peak, too much stress clearly impairs performance. Chronic high levels of stress are also just really bad for us and can cause illness, including diabetes, heart disease, high blood pressure, hyperthyroidism, irritable bowel syndrome, and ulcers.[7] So, too much stress should be avoided. Having others around us who are part of our in-group reduces stress and keeps it under control. In fact, hanging out with a good friend is better at reducing stress than any available medication.[8] I will repeat that because it is so important—hanging out with a good friend is better at reducing stress than any currently available pill!

Another important aspect of spending time together is the support it fosters. Just having other people around, who you know will care for you if you are unwell, physically injured, or just feeling down, can be very reassuring and results in lower stress. We feel safe and secure when others from our in-group are around us. This makes perfect sense from an evolutionary point of view as there is safety in numbers. And we have evolved a mechanism to facilitate this connection—we talked about it earlier: smiles are contagious. Seeing someone smile results in our mimicking that smile without even knowing it. And smiling results in the release of dopamine, another happy neurotransmitter that activates areas of our brain involved in feeling pleasure and comfort. This is yet another piece of evidence that we have evolved to be super connected. All our senses drive us to connect, to find joy in the company of others, and that joy keeps us both physically and mentally healthy.

Many years ago, I volunteered at a palliative care hospice. It was for patients in the last stages of terminal illness. It was very unsettling but extremely rewarding. The training was intense. We spent a lot of time learning how to connect with people. We were a mix of medical and psychology students, all very interested in helping others. An unexpected feature of the training was that it involved multiple sessions learning how to massage each other's hands and feet! This was a little strange to begin with. I thought we were going to be taught how to discuss grief, how to respond to anger, sadness, frustration, and the many other emotions involved in the process of dying. Brendan Murley, our trainer and supervisor and an all-around wonderful human, explained that the people we would meet would be in many different stages of grief. They would need someone to talk to and someone to listen without being judgmental or emotional. But to open up they needed first to connect, and the best way to connect is through touch. Going into a patient's room and asking them or their family if they want a hug would be difficult and awkward. However, asking someone if they would like a hand or foot massage is much easier and more comfortable. And he was right! The simple act of massaging a person's hand resulted in some amazing conversations and highlighted to me the importance of touch in creating a connection.

In her 2001 book *Touch*, Professor Tiffany Field from the University of Miami suggests that, in many circumstances, touch is stronger than verbal contact.[9] Touch is critical for children's growth, development, and health, as well as for adults' physical and mental well-being. And touch is involved in the process of driving us to find and preserve a group.

In all cultures, there is a ritual around greeting, and it almost always involves touching. Many Europeans kiss on the cheek, and the Inuit and Maori touch noses—a process that brings the two people close and allows them not only to touch but also to smell the pheromones given off by each other. In more stoic countries like the United States, England, Canada, and Australia, we shake hands. This still involves touching and bringing the person close enough to smell their pheromones. We also engage in grooming (and I do not mean in the despicable child-manipulating sense), which involves cleaning and maintaining another's appearance. Touching and grooming evolved so that we would seek it from those within our in-group, and it is a powerful way to connect.

If you look at any primate species that live in groups, grooming is very common and a way of establishing rank and order (as well as removing parasites). We still have the drive to do this, and in fact we have special sensors in our hairy skin called c-tactile afferents to make touch extra special. These sensors are fine-tuned for a soft touch, and they directly stimulate areas of our brain involved in pleasure.[10] And, amazingly, infant monkeys given the choice of having either this type of soft touch or food will choose soft touch to the point of starvation.[11]

We are that driven to want the touch of others, especially when we are young.

Touch is the first sense to develop and the primary means of providing love to a baby. Babies crave cuddling, stroking, and just being touched. We have known for many years now that skin-to-skin touch between babies and their caregivers has significant benefits for attachment and brain development.[12] Babies who get regular touch and cuddling are calmer and have better emotional control.[13] Touch also reduces stress levels in the caregiver as well as significantly improving mood and sleep patterns, which any parent will know is essential in those first few years. What does this tell us about our evolution? It highlights the importance of touch in our connections and relationships.

Professors Alberto Gallace and Charles Spence from Oxford University have studied the effect of touch in modern societies.[14] They suggest that touch can even have an impact on the decisions we make. For example, customers are more likely to test or purchase a product in a supermarket when they are touched by an experimenter posing as a store assistant. Also, bus drivers are more likely to give a passenger a free ride if they are touched as the request is made. And individuals who have been touched by an experimenter are more likely to agree to participate in an interview. Simply touching someone's arm makes them like and trust us. Let's not tell the big corporations this though, or before we know it, they will be hiring people to go around cuddling potential customers to get sales up. It could get a little awkward! But the effects are real, and just touching someone's hand, arm, or leg will make it significantly more likely that they will trust you, and trust is a major factor in the decision-making process.

If we return to those neurotransmitters, it is not surprising that touch increases trust and alters our decisions. Touch results in the release of the hormone oxytocin, which helps us form an emotional connection to one another. It gives us a sense of well-being and happiness. Oxytocin also generates feelings of compassion during interactions, which may contribute to an expansion of trust among individuals during social situations. Work by Professor Michael Kosfeld and colleagues from the University of Zurich showed that when participants snorted oxytocin, they were more likely to trust strangers and even lend them money.[15] It has even been suggested that oxytocin may help inspire positive thinking and an optimistic outlook on the world. Increased trust, emotional connection, positive thinking, and optimism are all going to affect the decisions we make.

Given that touch can impact our decisions, let's now consider some of the common situations that we find ourselves in. Some situations are set up, knowingly or not, to either facilitate touch or avoid it. For example, during court proceedings, judges are always well away from the accused, and there is no chance of touching. Of course, there is an obvious safety issue here, but perhaps our courts would be more inclusive and less stressful if under certain circumstances the judges were more accessible. And then there is the reverse situation with politicians, who like nothing more than to get out and "press the flesh" and kiss a few babies. Do they know that getting face-to-face with people and touching them results in trust and inclusion? Donald Trump insisted on continuing with his face-to-face rallies during the 2020 presidential campaign, even though Covid-19 was rampant throughout the United States. Did he or his advisors know the importance of this move? Maybe we all need to be a little more aware that when people touch us, perhaps they are trying to alter our view.

You might now be considering the impact of Covid-19. Many countries went into different types of lockdown, where people were restricted in their movements and whom they socialized with. We were all told to wear masks and keep our distance. And no touching! Is it any surprise that mental illness skyrocketed? That suicide rates more than doubled in some areas? More about these issues later, but I think you can see that we can't overturn millions of years of evolution in a single year due to a pandemic. Yes, we needed to be cautious, and we needed to respond to the situation, given that so many people were dying, but this cannot be the new normal. We need to connect, and that involves touch and real, live face-to-face communication.

Without touch and real time spent with real people, we suffer. This is highlighted by the devastating mental and physical health issues that occur when people are lonely or isolated. We crave the support of others, time spent with loved ones and friends, and the feedback we get from seeing their faces, watching their body language, and feeling their touch. The happy neurotransmitters that are released help us to feel relaxed, open, happy, safe, loved, and connected. As the connected species, we need real connection to stay mentally and physically healthy.

In summary:

- Hanging out with a good friend is better for reducing stress than any available medication.
- Spending time together with people we trust results in the release of neurotransmitters that result in feelings of joy, trust, openness, connection, and calm.
- Touch is an important part of greeting and cements bonds, increases connection, and even affects our decisions.

TIP OF THE CHAPTER

The best treatment for stress and anxiety is socializing with those we feel connected to. Make sure you are spending time with friends on a regular basis. Make sure it is face-to-face where you can see, smell, and feel them. You want that swarm of neurotransmitters released.

Part III

THE NEGATIVE CONSEQUENCES OF OUR DRIVE TO CONNECT

"A stereotype may be negative or positive, but even positive stereotypes present two problems: They are cliches, and they present a human being as far more simple and uniform than any human being actually is."

—Nancy Kress[1]

Part III

THE NEGATIVE CONSEQUENCES OF OUR DRIVE TO CONNECT

· 8 ·

Racism, Sexism, and Other -Isms

*T*he year 2020 was dominated not only by Covid-19 but also by several other significant events. There were worldwide mass gatherings in support of the Black Lives Matter movement, rallies in response to the #MeToo movement, and the appearance of Far Right groups like the Proud Boys and QAnon and Far Left groups like Antifa. Many of these groups and movements already existed, but they seemed to come to a head in 2020. And then there was Donald Trump's Make America Great Again (MAGA) movement, which buoyed the Far Right and incited the Far Left. What do all these groups and movements have in common? Whether justified or not, right or wrong, they are examples of the in-group versus out-group mentality that is part of our DNA. We are driven to create groups so that we feel safe in a common cause. When we do, we stop listening or even hearing what the other group is saying, and reasonable debate ceases. The year 2020, for me anyway, will be remembered as the year our group mentality went into overdrive.

The US Capitol riot was an excellent example of this group mentality. Trump spent much of his political career creating a strong in-group and, as a result, many out-groups. He did so with the utmost precision by invoking both nationalism and ideologies. It started with the "Make America Great Again" tagline. Of course, this statement suggests that America is not currently great and that someone is responsible for this decline. Who? He quickly started pointing the finger at other politicians with his "drain the swamp" rhetoric, the "Left," immigrants from south of the border, foreign countries and imported products, the media, science, and so on. He very quickly established an "us versus them" mentality and made sure the circle encompassed people who would rally behind him. And he made that border between "us and them" concrete by starting to build a wall. He then refused to concede defeat. He blamed all and sundry for cheating his in-group out of the election. He announced that he would not attend the inauguration of his competitor, Joe Biden, and rallied his in-group with an inspiring speech. He then sent them off to protect the group. The Capitol riots were the result of an influencer utilizing the connected species' drive for an in-group to attempt to maintain power.

I don't know whether behavioral scientists were advising the Trump organization on how to create an in-group or if one simply grew organically out of its marketing strategies. What I do know is that this period will be studied and written about from many different angles for years to come. However, it is not the first time that a politician has used the in-group mentality to such an extent. Politics is all about in-groups and out-groups. It is about creating a movement that people who support your policies and agenda can get behind and feel a part of.

What was different about the Trump version, in my opinion anyway, was the extreme faith that many of his supporters put in his every word. Even when the facts completely opposed his statements and he contradicted himself, they continued to believe. Looking at the pictures of the Capitol riots, "his people" were not only angry but willing to risk their lives. Such extreme levels of dedication and faith are usually reserved for religious groups and cults, where one's soul is invoked and eternal damnation threatened for not supporting the leader. However, in this case, it was simply another politician taking control in a system where the federal government doesn't have much control over the day-to-day lives of ordinary citizens anyway. So how did the Trump organization create such a following?

One thing Trump did extremely well was target and alienate already established groups. For example, he started by targeting the politicians themselves, which was an interesting tactic. The "drain the swamp" battle cry targeted both sides of the political spectrum, Democrats and Republicans. Yet, he was running as a Republican! How could he move Republicans to the out-group while not losing his in-group? Well, he wasn't a politician or a Republican; he was a businessman and a TV personality. Not a politician at all and therefore not part of that group, he could create his own group. The hardcore Republican voters would continue to support whoever was the Republican nominee. He created a new group of voters who previously weren't hardcore Republican but became hardcore Trump supporters. Remember, he significantly increased the Republican vote in both elections. And this is now a huge problem for the Republican Party because not all the Trump supporters are dedicated Republican supporters. They are Trump supporters. His effective "drain the swamp" battle cry played on the lack of trust in the existing political groups, including Republicans, and so many of the Trump supporters still won't vote for those they deem to be politicians. Trump alienated existing groups to create a very strong in-group of his own: MAGA.

Let's turn now to how Joe Biden managed to win when Trump had created such a loyal in-group. Biden also had a battle cry and created a loyal in-group. His campaign admonished voters to "join in the battle for the soul of the nation." Again, this pitted one group against another, creating an in-group and an out-group, dividing people into "us and them." If you are having a battle, then there must be an enemy, someone you are battling against. Does the soul of our nation belong to them or us? Join us if you believe in these ideals or if you don't belong to their group. And again, millions of years of evolution, of living in groups to survive and thrive, results in active, innate, implicit neural responses. Biden, once he was elected, changed this discourse very quickly and started talking about healing and everyone coming together. He then tried to widen the circle with statements about working tirelessly for those from both sides and bringing them together. This is an important move as a politician in a democratic society because he needs unity. But make no mistake, Biden's in-group was created by alienating Trump's in-group.

Let's move on from politics to some of the other huge events that happened in 2020. The Black Lives Matter movement developed significantly, sparked by another black man being killed by a white policeman in the United States. This quickly escalated and resulted in both peaceful protests and riots all over the world. The Black Lives Matter movement started in 2013 after George Zimmerman, a policeman, was acquitted of charges related to the shooting death of a black teenager. However, it was revitalized (for lack of a better word) in 2020 when George Floyd was killed by another white police officer, Derek Chauvin. The United States is not the only country in the world where black men die in custody more frequently than white men.[1] In Australia, Aboriginal and

Torres Strait Islander people are significantly overrepresented in incarceration, and the percentage of deaths while in custody is significantly greater as well.[2] Similar statistics are evident elsewhere, including the United Kingdom.[3] Why does such racism and discrimination exist?

I think the first thing we need to consider is that discrimination is not always against people of color. And I say this not to diminish the awful treatment of people of color both past and present but to frame this as a more universal phenomenon that has disproportionately affected certain groups—for example, the well-documented racial cleansing of Uyghurs, who are native to Northwest China, by the Republic of China or the treatment of the Romani people in Europe, ethnic pygmy populations in Central Africa, and Bantu people in Somalia, to name a few. Racism, sadly, has occurred and continues to occur all over the world. Can we identify why? And then can we develop methods to stop it?

Racism is a sad consequence of our evolution. Racism occurs because there are races: physical differences between groups of people. And the evolution of races occurred because of our drive to connect. Different races evolved because we, as the connected species, created groups that we belonged to. This meant that when we spread out around the world, we maintained these groups and evolved within them. Separation between groups resulted in slight differences in our evolution due to local environmental forces and niches that we exploited. I have white skin because the majority of my ancestors came from colder climates. My niece and nephew have brown skin because half their ancestors came from the tropics. Different races evolved due to our spreading around the world combined with our drive for connection.

We have already discussed the effect of this drive to live in groups: the capacity to automatically identify and empathize with those in our group and the tendency to believe what they say and feel comfort and safety when they are close by. Sadly, the other side of that coin is that we automatically identify those who are not part of our group, distrust them, misinterpret what they say, and feel stressed and cautious when they are close by. This process is automatic and innate. We are often completely unaware we possess these feelings and biases. And then remember the fact that we all engage in confirmation bias. We notice when we see something that confirms our stereotypes, and we are less likely to notice things that contradict our worldview. These processes that result in racism are innate. This is not an excuse but a first pass at understanding the consequences of our evolution, so that with constant questioning and reflection, we might override them.

In understanding racism, we need to factor in our face-perception mechanisms. In chapter 3, we discussed how we automatically orient or attend to faces of cross-races faster than our own race—the "cross-race effect." Interestingly, Professor Gang Sun and colleagues showed that if participants are from a place with a homogenous population, in this case China, then the subjects show a strong cross-race effect.[4] When the participants are from a more heterogenous mixed-race population, such as Israel, those effects are diminished. This study suggests that being part of a group of mixed races decreases your automatic bias to detect a race other than your own. The crucial thing about this research is that it shows our automatic face-perception abilities are altered by experience.

The influence of experience on our face-perception abilities is highlighted by incidents in Australia. The indigenous population represents only about 3 percent of the population, and racism toward Aboriginal people and Torres Strait Islanders in Australia remains a major issue. This was brought to light in all its infamous glory when a legend of our homegrown sport of Australian Rules Football, Adam Goodes, was named Australian of the Year in 2014. He was brave enough to call out racism when a thirteen-year-old girl in the crowd called him an "ape." Much of the Australian media portrayed Goodes as the aggressor, and he was then taunted by crowds at virtually every match he played from that point on. He retired as a result of the impact this had on his health and well-being. A documentary called *The Australian Dream* covers Goodes's life and shows the racism the Australian public and media perpetuated. Unfortunately, this is not an isolated incident and doesn't happen only in Australia. There are many factors contributing to racism in Australia and elsewhere, but the fact that indigenous Australians make up such a small proportion of the population and are rarely seen in the media could impact our face-perception template, leading to racist behavior.

The suggestion that living in a multiracial society can alter our face-perception template and affect racism becomes even more interesting when we consider some of the studies from the United States. Although there have been mixed results, the most consistent finding is that white participants detect African American faces faster than they detect white faces in visual search displays. In contrast, African American participants don't show the reverse: instead, there is no difference in their detection of white or African American faces. Further, a series of studies by Jennifer Eberhardt, a professor at Stanford University, showed that priming white participants with a picture of an African American resulted in faster perception of a gun relative to other primes.[5] Eberhardt briefly flashed a photo of an African American face, a white face, or a simple shape and then showed a series of blurred images that became less blurry over time. Note that these faces were presented subliminally (really quickly and in the periphery), so the participants did not "see" them. When the images were preceded by the African American face, the participants saw a gun faster than when a white face was presented. Participants also showed the reverse effect. When they were presented with a subliminal image of a gun, they were then faster to see an African American face than a white face. These results are provocative and informative because while these individuals live in a multiracial country, clearly their face-perception template still shows a bias—white faces are perceived more positively than black faces.

If seeing many examples of different races can overcome the cross-race effect, why then is racism still systemic in countries where there are lots of different races? Obviously, there are many facets of racism, and I am not silly (or arrogant) enough to think that I have all the answers. But I think we can look at what people are getting not just from those they interact with directly but in the images and messages they receive from society. A lot of our experience is now based on what is presented to us on screens and billboards. If we look at the biases in the entertainment industry, the media, and advertising, we see that a particular group or race is usually favored in most countries. In Japan, a country that has been criticized by the United Nations for its deep-rooted racism, if you turn on the TV, you will see Japanese faces in all the programs, except the dubbed movies from the West. Most of the billboards and other advertising will be of Japanese people. Japan is very homogeneous in its population as well, so this is not unexpected, but disturbingly, the same pattern can be seen in more heterogenous countries as well—sending strong messages about which race is "proper," and it's usually the dominant one.

The United States is often called a melting pot. According to the US Census Bureau's 2019 estimates, the population is 60 percent white, 19 percent Hispanic and Latino, 14 percent African American, 6 percent Asian, and 1 percent Native American. So, one would think American

TV would reflect that melting pot, right? Wrong. A study by Nielsen looked at the cable TV shows in a range of major categories. In an analysis of diversity and inclusion among those programs in the 2020–2021 season, they found Native Americans and Latino people were among the most underrepresented groups relative to their numbers in the general population.[6] They used a metric called "share of screen," which is the percentage of time specific groups appear as recurring cast members. They suggest this is a good measure of how often TV viewers see these types of people. And the diversity did not match the real-world ratios: Hispanics were only on the screen 3.6 percent of the time and Native Americans just 0.1 percent of the time. Although the United States may be a melting pot, what is viewed on TV is not.

There is hope though! An important aspect of all of this is that this cross-race effect can be altered. Professor James Tanaka and his colleagues from the University of Victoria have shown that, through training, our face templates can be manipulated to incorporate other races.[7] They have shown that our ability to identify people of our race better than people of other races develops in the first twelve months of life—and it's due to exposure to the faces of a particular race. Incorporating cross-race faces in books and games that the infants see in those early years can improve the situation. Tanaka's research has also shown that even adult training can reduce the bias.[8] Experience and training improve the cross-race effect—we could all train our automatic face-detection system to treat everyone equally.

With an evolutionary lens, the adaptability of our face template makes perfect sense. We would want to determine our in-group through experience. If this mechanism were hardwired, it would require the gene associated with the trait to be linked to the gene that determines race. However, there is no single gene that determines our race. Instead, much as with language development, our genetic blueprint for being connected drives us to consolidate an in-group based on experience. The take-home message from this is that, through training, we can potentially overcome the cross-race effects and perhaps reduce our implicit biases around other races—a first step toward eliminating racism.

Not only do we need to see people of different races to train our implicit recognition of the different faces, but we also need to incorporate them into our in-group. This means that the diverse characters we see in the media must be in roles that are part of our in-group.

People we would want to hang out with. Or perhaps even a hero! If we delve into the social messages in the media further, what we see is the impact of more bias. Most films that come from Hollywood have white (male) heroes. Black heroes are rare, and when they exist, for example, in *The Matrix*, they are usually secondary to the main hero, a white male. Professor Richard Dyer discusses this in depth in his book *White: Essays on Race and Culture*. The main point he makes is that "in western representation, whites are overwhelmingly and disproportionately predominant, have the central and elaborated roles, and above all are placed as the norm, the ordinary, the standard."[9] If we bring this back to our in-group identification, the white person is depicted most often as the member you want in your group, and all other races are the villains or protagonists, members of the out-group. We need to start focusing on creating an in-group that encompasses all members of our society. What we are exposing our children and ourselves to through the media and the cinema could actively help reduce racism by incorporating all races in all roles to retrain our implicit biases and recognition system.

Will this fix the widespread problem of racism? I wish it could be that simple, but of course it is not. Confirmation bias is a major obstacle to overcoming racism because we notice when behaviors or actions confirm our bias. If you believe that a particular race is rude, then every time you see a person from that race being rude, you will attribute that behavior to their being of that race. Conversely, you won't notice all the times you interact with people of that race who are polite, kind, and friendly. You will also be less likely to notice the times you interact with people of your own race who are rude. What we need to remember is that while confirmation bias is innate and automatic, the stereotypes and beliefs we have about different races are learned. So what we need to do is *change* our stereotypes. We need to change our beliefs about different races. If we can set more positive stereotypes about other races, then our confirmation bias will be confirming positive rather than negative ideas and beliefs.

Let's move on from racism to another awful -ism: sexism. When it comes to sexism and negative ideas and beliefs, I always find it difficult to reconcile our current situation. In his classic song "Real Men," Joe Jackson sings, "And if there's war between the sexes, then there'll be no people left," a beautiful line in a beautiful song that is bleedingly obvious. But it does make me wonder how sexism ever came about. From an evolutionary point of view, it doesn't make much sense. I mean you need (technology aside) both a man and woman to at least get together momentarily to produce offspring. And as we have spoken about, to ensure survival we have evolved a brain that seeks an in-group—a brain that implicitly detects, and drives us to maintain connection with, members of our in-group. And that brain evolved to enable us to rear young and survive. So how did we end up in a situation where the sexes are separated into "us and them?" How did patriarchy ever come to exist in a species that is driven to connect for mutual benefit?

My friend Gunter Swoboda, a psychologist and the author of *Making Good Men Great*, has explored patriarchy and its role in sexism.[10] He suggests that the growth of patriarchy, and therefore the relegation of women and children to a lesser status, occurred only in the last few thousand years or so. Sexism—which, let's be honest, is really about the subjugation of women for the benefit of men—is about power and privilege. And if we think about it like this, then it too can be seen as a consequence of this drive for an in-group. But it is *not innate* and has occurred very recently in evolutionary terms. When compared to racism—which, based on records and the fact that we have clearly defined races, has probably occurred for hundreds of thousands of years—sexism is a recent "man-made" phenomenon. If we look at most ancient human groups, such as Australian Aboriginals, Kalahari Bushmen, Native Americans, and so on, we find that sexism did not exist in most cases until Western society and patriarchy arrived.

For example, many Native American traditional societies were either egalitarian or matriarchal in structure. Professor Alice Schlegel from the University of Arizona, who studied the Hopi for many years, found that the larger clans have a male and a female head who lead together, and individual households are run by the female.[11] Patriarchy is a new phenomenon that was forced upon them. For example, the term *squaw* was used as one way of instilling patriarchal values in Native Americans by Western society. The term is a label used by non-Natives and is considered offensive, derogatory, misogynist, and racist by Native Americans.[12] The high level of domestic abuse in many Native American communities as a result of the destruction of their traditional values is horrifying and recent.[13]

If we look at many older societies, they held "the woman" in high esteem. The Yangshao civilization in China is thought to have been a

matriarchal society, and both the ancient Mayan and Persian civiliza-
tions treated men and women equally. The pharaohs of ancient Egypt
were both male and female. We have all heard of Queens Nefertiti and
Cleopatra, who were very powerful. The terms *Mother Earth* and *Mother
Nature* are believed to come from pagan societies, which had many rituals around childbirth and the importance of the woman. Across multiple
societies, it seems to be the arrival of patriarchal values that marks the
shift from an inclusive society (at least regarding men and women) to a
society in which the man is the boss.

This shift seems to coincide with the formation of several organized
religions that also place man as the leader. This creates an elite group,
men, and encircles that group. Members of that group want to protect
the group from members of the out-group—in this case, women. The
ramifications of this have been extreme. In some countries girls are not
allowed to attend school or leave the house without a male escort. And
the rate of domestic violence and sex-based murder around the world is
horrifying. The talk of equality between the sexes should be about creating an in-group that encompasses everyone. Focusing on that ideal, I
believe, will help in our discussions around this difficult topic so we can
move back to a society where women and men are equal.

Why do we need to encompass both men and women within the
same circle, the larger in-group? We already talked about automatic
detection of male versus female faces and that we orient toward male
angry faces faster than female angry faces. Angry men get noticed! We
also have a whole bunch of stereotypes associated with males versus
females that continue to reinforce the separation between the groups.
Remember, confirmation bias is based on our stereotypes and is automatic. I bet you could list off many of the common stereotypes: men are
stoic, strong, mathematical, analytical, and brave; women are emotional,
caring, nurturing, and talkative. I will skip the negative ones, but I'm
sure you are aware of them. And if these are our stereotypes, then they
are the behaviors our automatic confirmation bias is going to highlight.
We will notice when a man is analytical, logical, and brave, and we
are less likely to notice when a woman shows these same qualities, for
example. We need to increase the circle to envelop us all and modify the
stereotypes to start the process toward treating everyone equally.

The first step to eliminating these stereotypes is to realize that there
is no "male brain" and no "female brain." There are just human brains.

Yes, that is correct—there is no evidence of a difference between the brains of men and women. All those books you might have read on how women are from Venus or claims of a "female" brain just don't stand up to rigorous scientific analysis. In fact, a meta-analysis published in 2021 that looked at the huge amount of research conducted over the past thirty years found the only difference was the overall size.[14] And in relation to brains, size doesn't matter—if it did, then elephants would be vastly more intelligent than we are. Males' and females' brains are the same.

The effect of male/female stereotypes has been shown in many different circumstances. For example, physicians treat men and women differently for the same symptoms. You would think that physicians would be objective and treat symptoms, but studies show that when they are aware of the sex of the patient, they make different diagnostic decisions.[15] Research shows teachers treat male and female students in their classrooms differently,[16] and similar effects have been shown for police officers[17] and paramedics.[18] These are all professions in which objective, rational decisions should be made based on behavior and situation. But the decisions are impacted by sex stereotypes, which are reinforced by confirmation bias. We need to increase the circle and create an inclusive group that encompasses everyone.

A glaring example of sex stereotyping occurred at the March Madness college basketball event in Indiana, in the United States, in 2021. March Madness is a billion-dollar event organized by the National Collegiate Athletic Association, showcasing the best male and female college basketball teams. Ali Kershner, a coach at Stanford University, posted images to Instagram of the discrepancy between the weight rooms provided to male and female players. While the men had access to an extensive training area set up with weights and benches and everything else they needed, the women had access to just one rack of small dumbbells and yoga mats. Sex stereotyping still exists and affects so many aspects of our lives.

There are lots of other -isms we could talk about, but I will leave that to others with greater expertise in those areas. Hopefully you can see from these few examples that our brains' evolution to enable connection plays a major role in the issues we so often see in our society today. By creating an in-group, by definition, we are also creating an out-group. To be a group we need to create a sense of what it means to be a member of that group, who belongs to the group and why. These members then have common goals, attributes, and reasons for being part of the group. And those who are not members, therefore, don't have those same goals, attributes, and reasons. Our automatic face perception and our confirmation bias then take over, and whether our beliefs are true or not, we focus on instances when members of the group show behaviors that reinforce membership. And we notice and highlight when out-group members' behavior demonstrates and reinforces the reasons why they are not a member of the group. As the great psychologist William James said, "A great many people think they are thinking when they are merely rearranging their prejudices."[19]

But there is hope! We know that many of the underlying processes are influenced by experience—developed by infant and childhood exposure and moderated by further exposure in adulthood. We can use these foundations to develop effective methods to combat at least some of the sources of racism, sexism, and other -isms. We can increase our circles, our in-group, to encompass everyone. Next, we will discuss another consequence of our drive to connect: pandemics!

In summary:

- Politics is all about creating a large in-group that creates division.
- Racism is a consequence of our drive to connect and maintain groups; however, our face template is flexible, and stereotypes can and should be challenged.
- Sexism is not innate and has not existed for as long as racism.
- We need to work on our stereotypes and biases.

TIP OF THE CHAPTER

How broad is your face template? Our template is the average of all the faces we see every day—if we see a narrow range of faces, we will be more likely to have negative responses to people from other races. Just looking at faces in a book or magazine can widen our template. Spend time each day looking at a range of faces to improve your automatic face response system.

· 9 ·

Viral Viruses

*Y*es, 2020 was a crazy year, to say the least. Not only was our group mentality getting a serious workout, but Covid-19 hit the world stage with vengeance. Pretty quickly we were all talking about socially isolating and organizing virtual gatherings for work and social events. Schools were closed for face-to-face teaching, and we all had to learn how to manage our work lives and our kids' schooling from home. Within three weeks I had to shift my first-year neuroscience course from face-to-face lectures and lab sessions to 100 percent online learning—without disappointing approximately one thousand students. My experience was nothing compared to the plight of those who lost their jobs or, even worse, loved ones due to the pandemic. Yes, Covid-19 really turned the world upside down (although the world is a sphere floating in space, so there isn't really an up or down!).

But how did a minuscule particle that we can't see with the naked eye send the entire world into panic? There are several interconnected reasons why we as the connected species are so affected by this and other viruses. First, viruses need hosts and need to be transferred from one host to another. This requires close contact between hosts, and as we discussed, humans rely on close contact. Second, we are more connected now than ever before, with international airflights at a peak in 2019. Third, to stop transmission we need to isolate from one another, and isolation brings a multitude of both mental and physical health problems. We tried to connect online, but it's just not the same as real connection. But it was also our connection and our ability to cooperate on a global scale that resulted in the delivery of multiple vaccines in record time.

Covid-19 threw us a curveball, exploiting our connection, but it was also our connection that saved us.

Now, this was not our first global rodeo when it comes to pandemics. They have happened before, and they will happen again. Airline travel probably exacerbated the issue in the current situation, but several societies in the past were annihilated by rampant disease. For example, in 1520, the Aztec Empire was completely wiped out by a smallpox infestation brought to the region by the Spanish.[1] Before the arrival of the Spanish, the Americas had been isolated from Europe, and many of the viruses that had already traveled around Europe had not yet made it to America. When the Spanish arrived, the locals had no immunity to smallpox, so they suffered.

A few years ago, I was visiting a good friend who lived in Greenwich Village, and we sat in Blackheath Park, a beautiful, large, open green space in Central London—albeit one with a sinister past. During the Black Death, this was one of many areas used to dispose of the bodies of plague victims. The Black Death was a bubonic plague that killed one-third of the world's population in the fourteenth century.[2] And it occurred again in the seventeenth century. It was carried by rats and spread quickly because people were living in large cities without proper sewerage or sanitation. As the death rate was so high, the bodies were dumped in several mass graves, including in what is now Blackheath Park.

Living in large groups helped spread these diseases, but cooperating in large numbers has helped us combat them. Based on genetic tracing, we know that transmissible diseases have been around for millions of years, but these diseases would have been primarily isolated to small groups.[3] When we started living in larger communities, we gave these transmissible diseases the upper hand. They require close contact and large numbers of hosts to thrive and mutate. Our large towns and cities are fertile ground for these diseases to spread. However, through our connection we have discovered ways of tackling the diseases head-on. Through scientific endeavor and ingenuity, we now know how diseases transmit and that sanitation and disinfection can slow and even stop their spread. And in cases where this is not enough, we have developed antibiotics, vaccines, and other drugs to combat them. None of these scientific discoveries would have come about without us working in diverse yet interconnected specializations. While connection has increased the spread of these diseases, connection has also enabled us to combat them. It is a double-edged sword that we could not discard even if we wanted to.

So what is it about viruses that make them so hard to stop? Well, viruses are tricky because they have evolved to take advantage of our and other species' drive for connection. There are three important aspects of a virus: its virulence, its incubation period, and its infection rate. Virulence is its ability to cause disease in the host. The incubation period is basically how long you have the virus before you have symptoms. The infection rate measures how easily it is transferred from one host to another. And there is an interesting relationship between these attributes that means social species, like us, are susceptible to pandemics.

You see, a virus "wants" to be passed on from one host to another. Covid-19 was so successful because it has a relatively long incubation period. That is, there is a reasonably long period between when people contract the virus and when they show symptoms. And if you are not showing symptoms, then you don't know you are carrying the virus, so you pass it on to other hosts. It is also virulent in only a subset of the population. In most cases only the elderly or those with preexisting medical issues are susceptible to severe illness or death. So, a large majority of the population can contract the virus and carry it around, passing it on to others. And it is very infectious, transmissible via tiny particles in the air, possibly even via air conditioning. All of these aspects made it an extremely successful virus for a species that is now connected across the world and loves nothing more than traveling long distances. It passed from person to person, easily spreading across the globe.

Combating Covid-19 required many countries to instigate lockdown measures that affected many peoples' health and well-being. It was an extremely successful virus because it didn't require direct contact between individuals but was transmissible via aerosol (our breath). This meant that unlike with many other viruses, just washing hands and keeping others at arm's length did not suffice to stop the spread. We needed to instigate quite strict measures, such as mask wearing, a lot of testing, and in many cases lockdowns or isolation. The impact of these measures was very effective in slowing the virus in many countries around the world. Countries that were slow to act saw hospitals and emergency wards overwhelmed and many more deaths. But there were also negative impacts on our health and well-being in the countries that underwent lockdown measures, which will be evident for years to come.[4]

I think the term *social distancing* was a misnomer that possibly impacted stress and anxiety levels. We were actually being asked to practice "physical distancing." We were allowed to socialize, and as social animals, we needed to socialize. As already discussed, a large percentage of our brain has evolved not only to enable us but to require us to socialize. We know that people who are socially isolated become depressed very quickly. Socializing is extremely important, especially in times of stress. To stop the transfer of the virus, we needed to stop physical contact. The term *social distancing* sent the wrong message.

The physical distancing and lockdowns have had quite a profound impact on people's mental health. In all countries where lockdowns occurred, there has been a significant increase in mental illness, including anxiety, depression, and suicide. There has also been an increase in domestic violence, separation and divorce, and alcohol abuse. We are not a species that handles isolation very well at all. Professor Daisy Fancourt from University College London tracked some of the effects of lockdown in the United Kingdom.[5] She had more than seventy thousand participants fill out weekly online surveys about well-being, mental health, and coping strategies. She suggests that the lockdowns all around the world had effects similar to incarceration.

So why did we see such an impact on well-being during the lockdowns? As we've discussed, enforced isolation such as solitary confinement, or in this case lockdown, is detrimental to social animals. We see increases in anxiety, stress, depression, and feelings of not coping. In extreme cases, we see suicidal thoughts, psychosis, and paranoia and even structural changes to the brain. Why? Being isolated or locked down is against our very nature and results in pain and suffering.

Of course, we weren't completely isolated. We had the internet, and we had our devices. We could watch TV, or Netflix, or Stan, or Disney; we had Facebook to see what everyone else was up to; we had Pinterest and LinkedIn and Twitter to keep up with the latest trends and controversies; we could chat or text with our friends. We could even Zoom, or Skype, or FaceTime, or use any of the hundreds of other ways to chat with someone over cyberspace. We were all working from home, schooling from home, entertaining from home, and doing everything else from home. I attended Thanksgiving at a friend's house in the United States, something I hadn't experienced since I lived in Boston. I visited regularly with friends in Cambridge and Liverpool in the United

Kingdom. I went to many birthdays with friends overseas whom I hadn't seen in years. But I was still lonely and isolated. Why? All this was done in cyberspace. We have not evolved to connect through a device. Ten years of using devices does not override millions of years of evolution. We were isolated from what we really needed.

Remember my previous metaphor about connecting over the internet being akin to eating fast food? It's like that rewarding short-term sugar buzz that lacks the nutrients of a healthy home-cooked meal. So, even though we all thought this "new normal" (I despised that phrase because there was nothing "normal" about it!) meant that we were more connected than ever, we felt lonely, stressed, depressed, and isolated. We need to connect on a real, not a virtual, level. We need to be able to see the whole person. We need to be able to touch and communicate without a screen between us. Why is it that being on a device increases our stress levels, makes us more distractable, and is not the same as being with someone in person? All the important brain mechanisms we've been talking about evolved in the "real world" to automatically process information to foster connection. Online, either that information is not available or it is distorted, resulting in us often making incorrect interpretations during cyber communications. Let's look more deeply at a few of these issues.

As we talked about in chapter 7, touch is an important part of greeting a friend or loved one. Most cultures have specific rules or standards for proper greeting, which usually involves touch. And loved ones and close friends are usually touched more than strangers or new acquaintances. Over a screen and through the distance of cyberspace, we lose that important link and fail to receive the flush of important neurotransmitters that are released when we are touched. This was even an issue after lockdowns ceased as we were told not to touch other people—to keep our distance from each other. If we had to touch, we were to use other greetings such as a foot or elbow tap. Again, we lost an important opportunity to touch when greeting a member of our group. We were missing out on all those happy hormones and neurotransmitters that make us feel connected when we greet.

The next issue with trying to connect over cyberspace is that body language is difficult to read because we only see the other person's face (and perhaps shoulders). As we have discussed, we automatically gain a huge amount of information from body language. We connect by mirroring each other's movements. We understand how others are feeling and if their mood changes via their gestures and posture. These are vital aspects of communication, and although most of us don't realize we are doing it, we are, constantly—but not over cyberspace.

Another issue with the "new normal" is taking turns. When we are really with each other, we automatically know when to talk and when to listen. We do this based on body language, eye gaze, head nodding, and so on. This is especially true when more than two people are talking. When everyone turns to a particular person, that person knows it is their turn to talk or that they are expected to talk. When someone wants to talk, they will try to catch people's eyes through small gestures and eye contact. All of that turn-taking information is lost when we are on devices. We are all looking straight at a camera or a screen, and everyone is looking directly at us (or even worse, not looking at us because of their screen position!). It is impossible to know whom someone is looking at and to use these subtle cues to attract attention or indicate your turn. We lose all these important turn-taking cues when we are on a device.

We also have the issue of not knowing what the other people are doing. Often people's cameras won't be placed where the screen is. So even though they are looking at the screen and therefore at you, it looks like they are looking away. We automatically read a lot from where someone is looking. It is one of our oldest and strongest abilities to attend to or understand where other people (and animals) are looking. When we are talking to someone, we expect them to look at us. And even though they may be gazing raptly at us via another screen, the perception that they are looking away and ignoring us is stronger.

Of course, sometimes they might actually be doing other things! People will often check email or text while on a cyber call, something they would not do if you were talking to them in person (although, worryingly, that is a increasing trend too—we'll talk about the impact of devices on our conversations and connection later on). If the camera is on, we can see them not attending. If we are talking, we get the message that the person isn't listening (and they probably aren't). Even worse, many people turn off their cameras so you can't see what they are doing, and we (or at least I) assume they are not listening and don't care. This is an assumption, and they may have a good reason for turning off the camera, but again, our assumption, when we lack the usual cues that someone is engaged, is that they aren't. Over cyberspace we don't actually know what another person is doing, but we automatically make assumptions based on our millions of years of communicating in the real world.

From what we've covered so far, you know that we have evolved to enable ourselves to live in groups, to communicate, to collaborate, to benefit from the positive response we get from being around other people. A large percentage of our brain is dedicated to a gamut of automatic and implicit processes that enable us to read people's minds based on their body language, eye gaze, and facial expressions. We also have interconnected processes that automatically control or respond to these cues to further our connection to people within our in-group. When we talk on devices, at best we lose the ability to use many of these abilities; at worst the situation is misinterpreted, and we read messages incorrectly, causing us to feel frustrated and disappointed. We need to connect in real life, just like we need a wholesome home-cooked meal.

Face masks also impacted our ability to connect and added to feelings of depression, anxiety, and stress. I understand why they were necessary. I believe we should wear them if there is any chance that we are infected or if there is infection in the society in which we are moving. But they do impact our connection (and I'm not referring to the fact that they are bloody uncomfortable and always make my glasses fog up!). No, I'm talking about the fact that wearing a face mask covers up a large part of one of our communication devices.

About 40 percent of our ability to understand what someone is saying comes from lip reading. The McGurk effect (check it out on You-Tube!) is a great example of this fact. If I show you a video where the audio is presenting one phoneme (e.g., "ba, ba") but the visuals show someone mouthing a different phoneme (e.g., "ga, ga"), you perceive a third phoneme entirely (e.g., "da, da"). This demonstrates the impact of lip reading on speech perception.[6] Professor Rajka Smiljanic and her colleagues from the University of Texas showed that mask wearing significantly affects participants' word recognition and memory, especially when the conditions are less than perfect.[7] If we are not able to read lips, we are missing important information, making it harder for us to understand others. (This is even harder for people with any degree of hearing impairment.) Second, facial expressions indicate how others are feeling. It is difficult to read facial expressions hidden behind a mask. And finally, remember, we mimic the facial expressions that we see, which tends to make us feel what others are feeling. By seeing another person smile at you, you also smile, and this releases those happy neurotransmitters to brighten our day. However, Professor Till Kastendieck and his colleagues from Humboldt-Universität zu Berlin found that people don't automatically mimic a person's smile when they are wearing a mask.[8] If we don't see others smile, then we don't smile back, and we don't get those happy hormones!

Soon after the face masks became compulsory in hospitals, staff noticed that patients were not coping as well because they couldn't tell what nurses and doctors were thinking. When some hospitals moved to clear face masks so that patients could see the faces of their caregivers, staff reported that the issues resolved. In support of this anecdotal evidence, Professor Felix Grundman and colleagues from the University of Groningen showed that wearing masks negatively affects emotion recognition, perceived trustworthiness, likeability, and closeness.[9] Face masks cover our mouths, which are a very important part of our face for communication and connection; losing these cues impacts our mental health.

Overall, 2020 will be remembered for a number of reasons, but Covid-19 must be among the most infamous. It was not the first time the world has dealt with a severe pandemic, nor was Covid the deadliest disease we have had to tackle. But by taking advantage of our astonishing global connection, it did spread worldwide faster than any we have experienced before. Airline travel was at an all-time high, resulting in the disease spreading both within and between countries extremely quickly. The long incubation period, high infection rate, and low virulence in much of the population made it a very successful virus. Sadly, not only did we suffer the direct health consequences of the virus, but lockdowns, physical distancing, and mask wearing meant that we, as the connected species, suffered as a result of the isolation as well. However, cooperation across the world meant that multiple vaccines were created, tested, and approved within record time, resulting in many lives saved!

In summary:

- Viruses spread through our species, causing illness, because we are connected and they require hosts.
- Air travel, long incubation period, high infection rate, and generally low virulence exacerbated Covid-19's effectiveness.

- The lockdowns, physical distancing, and face masks affected our mental health in ways we will continue to feel for some time.
- Our connection and ability to collaborate and cooperate across the world meant multiple vaccines were developed in record time.

TIP OF THE CHAPTER

Nothing compares to connecting in real life with friends and loved ones. Organize regular catch-ups with those who are important to you.

· *10* ·

A Crowded Room

$\mathcal{A}$s I mentioned earlier, I grew up in a small country town in Australia. Our home was only a couple of streets from farmland. We often went into the forest, picking blackberries and mushrooms. It was anything but overcrowded. I remember vividly when I was young and my mother took me and my siblings to visit her half sister in Melbourne. That night my mother took my sisters out for dinner and a movie, and my younger brother and I stayed with my aunt. She lived in an apartment block. There were no apartment blocks where I lived, and my memory of the evening is of feeling very cramped and scared. I was sure that someone would break in and hurt us. I could hear traffic outside and people in other apartments. It terrified me, and I still remember the sense of anxiety and dread.

Why did I feel that sense of dread? One reason was simply exposure. I had never been to a large city before, and the sheer size was overwhelming. However, there is more to it than that. When I worked at the Massachusetts Institute of Technology, I used to love going to New York City on the Chinatown bus for the weekend. It was always great fun and quite a buzz, but it wasn't relaxing. When I want to relax, when I want a break, I go to places that are quiet and don't feel crowded. It is an interesting juxtaposition that we are the connected species, and we love to be around our in-group—and yet we need time alone too. We get joy out of connecting and socializing, but there is a limit to the amount of socializing or the size of the group that feels safe.

It turns out, there is good evidence that there is a limit to the density of groups in which we find comfort. Although we suffer when we are isolated or alone, we also suffer when we feel overcrowded.

Overcrowding causes a range of mental and physical illnesses in both humans and other social species. And overcrowding in humans usually happens in urban environments that are uniquely different from the natural environments in which we evolved. Urban environments add to our discomfort as they put stress and strain on our perceptual system. These overall feelings of distress result in higher levels of anxiety and increased vigilance. Parents are often more cautious with their children, resulting in restricted opportunities for free play, which is essential for children to learn important social skills. And with the increased number of faces in crowded urban environments, our automatic face and facial expression perception is in overdrive, adding to our anxiety. There is a limit to our drive to connect and the size of the cities that we feel comfortable living in.

In fact, when populations become too crowded or dense, there is a negative impact on society. In a 1962 piece published in *Scientific American*, Professor John B. Calhoun coined the term *behavioral sink* to describe the decline or collapse in societal behavior resulting from overcrowding.[1] Calhoun conducted a series of experiments in which he gave groups of rats all the food and water they needed. This "rat utopia" enabled uncontrolled breeding and population growth. However, Calhoun and his colleagues observed a complete breakdown of these groups once the population numbers got to a critical level. Many of the female rats were either unable to carry a pregnancy to full term or died during delivery of their litters. Those that were successful at childbirth failed to show normal maternal instincts to care for the pups. The male rats showed severe behavioral disturbances, including sexual deviation, cannibalism, overactivity, and withdrawal. These studies have been argued to provide insight into the potential collapse of our societies if populations become too dense.

I know what you are thinking: rats and humans are very different species! And you are right—the extrapolation is great indeed. Several research groups have tried to test for similar results with human populations. Of course, overcrowding is a difficult situation to replicate scientifically with humans due to ethical considerations. Placing a group of humans in a "human utopia" and observing what happens when population growth results in overcrowding would not get past any ethics review board I have ever dealt with. Therefore, studies in humans have used very different methods and have had quite mixed results.

Some researchers have used these human studies to dismiss Calhoun's work as irrelevant, but the studies were never really comparable. For example, Professor Jonathan Freedman and his colleagues from Stanford University tested students' memory or creativity under different levels of crowding for four hours at a time.[2] They showed no effect of crowding under these conditions and argued that Calhoun's work was therefore not relevant to humans. However, Professor Morag MacDonald from Birmingham City University has shown that, in keeping with Calhoun's work, overcrowding in prisons results in severe mental health issues and increased violence.[3] Although prisons are not "human utopias," they are environments in which the human subjects are enclosed and monitored closely, like the rats in the original studies.

In support of Calhoun's original work, recent studies in a range of animal models, including primates, have also shown significant effects of crowding on stress levels and social behavior. They have also highlighted significant structural and functional brain changes in the part of the brain known as the prefrontal cortex. The prefrontal cortex is a key area involved in learning and understanding our behavior and the behavior of others, especially in a social context. Damage to this area of the cortex has a serious impact on social interactions and stress. These animal models provide strong support for Calhoun's original concerns.

I remember many years ago being at a music festival, and Nirvana was playing. The group had only very recently become famous, and the crowd was way too large for the venue. During the concert I was absolutely enthralled by the band. Kurt Cobain had the crowd eating out of his hand and was absolutely mesmerizing. The Violent Femmes played next and continued to entertain like only they can. It was when the band left the stage and the event was over that stress levels went up very quickly—there were too many people in the venue and not enough exits.

Have you ever noticed that some people start feeling anxious in crowded situations that you are happy to enjoy? Or perhaps you have felt overwhelmed in a crowd where your friends have been enjoying themselves?

Crowding, especially in humans, is an important yet complicated beast. It has been suggested that crowding may not be simply a physical phenomenon but rather a subjective experience of an individual. There is now a distinction made between "density" as a physical measure and "crowding" as a subjective response. "Crowded" is now classified as a feeling (rather than an absolute), and therefore different people can feel crowded under different circumstances. These factors change from one individual to another and include an individual's need for privacy, ability to control a situation, or social role. The argument is that increased density might be inevitable, but human beings are capable of coping with crowding under the right conditions.

There has been quite a bit of work in how to design cities, apartment blocks, and other high-density housing to enable privacy and perceived control to minimize any negative effects of crowding. Just because a city is densely populated doesn't mean it has to feel crowded.

Let's go back to New York City! When I visited, I felt in control. The naming of the streets is systematic and logical, and the layout of the subway system is relatively simple. Yet, after a while, I did start to feel overwhelmed. And it is not just NYC; the same happens in other large cities. I have many friends who have spent extended periods living in a large city and then moved to the suburbs or perhaps embarked on a sea change experience. They usually say it was time and felt like a weight was lifted off their shoulders. And as I mentioned before, people who live in large cities—in fact, most of us—take a relaxing holiday somewhere quiet, somewhere remote, somewhere away from the hustle and bustle of the big cities. We might head to a big city for an experience, but we head to a quiet location for relaxation.

Why do we feel more stressed and anxious in a big city as compared to on a tropical island or in a small village? As it happens, both "low-level" sensory and perceptual level issues (triggering core, basic brain mechanisms) and higher-level social issues impact our automatic responses. Let's now discuss some of the low-level sensory and perceptual issues with urban high-density living.

Our visual system evolved in a natural environment with trees, grass, hills, mountains, and so on. We have only started living in buildings and using straight roads in the last couple of hundred years. There is a big difference between the information our eyes receive when we are in a natural versus an urban environment. One way to measure the information received by our eyes is to look at the spatial frequency of the light. In a natural environment, the spatial-frequency information is primarily low. You could think of this as smooth or rounded with no sharp edges. On the other hand, urban environments are dominated by high spatial-frequency information: straight lines and hard borders. Think of the edges of buildings or signs, straight roads, and the square boxes that make up the rooms we live in. And our visual system is most in tune and able to process low spatial-frequency information. So perhaps it makes sense that we are more relaxed in these environments: nature puts less strain on our visual system than urban environments do.

Art is a great illustration of how nature is preferred (nice pun too!). A colleague, Professor Branka Spehar at the University of New South Wales, studied whether art is popular based on its relationship to our visual systems' evolution. Branka and her colleagues found that the paintings of the most successful artists are closer in spatial frequency to the natural world than to our urban environments.[4] Now you are probably rightly thinking of artists like Vincent van Gogh and Claude Monet. They often painted pictures of nature, and so perhaps not surprisingly, their paintings have the same natural spatial frequency. However, the researchers showed that even paintings by popular abstract artists like Jackson Pollock used a similar spatial-frequency profile to nature.[5] And they went on to show that a person's visual sensitivity to simple visual patterns is highly correlated with their visual preferences. We get enjoyment from pictures that mimic nature and put less stress on our visual system.

This idea is further supported by the fact that the closer children live to an open, natural area, the lower their levels of stress and depression and the better their grades. For example, Professor Kristine Engemann and her colleagues from Aarhus University showed that the more green space in their environment, the less likely children are to have a mental illness in adulthood.[6] The high spatial-frequency information in urban societies puts stress on our visual system. The low spatial-frequency information in nature is calming and relaxing. In childhood, then, nature and green space result in calmer and more relaxed children who are ready to learn.

Living in a dense urban environment also puts a greater strain on our attention. Currently I have a tradesperson working just outside my office making an absolute racket. Ironically, I am having trouble concentrating on writing about attention because their banging is capturing mine! As we talked about in chapter 2, the ability to look at or notice different things in our environment is controlled by attention, and our attention is limited. If you haven't already seen it, check out "The

Monkey Business Illusion" by Professor Dan Simons on YouTube.[7] It is a great example of how our attention allows us to focus on one aspect of a scene and blocks out everything else. But our attention requires effort, and the more things we need to block out, the harder our brains must work. In an urban environment, the number of distractions increases, with traffic noise, people, billboards, and advertisements working hard to capture our attention. So we end up under more stress with higher levels of anxiety because of the myriad distractions that drain our capacity to concentrate.

In urban environments, we also tend to have more people around. We discussed previously the evolution of automatic detection of faces and facial expressions. Think about this in the context of a crowded place. Your brain, without your conscious knowledge, is detecting faces in the environment and determining if they are known or unknown, if they belong to an in-group or out-group member, and if they are angry or fearful. Your brain also tries to capture your attention and get you to attend to those faces. Now, this would have worked well and continues to work well in relatively small groups. However, what happens in large groups when you physically can't attend to each individual face? If we are not able to attend to everyone and therefore are not "aware" of each individual, our brains are doing a lot more with those faces than we are aware of. The number of people around us in large cities must cause overstimulation of this unconscious processing system.

Now recall that the amygdala is the driver for the automatic detection of facial expressions and *also* the key to our fight-or-flight response. Activation of the amygdala results in an increase in heart rate, pupil dilation, increased blood flow to our muscles, and the feeling that we need to react in some way—essentially an increase in stress. This response continues until we can attend to the face that is causing the response and assess whether it represents a threat or not. And overstimulation of the amygdala is associated with anxiety and depression. I don't think it is a huge leap to suggest that living in an environment in which there are so many people that we are unable to attend to everyone may impact our mental health.

It is also important to remember that processing negative facial expressions and body language results in a similar negative emotion in ourselves. The mirror neuron system enables us to understand how others are feeling by mimicking the same response. Now consider cities where the effects that I have described so far are creating a large group of anxious and depressed individuals. Facial expressions and body language are contagious.

Not only do we have an increase in mental illness in large cities and crowded environments, but we also have an increase in fear. I will give you one compelling example that I believe highlights our exaggerated fear in Western societies today. In 2008, Lenore Skenazy wrote a piece for the *New York Sun* in which she described her decision to let her nine-year-old son take the New York City subway home alone. She had done everything that I think a sane and caring parent would do to ensure her son was safe. He knew which stop to get off, she dropped him at the entrance to the subway, he knew how to get home from the subway, his father was at home to greet him when he arrived, and so on. The response to the article was swift and harsh. Skenazy was called the "world's worst mum," a label she now wears with pride, and the story went global.[8] Skenazy now has a very popular blog, a book, and a movement called "Free-Range Kids." Her story is a fantastic example of the fear many in society now hold not only for their own children but everyone else's children as well.

When I was young, I didn't have any organized activities after school. I finished school, walked or rode home, dumped my bag, shoved some food in my mouth, and headed off to either a friend's house or some other place we had arranged to meet. There were no adults there to sort out our problems. There was no one to turn to when an argument started or someone was upset or angry. We had to deal with issues ourselves. Sometimes the outcome wasn't ideal, and someone went home upset. But we learned what was appropriate and what we needed to do differently next time. We had an opportunity to experiment with negotiation and compromise. Today, most children in developed countries spend most of their time in organized or supervised situations. Even during recess and lunchtime, there are teachers or supervisors around to sort out any conflicts or possible misunderstandings. And after school or on weekends, there is organized sport, or tutoring, or band, or some other ordered activity. If there are always established rules and an adult to intervene when the rules are not obeyed, when will children learn how to socialize and negotiate?

In *The Coddling of the American Mind*, Professors Jonathan Haidt and Greg Lukianoff talk about the fear culture in the United States and across the Western world and its impact on children's development.[9] They suggest that by overprotecting children, we end up harming them—that children need to learn how to thrive by experiencing and experimenting with life and relationships. And their premise rings true. Today's kids have less freedom and less time without parents, teachers, or caregivers than ever before, despite being safer than at any other time in history. Haidt and Lukianoff suggest this hypersupervision has come about through constant bombardment by the media and government agencies about stolen children and other awful events. This has been paralleled by the rise of carefully scheduled play and skill-development activities with the resultant loss of time to just play. I would argue that the impact of living in large cities on our stress levels is also a contributing factor. Unfortunately, supervised activities don't allow children to learn important skills such as negotiation without an authority figure, empathy for others, how to self-care, and how to ask for help when needed. We need to challenge ourselves to extend and reinforce our abilities. Haidt and Lukianoff suggest that we need to work toward "antifragility," and I agree. Many of the university students I see today are too fragile. One factor in this is the fear culture stifling the development of important social skills.

Although most of our brain is dedicated to connecting and communicating with other people, we need to learn how to do so. This requires practice and a lot of getting it wrong. We need to learn to socialize by socializing. This requires experiencing both positive and negative reactions to our behavior so that we learn what is appropriate and what is not going to be tolerated by others. We also need to experience other people's behavior, both good and bad, to learn what we are willing to tolerate and what we find intolerable. These experiences are important for learning the boundaries that others will accept and what we are willing to accept. One major contributor to current societal challenges is that our children and teenagers don't have the opportunities that previous generations had to learn these important lessons.

I understand the many reasons for this constant supervision. We want the best for our children, and we want them to have the opportunities we didn't have. I struggle with this myself. I run the surf lifesaving program for my daughter's age group because I want her to have a great experience and I want her to love the ocean. Both my kids play a musical instrument and are in school bands—things I never had the opportunity to do but would have loved. And I worry that my children won't get the marks to get into the right course at the right university. But I'm also concerned that they don't get enough time to just hang out with friends. With constant supervision they won't have the opportunity to learn how to be independent, brave, and resilient.

Fear is the other side of this constant supervision. We are scared that something will happen to them in this crazy, violent world. Large cities are dangerous and full of criminals. And fear, especially in Western societies, has grown exponentially over the past fifty years despite the statistics showing we are safer today than at any time in history. In *The Better Angels of Our Nature*, Steven Pinker of Harvard University explains that violence has declined both in the long term and in the short term.[10] So why is it that we are more afraid than we ever have been?

One obvious reason is the media and the internet. We are constantly bombarded with clickbait—sensationalized headlines to get us to click—from all over the world. The competition for our attention on the internet has created a twenty-four-hour news cycle. And anyone with a Facebook page or Twitter account can create news. Today the competition for clicks, likes, retweets, and so on is insane. We are constantly hit with overdramatized and sensationalized headlines that make us feel like awful things are happening everywhere—we live in fear and hold on to our kids tightly.

During the height of the Covid-19 pandemic and the first lockdown here in Australia, I must admit I got sucked into the void of shock and awe on the internet. For a few weeks, as the virus spread and the so-called predictions and alternative theories were coming out, I was trawling the internet and watching the news feeds constantly. I was feeling depressed and overwhelmed. I remember reading one article claiming that the symptoms from Covid would last up to five years. Five years! This was at a time when the virus had only been discovered about six months earlier. How could a so-called expert be claiming the symptoms of a virus that had only been around for six months would last for five years? It was that article that made me call bullshit! It was nonsense, and I needed to turn off and get back to life. The media need to stop chasing clicks and likes and return to proper investigative journalism again, because sadly there is very little left. We will discuss the constant barrage of (mis)information from the internet and the media in the next chapter. The shock and awe on the internet are causing a pandemic of fear.

Our feelings of media-fueled fear and our automatic face-detection system in overdrive in large cities are creating an unhealthy level of anxiety. This, combined with increased stress as a result of our perceptual systems, which evolved in a natural environment, and our need for perceived control over our environment, makes living in crowded cities stressful. Many children do not have enough time in unsupervised play and therefore don't have the opportunity to practice negotiation, collaboration, and compromise during these formative years. We need to recognize that we are safer today than we have ever been and that children need unsupervised play to develop crucial social abilities. And we all need to relax, take a deep breath, and maybe head to nature regularly to reset.

In summary:

- Although we suffer when we are isolated or alone, we also suffer when we feel overcrowded.
- Overcrowding in humans usually happens in urban environments, which are uniquely different from the natural environments in which we evolved. Urban environments lead to stress and strain on our perceptual system.
- With the increased number of faces in crowded urban environments, our automatic face and facial expression perception is in overdrive, adding to our anxiety.
- Parents are often more cautious with their children in urban environments, resulting in restricted opportunities for free play, which is essential for children to learn important social skills.

TIP OF THE CHAPTER

Get into nature on a regular basis. Go to a park, sit, and relax. Look at the trees and the bushes. It is a good reset for your brain. Or maybe climb a tree if you're feeling adventurous. If you have kids, consider ways you can let them have unsupervised play.

Modern Technology Thrives on Connection

*I*f you've seen one of my blog posts or talks on how smartphones are making us dumb, you won't be surprised to hear that I believe one of the biggest threats to the connected species is the impact of modern technologies on how our brains develop and adapt. Let me explain why we should all be concerned about their impact. Today many people treat their smartphone as more important than a real person standing right in front of them. They attend to their phone as though it were an infant in need of their constant attention. They stress if it is not close by, and they immediately respond to it whenever it shakes or cries out. They will interrupt a real conversation with a real person in real life to "check" an incoming notification. The virtual world is subsuming their real connections, and they no longer have time for a good-old "home-cooked meal" of real connection between two real people.

What is the first thing you do in the morning and the last thing you do at night? Do you ever go anywhere without your phone? Do you feel anxious when you don't have your phone close by? Have you ever looked at your phone while having a conversation with a loved one? Do you interrupt real conversations to answer notifications on your phone? Do you spend more time on a device than with real people?

There is now overwhelming evidence that the way we use smartphones and other devices is having a negative impact on our relationships and our mental health. Work by psychologists like Professor Jean Twenge and many others has shown alarming increases in anxiety, depression, and suicide that strongly correlate with screen use.[1] Even more concerning is the work by Professors Tzipi Horowitz-Kraus and John Hutton, from Cincinnati Children's Hospital Medical Center, showing significant decreases in brain white matter tracts associated with early screen use in children.[2] White matter tracts are like the freeways or rail networks in the brain that connect the different brain regions and allow them to communicate. These tracts are crucial for normal function—including our ability to communicate, understand, reason, problem-solve, and empathize. And screen use at an early age is impacting the development of these crucial networks.

It's not that I think we should throw this new tech out the window, but we are in the middle of a global experiment, and the preliminary findings are horrifying. As Todd Sampson, director of *Mirror Mirror: Love and Hate*, stated, "I think that we are on the cusp of a global crisis. So you can call that alarmist. I just call that reality." We need to get a better understanding of the impact of devices on the brain and at least restrict the exposure of the developing brains of children and teenagers.

Our brains constantly change and adapt throughout our lives, which is called *neuroplasticity*. Your brain today is ever so slightly different from the brain you had yesterday. Some connections have been made stronger, and unused connections have been weakened. This happens constantly—based on what we are doing both mentally and physically. It is how we learn. This is a great thing for those of us past our prime because it means you can teach an old dog new tricks. It is important for everyone to understand this as it means our abilities today don't need to define who we will be tomorrow, no matter what our age. On the flip side, it is also how we forget. Ever heard the phrase "use it or lose it"? It works for the brain as well. Abilities that you work on become stronger, and those you neglect become weaker. We need to be exercising our entire brain regularly to keep it strong and healthy. And we need to be doing a range of things that work (activate) a large percentage of our brain regularly. Focusing on one discreet ability to the detriment of others is not ideal. It will strengthen that ability, but other important functions will be negatively affected.

The problem is that modern technologies like smartphones are now doing a lot of things we used to do for ourselves, which means we are losing those abilities. We don't have to navigate, remember, calculate, consider, imagine, or interact with the world and others. If we don't use abilities, we will lose them. Even more concerning is the fact that if younger people don't develop these abilities, they will never have them. The earlier a child is introduced to a smartphone, the more likely they are to be diagnosed with ADHD.[3] And the more time a teenager spends on a screen, the more likely they are to have ADHD symptoms.[4] Smartphones are designed to steal our attention. The prefrontal cortex, an area of the brain involved in controlling our attention, is not fully developed until we are approximately twenty-five years of age. It is being rewired in all of us, but in the younger generation, those on devices regularly, this important ability may never be fully functional.

Now, I don't for a minute believe that it is the smartphone itself that is making us dumb. It is the *way we use* these devices that is making us unsociable and affecting our intellectual capacity. In part, this has come about through the invention of "apps" and the genius thinking that created the app stores. Applications for smartphones are fairly easy for a good developer to create. And the app stores allow them to sell these apps to anyone, anywhere. So now any reasonably good developer with a reasonably good idea can create an app and make it accessible to the world.

However, there is always a catch to an ingenious idea. The first issue is that a lot of developers are making apps and uploading them to app stores. And when I say "a lot," I mean millions. A recent report in *Forbes* suggested there were 8.9 million mobile apps available in 2020, so the competition is red-hot.[5] The second issue is that apps are usually free, which means advertising on the app is the only way the developer can make any money. Or they cost very little per app, which means it needs to be extremely popular for a developer to make even a modest amount of money. Either way, this means they need their apps to go viral.

How do you make an app go viral and get people to not only download it but to use it and recommend it? Well, the easiest way is to make it addictive. Make people feel like they cannot live without it. Make them feel like they will miss out if they don't have it. Make them feel like everyone is using it. Make it more important to them than the person standing right in front of them. Eyes on screen is the name of the game. And FOMO (fear of missing out) is rampant, but not fear of missing out on real-life experiences—fear of missing out on viral social media posts. Tech entrepreneurs, from small-time app developers working alone to Facebook and Google, all want your attention, and they want it constantly. They want you to feel like you belong on their app more than you belong in the real world. Over 85 percent of smartphone users will check their device while in conversations with friends and family. Is it any wonder it's called "going viral" when something spreads so contagiously?

To be honest, the dumbphone addiction issue drives me a little nutty. I am a volunteer lifesaver, and during the patrol season I am in uniform on the beach about once every three weeks. It is a beautiful beach, and it makes me sad/mad to see so many people sitting on the beach staring at their phones. Teens sitting with a group of friends scrolling their Facebook or Instagram feeds. Parents checking emails or LinkedIn posts while their children play. I had a bizarre experience a few years ago at a family gathering. My teenage nieces and nephews were all sitting in the lounge watching a movie. And they were all busily scrolling and tapping away at their phones and laughing. I asked them what they were doing. I got the usual blank stare to begin with, but after a moment my niece explained that they were all sending comments to each other via a chat group while watching the movie together. They were communicating with each other via the dumbphones when they were all in the same room. What?! In fact, a report by Common Sense Media found that teens spend an average of seven hours and twenty-two minutes on their phones every day. How much time are they really spending with their friends?

I know, I need to get with the program, right? What is so wrong with a world in which we are all online and communicating via chat groups? Why is it such an issue that teens now prefer to sit in their bedrooms and text rather than hang out with friends? Times change, I hear you say. But this change is affecting us in profound ways. Let's start with the lack of information—information that we as the connected species evolved to use when communicating. My father used to hate talking on the phone. He would say, "Never have a serious conversation with someone if you can't see what they are thinking." And it is the best piece of advice he gave me. We obtain so much information when we look at each other, both consciously and implicitly through the automatic analysis of the other person's face and body. We can infer what someone is thinking. What happens when we don't get this information and must rely on the written word? We're bound to misunderstand each other.

Not only do we lose the important cues from the face and body online, but we also don't have the touch that is important for connecting and making each other feel welcome. And as a result, we don't receive those neurotransmitters, the happy hormones that relax us and make us feel connected. And we don't have reciprocal or mirrored movement and gesturing that help with understanding the mood and feelings of the conversation. Without all of this, we can't easily put the conversation into context or relate to the other person. Is it any surprise that people are more likely to have misunderstandings and conflicts online? Is it any surprise that people are more likely to be nasty or inappropriate online? Is it any surprise that shaming, bullying, vitriol, and abuse are rampant online? People readily agree that many of the things they are willing to say online they would never say to someone's face.

So why are we so willing to give up face-to-face socializing and sit at home on our phones instead (or even ignore someone sitting beside us and text them instead)? Well, for kids and teens (and probably many adults), it feels safe! Being with people, although there are innumerable positives, can be challenging. And all our socializing abilities need to be learned and practiced regularly. In 2019, my then eight-year-old son had an epiphany. It was his first time snowboarding, and he had just started to get the hang of it. We were on the chair lift when he turned to me and said, "I just realized something, Dad. It's really fun to scare yourself a bit. And it helps you get better!" I was so proud because he was completely right, and it is an important lesson to learn. We need to scare ourselves, take ourselves outside our comfort zones just a bit, to learn and progress. When we are young, we need to socialize, to get into arguments, to apologize occasionally and stand our ground at other times, to learn how to negotiate and collaborate. Sitting in our rooms and communicating via text seems easier, but it results in more misunderstandings, and we miss important opportunities to learn and connect.

There is now a huge amount of research to back up the idea that our smartphone use is a real issue. For example, Professor Yalda Uhls and her colleagues from the University of California, Los Angeles, showed that simply taking grade-six kids to camp for five days without access to devices improved their ability to recognize facial expressions.[6] Just think about that for a minute. These were average kids with "normal" screen time, and they didn't do any special cognitive training; they just went to camp! But a camp without devices means time socializing and interacting in real life! The fact that this improved their emotion perception tells us that their starting ability must be below normal.

Even more concerning is that twelve-month-old children whose caregivers use a smartphone show impaired facial expression perception.

Professor Jenny Radesky and her colleagues from Boston Medical Center have shown that a caregiver using a smartphone does not respond appropriately to the child.[7] The child falls, and the caregiver doesn't look concerned, or the child does something positive, and the caregiver doesn't smile. These cues are important during our early years as they help us understand the right response for different actions. This mounting research suggests children are missing out on important social lessons because of our addiction to smartphones.

In the past we had no choice but to brave potentially challenging social interactions. Now the smartphone gives us another way to communicate. The issue is that we can't develop the know-how to navigate the complex dance of social communication on a device. We need to develop an understanding of subtle signs, body language, facial expression, prosody and vocal intonation, pecking orders, and what is "rad" and what is not (and yes, I know, saying "rad" is not cool anymore). Although our brains process all these cues automatically, we need to cognitively understand what those cues are telling us. If we don't learn what these signals mean, we won't know what to do when they occur.

Social communication needs to be learned, and it is during childhood and teen years that most of this learning and exploration occurs. During this vital period of development, our youth need to establish their personalities and emotional intelligence. Instead, this generation is growing up looking at a screen and sending emojis. Like my son so insightfully realized, we need to scare ourselves a little bit to get better at something. Without our children and teens actually interacting, we may be growing young people whose brains literally lack the pathways that allow them to socialize, collaborate, participate, and connect.

This global experiment is going to have consequences. We already know that without socializing, we feel depressed, anxious, and stressed, leading in extreme cases to mental illness and psychosis. As Professor Brené Brown said, "We are hardwired to connect with others, it's what gives purpose and meaning to our lives and without it there is suffering."[8] And unfortunately, connecting online is not the same as connecting in real life. Lacking those important cues that we use to interpret others' feelings and losing those important bursts of relaxing and happy neurotransmitters that are so important for our health and well-being, we end up with a weak and inadequate imitation of social contact. The more time spent on social media, the greater the likelihood of depression.[9] And we haven't even taken into consideration the effects of cyberbullying, which is on the rise. Without *real* socializing and *real* friends, we as the connected species suffer greatly.

What about adults? Is this all just an issue for our youth? Unfortunately not, because, as discussed, our brains are constantly changing throughout life. As with a muscle, we have to use it, or we lose it. If we use, or practice, certain abilities, the brain will alter, and we will get better at those abilities. But on the flip side, if we don't use a particular ability, then the brain changes to let that valuable real estate be used for something else, and we will get worse at the ability. Those of us who grew up in the twentieth century developed in an environment where we had time to socialize and learn how to collaborate and communicate. That means the pathways were developed—but if we now spend a large percentage of our time glued to our phones and not exercising our social abilities, we will lose them. And this is what appears to be happening all too readily. We have seen a steady increase in social anxiety in wealthy countries, and although millennials are the most affected, the increase is happening at all ages. We need to exercise our social abilities.

Perhaps you regularly meet up with friends and interact with others directly. You might be thinking, "Smartphones don't affect me!" Think again! When was the last time you went out for a coffee and a chat with a friend and there wasn't a smartphone sitting on the table between you? Or went to a meeting and there wasn't a smartphone sitting on the desk? The act of placing a smartphone on the table actually interferes with the depth of the conversation. Professors Andrew Przybylski and Netta Weinstein from the University of Oxford have shown that just placing a phone down on a table acts as a message to the other person: "If that phone buzzes, or beeps, or vibrates, I will interrupt our conversation and check it."[10] This reduces the intimacy and depth of conversations. People are less likely to ask important questions or bring up sensitive and important issues if the other person has their phone visible. Smartphones are creating an emotional rift between us, even when we meet in person.

We also know that there has been a significant drop in close friendships in workplaces—and it's possible to link this to the increased use of smartphones. There are fewer conversations about the weekend or our children or the latest headlines around the watercooler or the coffee station at work. Instead, everyone checks their phone. There are also fewer spontaneous conversations when people are waiting for a meeting to start.

Everyone checks their phone. There are fewer spontaneous conversations while waiting for the elevator, or waiting at the photocopier, or waiting for a coffee, or waiting for anything. Everyone checks their phone. And we are missing important opportunities to connect—which also means we are missing important opportunities to collaborate and innovate.

Let's now turn to the big issue of so-called social media, which links so strongly with the rise of the smartphone. I say so-called because it isn't "social" at all. According to the *Cambridge English Dictionary*, the word *social* relates to (1) activities in which you meet and spend time with other people and that happen when you are not working, (2) society and living together in an organized way, and (3) an event at which people can meet and enjoy themselves. All of these suggest spending time with "real" people. Social media does not allow us to spend time with people. It allows us to see what others are doing and enables us to communicate with people, but communicating over social media is not being social. It is communicating at arm's (or screen's) length. You don't get the wash of happy social neurotransmitters that you get when you physically interact with someone. It is a bit like watching a surfing video versus doing it yourself. There is no comparison to the real thing, and the experience on a device leaves us wanting more.

One potential outcome of using social media could be a social occasion, but that is the outcome, not the medium itself. In *Stolen Focus*, Johann Hari reflects on a chat he had with Tristan Harris (who appeared on Netflix's *The Social Dilemma*).[11] Tristan, who worked for Facebook, suggested that if these tech companies were really interested in being "social apps," then they would notify you when friends were close by. So if you were visiting New York, for example, you could tap a button to tell people on your friends list, "I want to meet up—who's nearby and free?" And then those who were close would be notified that you were around and wanted to get together. According to Tristan this would be extremely easy to instigate, but the social media executives won't. Why? They don't want us to meet up in real life; they want us lonely and on our phones. Sadly, many people have drunk the Facebook Kool-Aid and now use social media as a way of socializing. It's how they stay connected with friends and family, but it lacks the features we need to really fulfill our deep-seated drive to socialize and connect. It's a pale substitute for the real thing. Social media is not an alternative to actually socializing.

I remember visiting a local market where a kids' petting zoo was set up. A group of teens had paid to pick up the cute baby farm animals. They were not petting the animals or enjoying the experience. They were grabbing one cute animal after another, taking a photo, and moving on to the next. The focus was to get the perfect selfie shot. No time to experience the real moment. Isn't this sad? A petting zoo is now about getting the right image for our online persona to feed our addiction.

So why do we constantly feel like we need to update our social media? This feeling of wanting more arises because our need actually hasn't been fulfilled, which, in combination with a bunch of addictive features that manipulate our neurotransmitters, creates a desire to log on again and again and again. What are these addictive tricks? Well, let's start with the effect of the "like" button on your dopamine system. The "like" is a little reward similar to winning on a poker machine or in a video game. When we get a reward, our brain releases a bit of dopamine—which makes us feel happy. We want this feeling again, so we wait anxiously for another like and another hit of dopamine. Maybe we post another funny picture hoping to get more likes. In the case of teens, they may post a prettier picture, a more revealing picture, or a more dangerous picture, hoping for more likes and more dopamine. The apps or social media platforms help us with this. They notify us regularly to ensure we know who has commented on or who has liked our posts. As a result, we increase the time we are monitoring our feed and others' feeds. And any time spent in the real world gains an emphasis only in the context of how it might be shared on social media, working out and setting up for the next post.

And what happens when we get used to these hits of dopamine? We need more to get the same "high." Sound familiar? This is the story we hear about drug addicts and problem gamblers. The tricks and effects are not new. Poker machines and video games use the same methods. The difference is smartphones are with us all the time, which makes them more pervasive than anything that came before, and we are letting our children and teens experience them frequently and freely.

There are, of course, other issues with living our lives online, including the ease with which people can misrepresent themselves. In my example above, the teens were going to great efforts to portray themselves in the most perfect pose to present the best version of themselves. And then there are options for photoshopping and editing to always show a "perfect you." This type of misrepresentation is causing serious mental health issues in many who feel they cannot live up to the standard. But there's also active, deliberate misrepresentation that is much easier online and extremely difficult to detect.

A good friend of mine often catches the bus to work. One day, he was trying to do some work, and a group of teenage boys from a local high school jumped on the bus and sat behind him. Being teenagers, they were quite loud, and he happened to overhear their conversation. He also has three daughters, so there was probably a bit of fatherly interest in his eavesdropping! He heard one of the boys explaining that he had infiltrated an online girls' group by pretending to be a girl. He had spent months convincing the girls to trust him (or her, as they believed). Why? Because he was hoping to see things that he could then use against the girls in the future. To manipulate or coerce them. This is not unusual. Many teens have multiple online versions of themselves that they use in different situations for different reasons. They often have one account set up to share with family members, one for friends, and one to present an alternative version of themselves. And then there are the people online for illegal reasons, who are free to set up any type of account they like to lure unsuspecting people into their webs. Living online is far more dangerous than many of us realize.

Pretending to be someone you are not is so much harder in person (unless you are Mrs. Doubtfire!). We often exaggerate or embellish stories about our past, but most of the time we are what and who we say we are. Online, we can put up a picture from twenty years ago or a picture of someone else. We can pretend to be a thirteen-year-old girl from Vietnam or a sixty-five-year-old man from Italy. The phenomenon is so pervasive nowadays that there is even a name for it: catfishing. And it is extremely hard to tell truth from fiction unless we also know people in real life.

Another issue with our online lives is the groups that we can be drawn into. Social media puts our brain's desire to establish and belong to groups in overdrive! It is a big factor in social media's popularity. What groups are we members of and why? And social media groups, in particular, are often very polarizing. Professor Damon Centola and his colleagues from the University of Pennsylvania have studied the polarizing effects of social media groups and suggest that it is the "influencers" who create the extreme views.[12] In one study they placed Democrat voters in one online group and Republican voters in another and posed the same questions to both groups. They found that the two groups did not become more extreme in their views as often happens on the internet. Actually, after discussions within the groups, their opinions became more moderate and closer to each other—even though the groups were kept separate and were from opposing political affiliations. After some investigation, Centola concluded that it was not the groups themselves that created the extreme views; rather, the influencers within the groups drove the division.

InfoWars is a clear example of an internet group set up and run by an influencer with nefarious intentions. The founder, Alex Jones, claimed for years that the 2012 Sandy Hook massacre was a hoax and part of a government conspiracy to take away gun rights in the United States. In 2022 he was found guilty in two separate court cases and ordered to pay millions to the victims of his lies after the court heard how "strangers showed up at their homes to record them, and people hurled abusive comments on social media."[13] InfoWars is only one example of many groups on the internet that spread misinformation to drive division in communities.

Most groups created online are controlled either explicitly or implicitly by one or a few influencers. These individuals have access to the majority of members, and they usually have an agenda to push. Remember, they set up the network for a reason, perhaps one that is not evident to everyone. They are also the most influential (hence the term *influencers*) and the most prolific in their posts and activity. They push the community in a particular direction that supports their agenda. The influencers have a completely disproportionate impact on the conversation both within the communities and on the internet at large. This gives them an amazing amount of power: whereas individual members believe that all members of the group support the influencer's position, often only a small percentage are true believers. And of course, we already talked about all the strong evolutionary drivers that lead us to want to belong to the group and how confirmation bias limits our ability to see that we are possibly being misled or controlled.

Biased views will undoubtedly become entrenched in communities with powerful influencers at their center. So how do we remove the impact that influencers have on groups? The court decisions made against InfoWars and Alex Jones are a good start. However, court cases are expensive, and the information is already out there, so there needs to be a better way. I think the social media platforms themselves need to stand up and correct this issue. Of course, influencers often make money from being popular—in some cases a lot of money—so I assume these platforms are reluctant because of backlash. Influencers also attract attention, and given that these platforms make money from attention, they will be reluctant from that point of view also. However, we know that algorithms are used to decide what information you are fed and that these platforms are constantly working to "improve" these algorithms. Wouldn't it be nice if the social media companies used these algorithms for good rather than evil! And if they are not willing to, then governments need to step in and protect the young and innocent.

Another easy fix would be to remove the "like" button. This would decrease the drive for popularity as well as the impact of influencers. Of course, this will be difficult to achieve as it will impact how addictive these platforms are and therefore the amount of money these organizations make. However, it is worth pushing; as Centola stated in a piece for *New Scientist*, "The more equity in people's social networks, the less biased and more informed groups will become—even when those groups start with highly partisan opinions."[14]

Overall, then, there are clear dangers in our current use of social media, smartphones, and devices. Our children are not developing normal social and emotional processes, we are losing skills we need to interact in the world and society, and we are giving a platform to extremists. It's time to recognize the effect of smartphones on our interactions and our brains, limit our use, and really consider the impact on our young people.

We now turn to exploring how we can address some of the problems we are seeing in our communities and around the world.

In summary:

- Without the difficult yet crucial experiences of socializing in real life, children and teens are missing important learning opportunities, which will affect how they collaborate, innovate, compromise, and connect.
- So-called social media is not social at all.

- Influencers have a disproportionate impact on views and opinions on the internet and drive extremism.
- Addiction to "likes" and comments is altering behavior both online and in the real world. Removal of likes from social media and using the algorithms in the background to give everyone an equal say could help with some of these issues.

TIP OF THE CHAPTER

Download a screen-time monitoring app (yes, not all apps are bad!) onto all your devices and check out how much time you are spending on them. People often find it surprising how much time they spend on different apps. Knowledge is power.

Part IV

HOW CAN WE FIX IT?

"Can we fix it, yes we can!"

—Bob the Builder[1]

Common Humanity Perspective

In 2019, the worst mass killing seen in New Zealand's modern history occurred. A white supremacist attacked two mosques on the South Island, killing more than fifty people and wounding many more. The prime minister, Jacinda Ardern, responded quickly, stating that New Zealand was "a home for those who share our values. Refuge for those who need it. And those values will not and cannot be shaken by this attack. . . . We represent diversity, kindness, compassion." She spoke with empathy and caring for those affected but also embraced them as part of the larger group that is New Zealand. She visited the mosques wearing culturally appropriate attire, including headwear, to show her solidarity with those attacked. She focused attention on the people affected and not on the perpetrator. Her response is a beautiful demonstration of what needs to occur to curb violence.

How might we address some of the issues we are now seeing in our society because of our drive to connect? For some issues, we can actively work to expand our groups and create larger circles that encompass everyone. For other issues, there are toxic groups that cause harm and distress, and we need to work to dismantle them altogether. For groups to be effective, they need a way of identifying who is a member and who is not. If you cannot identify members and nonmembers, then there really isn't a group—so in some cases, simply removing symbols can disrupt the group. We also need to be aware of influencers' ability to manipulate the message within groups and the impact this can have on group members. We should all become aware of the implicit biases that occur when we are members of a group and ensure that we do not exclude others. We need to expand our circles.

Whatever a radical group's agenda or philosophy, the tactic is always the same: to create a divisive "us or them" mentality, an in-group and an out-group, to engender a sense of hatred. These groups highlight differences. This is essential for any radical group's success, as they need members to implicitly associate with the in-group and to hate the out-group. And to do this, members need to be aware of the in- and out-groups' memberships. As we have discussed, this results in distortions of empathy and understanding and even distorted perceptions of what is said and done. We listen to what those in our in-group are telling us, while we view what we hear from those in the out-group through a distorted lens. We feel empathy for those in our in-group but not for those in our out-group. We reward those in our in-group and punish those in our out-group. Implicit bias, combined with confirmation bias, serves to reinforce our in-group mentality. And all of this relies on us being able to identify who is in and who is out. There needs to be a clear boundary between in and out—or at least a perceived boundary.

This is why groups wear, carry, or get tattoos of icons or other clear signs that they are members of the group. We all do this. I have a drawer full of Geelong Football Club gear that I wear proudly to show I am a fan when I go to a game. I also have a couple of MIT sweatshirts from when I worked in the United States and several Sea Shepherd T-shirts to show my support for marine conservation. And then there are the band T-shirts and so on. I'm sure you have merchandise that signals some of your in-groups as well. Of course, there are more official uniforms that readily indicate group membership as well, including police, firefighter, and military uniforms. They are clear signs that indicate our membership in a particular group.

And there are other ways to signal your group membership. In the early 1990s, I had long hair and wore flannelette shirts. (Yes, it was a good look.) The majority of my friends did as well. We listened to all the latest grunge music. I grieved when Kurt Cobain died and still get excited when Dave Grohl announces a new album release. During this period I started to go bald, and rather than try to cover it up, I shaved my head. I will never forget approaching the share house I was living in at the time. A group of friends were hanging out in the front yard. I jumped the fence and started across the lawn as usual. In unison, they all stood and headed toward me with clenched fists. When they got close enough, they realized it was me and stopped in their tracks. A few were still wary though. You see, I hadn't realized that long hair was part of our in-group's uniform. By shaving mine off, I was signaling that I was a skinhead, an entirely different group that was often violent toward members of the grunge scene in the 1990s. Most groups have uniforms or signs to identify the members. Sometimes these signs are explicit, and sometimes they are subtler.

The British royal family and "the firm" (the organization behind the royal family) are an example of a very well-organized group with a well-defined uniform. There are the crowns and tiaras, the military uniforms and the British flag. There are the castles, the titles, the accent, the ceremonies, the tea parties, and the proper behavior. And members of the royal family are white and English. Royalists wear their support and love for the group with pride. The group and the institution go back many years, and it doesn't look like it will be broken up any time soon. And we have seen multiple times what happens if someone who doesn't fit the mold tries to join this very exclusive group. The latest example, Meghan Markle, was never going to fit in with the in-group. She did not fit the cookie-cutter image of a British royal. The majority of "royalists" in the United Kingdom would not accept her as one of them—because she wasn't one of them. She was an American woman of color without a title—and an actress of all things! The British tabloids, looking for clickbait, took full advantage of the situation. Now she and Harry have left the service of the royals. And the royal family and their in-group remain intact, for now.

There are also sinister groups with clear signs to indicate group membership. These signs are often banned to curb violence. The flag, emblem, and uniform of the Ku Klux Klan (KKK) are instantly recognizable by both in-group and out-group members. Similarly, the swastika and the Nazi crest are also used by radical right-wing groups and are also easily recognized. Given their association with barbaric behavior, these symbols are rightly outlawed in many places around the world.

In Australia, there has been a push to ban the colors and uniforms of outlaw motorcycle gangs. The violence and lawlessness of these groups in many states has resulted in special task forces to attempt to break them up. Taking away their ability to recognize friend from foe by banning the colors and emblems helps to eliminate the potential threat, especially as much of the violence is between rival gangs and the uniform is used to intimidate. If there is no way of identifying different gangs' members, then confrontation and intimidation are limited. Removing the symbols and uniforms means members and nonmembers cannot easily be identified, and violent confrontations are lessened.

Eliminating the ability to identify group members (both in-group and out-group) can help to curb violence and hostility; however, this also depends on the characteristics that define the groups. For example, in the case of the KKK, the out-group is anyone who is not white, so if Klan members want to target such individuals, they can quite easily do so. However, identifying who is a member of the in-group is much more difficult as just being white does not mean you are a KKK member. When the in-group and out-group are not defined by race, ethnicity, or sex, identifying the in- and out-group is much more difficult, which is why banning identifying paraphernalia is more successful with gangs and the like.

Sadly, this may also be one reason why religious groups who wear certain clothing or jewelry can often be the target of discrimination. The Jewish and Muslim communities, for example, have been targets of discrimination (and worse) in many different parts of the world. Their clothing is often distinct and identifies them as an in-group of their own within many communities. As such, the many aspects of in-group/out-group mentality can take over the thinking of others. This often happens during times of stress or strain in which a group that is easily defined and isolated can be used as a scapegoat, as happened in Nazi Germany.

Adolf Hitler very purposefully targeted the Jewish community. Germany was in a severe recession after World War I, and the people were suffering. He accused the Jewish community of using resources and not belonging to the in-group. They were easily identifiable and easily targeted. The Third Reich then marked out-group members with the Star of David on their clothing—and the outcome is as well documented as it was horrendous.

But we can't ban all groups and remove all symbols of group membership, and in fact we've seen how such membership can be crucial for health and well-being. We thrive within groups, and we need groups to feel a part of something, a sense of belonging, a sense of purpose. And most groups are not harmful. I'm sure you can think of memorabilia and sweatshirts with a sporting team or college logo on them that you wear with pride. Or a book club, or a community group, or a religion, or a yoga group. These groups are usually harmless and create a sense of community.

The issue is when the group's agenda serves the purpose of discriminating against members of the out-group. Certain groups are deliberately set up or manipulated for this purpose, and other groups become divisive due to the input of an influencer or dominant individual or individuals within the group. In cases where violence occurs or is threatened, I see no other solution than to outlaw the group and act quickly to do so.

In less violent situations, I think our need to belong and the in-group mentality could be used to decrease the impact of the group. We can do this by expanding the circle of the in-group to encompass members of the out-group. A fantastic example of this method was used by Anna Pauline "Pauli" Murray, an African American queer woman born in 1910. She became an American civil rights activist, a lawyer, a women's rights activist, an Episcopal priest, and an author. There is now a residential college at Yale named after her. In 1945 she wrote, "I intend to destroy segregation by positive and embracing methods. . . . When my brothers try to draw a circle to exclude me, I shall draw a larger circle to include them."[1] She included everyone in the group, which meant they could all listen, empathize, embrace, and thrive. By increasing the group to include everyone, we can use our in-group mentality to embrace all.

This idea of drawing a larger circle or embracing everyone within the group is not new. Some of our oldest texts are religious, and they often espouse inclusivity. For example, much of Buddhist teaching could be interpreted as not limiting oneself to a group. The idea that "hatred does not cease by hatred, but only by love" tells us to open up to all people. Or "to understand everything is to forgive everything." And throughout the Old and New Testaments, the Quran, the Hindi sacred texts, and so on, there is reference to the importance of unconditional love for everyone. Although segregation, isolation, and the most extreme versions of in-group mentality have occurred in the name of these religions, these consequences were the result of influencers within the group. The teachings within their sacred texts often call for inclusion and love of all people regardless of group. However, like so many groups, those with power or influence often distort the message and create the in-group/out-group mentality to isolate and segregate.

And we can all widen our circles if we wish to. I grew up in a Catholic family. My father at one stage during his childhood dreamed of becoming a priest. But if asked, I could say I grew up in a *Christian* family, which would embrace more people and is still true. Or I could say I grew up in a *religious* family. Or to widen that circle even further, I could say I grew up in a *spiritual* family. See how easily we can widen the circle to embrace more people and encompass everyone? Great religious leaders have done this during times of crisis.

Let's head back to New Zealand for a moment. Sheikh Gamal Fouda, imam of the Christchurch mosque targeted by the 2019 terror attack, spoke on the twelve-month anniversary. The imam described Prime Minister Ardern's address as a message of inspiration to fellow leaders around the world. He also said, "If you are Muslim, I would like you to visit a non-Muslim today and say to her or him: I love you because this is my religion. . . . [I]f you are a non-Muslim, I would also like you to go back to your country and visit an Islamic center and tell them that you love them and are ready to start a project with them. Do something human." These were amazing words, considering that only twelve months earlier he watched members of his mosque gunned down in cold blood. He was trying to widen the circle. To embrace all people. To stop the in-group/out-group mentality. To stop the hate.

Similarly, after a terror attack on a café in Australia in 2014 by an Islamic man, there was concern about Islamophobic retaliation. Many Muslims, especially women who can be easily identified by their head-wear, were afraid to catch public transport. When this became public, the #IllRideWithYou movement started and went viral. Non-Muslim people offered to accompany Muslims on public transport to help them feel safe. The simple act of sitting on public transport next to a person who might feel afraid, to show support, was an effective, inclusive act. This was a great example of expanding the circle to include those who may feel isolated or threatened.

Some of the great leaders of all time also embraced the idea of expanding the circle or encompassing everyone. Let's start by reflecting on those who have been able to create major positive societal change. People like Martin Luther King Jr., Mohandas Gandhi, and Nelson Mandela all had one thing in common. They didn't talk about "us" and "them"; they weren't about dividing or replacing; they spoke of including everyone. Essentially they all expanded their in-group to include more members (particularly members of the dominant out-group). For example, Nelson Mandela said in his famous trial speech, "I have fought against white domination, and I have fought against black domination. I have cherished the ideal of a democratic and free society in which all persons live together in harmony and with equal opportunities."[2] He didn't talk about how black people should be in control or how white people should be punished. He focused on all people being equal. He increased the circle of his in-group to encompass everyone—and this increased the extent to which he could be heard by everyone.

Similarly, in his famous "I Have a Dream" speech, Martin Luther King Jr. also expanded the circle of inclusiveness. "I have a dream that . . . one day right there in Alabama, little black boys and black girls will be able to join hands with little white boys and white girls as sisters and brothers."[3] This doesn't highlight his inner group but expands the circle to encompass both black and white people. Both groups fit within the circle, so they were more likely to hear the positive message.

We can also look at the opposite side of the political coin. Donald Trump's speeches were full of "we" and "our," "us" and "them." For example, on January 6, 2021, he said, "Our country has had enough. We will not take it anymore, and that's what this is all about. . . . We want to go back, and we want to get this right because we're going to have somebody in there that should not be in there and our country will be destroyed, and we're not going to stand for that. . . . We fight like hell . . . for our movement, for our children and our beloved country."[4] The emphasis is on him and his in-group; it's not about expanding the circle but strengthening the in-group mentality. The wall along the Mexico border was a physical manifestation of the mindset that created such a divisive moment in American history.

Great inclusive leaders use words that include and embrace everyone. The opposite can be said for leaders who use phrases like "You are either with us or you are against us" or "It is us versus them." These types of statements are divisional and make the incorrect assumption that there is good and bad or black and white, with no gray area. There is always a gray area, and there are always options that enable the out-group to be brought into the in-group.

Politics and religion aren't the only areas in which we can expand our in-groups. I live on the Northern Beaches of Sydney, and when I am elsewhere in New South Wales, that is what I will tell people. However, if I am elsewhere in Australia, I usually say I am from Sydney. When I lived in the United States, I used to say I was from Australia (although most people picked that up from my accent). If I am ever lucky enough to travel to another world with other beings, I will say

I am from Earth. The circle can easily increase or decrease depending on the situation. We naturally do this in some spheres, and we need to actively develop it in others, to embrace everyone.

And on the topic of travel, meeting people from different countries and especially different cultures is also a great way to expand our circle. I grew up in a small country town that was very much a monoculture. Since then, I have traveled all over the world, including most of Asia and Europe; North, Central, and South America; and Russia, but I would love to do a lot more. Experiencing new cultures and different ways of life expands our circle. It helps us understand that we are all part of this big, wonderful group, the connected species, with the same loves: love of family, of food, of freedom, of choice, and of connection.

Travel and spending time with people from other ethnic and cultural backgrounds can also reshape our face template. Remember, we discussed our implicit face-recognition system and how it is searching for anything that deviates from average. Ideally, the faces that we code would include the full range of faces that we will experience—if this were the case, then this system would have a much better setting for our current multicultural society. You could think of this as a sensitivity dial on a smoke alarm. If you have it set to too sensitive, the smoke alarm goes off too often and in situations that are not dangerous (e.g., your toast is burning). If your face-detection template is too narrow because most of the people you are exposed to are of your race, then it will activate for anything other than your race. We want to turn the sensitivity dial down. We want our face-detection system at a point that it doesn't activate for other-race faces and treats everyone as equal. To do this, we need to be exposed to lots of faces of varying races.

Not only do we need to be exposed to many faces from many races, but our exposure needs to eliminate implicit biases as well. Our implicit biases about race and gender (among many other things) are based on stereotypes we learn as infants and children. These biases are evident in the media we watch and the books we read. They are evident in the way we and others are treated by teachers, doctors, police, and, well, everyone. Confirmation bias then reinforces these implicit biases, as we primarily notice situations that reinforce our stereotypes. Removing these stereotypes from our societies is going to be difficult, but we are starting to hack away at some of these issues. The media is getting better but is not yet good enough. How many Asian superheroes do you see in Western movies? Children's toys are also getting better but are not yet good enough. How many indigenous dolls are available compared to white ones? We need to work hard to remove the stereotypes, and that means we all need to acknowledge and work on our own implicit biases.

You might be thinking, "Hang on, it's not that bad. Hollywood has changed a lot, and we see much more diverse representation in movies and on TV these days." Unfortunately, you'd be wrong! In 2021, the *Los Angeles Times* did a deep dive into the Hollywood Foreign Press Association.[5] This group is responsible for nominating and selecting the winners for the annual Golden Globes. This is a big deal for actors worldwide, and the influence that this organization has on what will become popular and what will get produced is not to be underestimated. The report found that there was not one person of color in the Hollywood Foreign Press Association. Not one! Surely, the group that makes decisions about who is nominated and wins at the Golden Globes should be representative of the audiences who watch the movies. It sounds like the Hollywood Foreign Press Association needs to expand its circle, and its members need to be aware of their implicit biases.

How do we work on our own implicit biases? Sadly, I don't have all the answers. I know I still have implicit biases, and when they rear their ugly heads, I reflect on how and why it happened. I ask myself how I would feel if the situation were reversed. I remember watching the film *A Time to Kill*, in which Matthew McConaughey plays a lawyer who defends a black man (Samuel L. Jackson) accused of murdering two white supremacists. He murdered them because they had savagely raped his ten-year-old daughter in Mississippi. In the lawyer's speech to the all-white jury, he asks them to close their eyes and then describes what the men did to the defenseless young girl. In the end, he says, "Now imagine that she is white." It is a potent example of how these automatic processes and our in-group mentality changes our feelings and empathy for others. I believe we all need to start imagining that everyone we meet is the same as us, a member of our circle, so that we treat them as a member of our in-group.

We also need to be careful not to condemn all groups. Not all groups are bad. Some groups are very important. We just need to be aware of the boundaries and why those boundaries exist. We need to understand the agenda behind the group. We need to be aware of group influencers and their agendas. And we need to be aware that groups, the influencers within them, and their agendas can change. Some groups are fantastic, creating a sense of belonging, community, and support, but we need to be ever wary.

We need to be mindful of all these aspects and reflect on why the group exists and why we are members. Groups like the Men's Shed are fantastic with a great agenda: men's mental health and the creation of strong support networks. However, such a group could potentially be swayed with the wrong influencer involved. What if someone like Enrique Tarrio, leader of the Proud Boys, became an influencer within a group like the Men's Shed? It could end up looking something like the Proud Boys. I am not trying to suggest that this will happen; it is simply a thought exercise. Groups evolve, and influencers can have extraordinary power over their agendas.

But like groups, influencers are also not all bad. There are many influencers who are doing great things to enable others who have expanded circles. Look at the positive movements and ideals of people like Oprah Winfrey, Shan Boodram, Brené Brown, Dwayne Johnson, Malala Yousafzai, and so on. They are people who inspire others to do good. Some things they all have in common include listening to others, seeking expert advice on topics of interest, being willing to be vulnerable, being honest and respectful, and inspiring love and inclusion, not separation. We need to be careful that all the groups we are involved in and support have influencers with these traits.

We also need to recognize that we all influence people within our groups. Sometimes we have a big impact; other times it may not be so obvious. But there are always people within the groups that we belong to who will be influenced by our actions. And we are not always aware of who we are influencing or why they are listening to us. I remember being quite surprised when a friend's son repeated something I had said several weeks earlier about a mutual acquaintance. I didn't even remember saying it when he was around, but he had been influenced, and I regretted my comment. Be careful about what you put out there, and remember that you may be influencing members of a group you might not even know you are a member of. You never know how wide your circle is.

On the flip side, not all influencers can influence all groups. This might seem obvious, but the idea is often neglected. How often have you seen an old white male politician trying to talk to a group of female indigenous leaders about equality? Or a black man trying to convince a group of white people that there is a problem with law and order and the treatment of minorities? To influence a group, you need to be seen as a member of the group. You need to be part of the in-group for members to listen and learn. That means we need white men within white male groups to speak up for those who are not favored by the current white patriarchy. We need indigenous people to lead change within indigenous communities. To establish change, we need people to be willing and able to listen and debate honestly and openly. We need positive influencers from within to have a voice because not all influencers can influence all groups.

We also need to be extra vigilant when people who are not part of the in-group are given power over the group. Some examples include a foreign army that occupies a country, white law enforcement officers in black neighborhoods, male judges in rape trials, and so on. In these and many other similar situations, we have seen poor decisions that show the influence of bias, inappropriate actions, and much worse. It is not always the case, and there are wonderful people who do not share characteristics with the group who have done some amazing things. But there are many more examples of these situations going wrong. People can be treated unfairly, and situations may escalate to outright discrimination and violence. There is a need for training in implicit and confirmation biases and very close checks and balances if these situations are unavoidable.

Training in emotional awareness, in how social systems and "groupthink" works, should be a priority for schools, law enforcement, politicians, the legal profession (especially judges), the media, and parents. Without awareness of these important issues, these problems will continue. As populations continue to grow and societies become more multicultural, these issues will become more evident. Now is the time to start investing in our future by training everyone to reflect on their biases and to do better.

In summary:

- Groups are an important part of our communities and help with connection and support. All groups have either explicit or implicit uniforms and ways of behaving to indicate membership.

- We need to expand our groups and create larger circles that encompass everyone.
- We need to be aware of the influencers within our groups and ensure their messages are appropriate.
- Not all influencers can influence all groups. We need groups to change from within.
- Training on how social systems and "groupthink" work should be a priority.

TIP OF THE CHAPTER

Consider all the groups that you are a member of and whether they are really inclusive. If not, then perhaps you could chat with other members of the group about how to be more inclusive—how to widen the circle.

· *13* ·

Get Real

*L*ast time I visited Bangkok, Thailand, I decided to catch a water taxi to a restaurant. Often tourists are taken advantage of, so I first checked where the restaurant was, asked friends how much it would cost and how long it would take, and then negotiated the price and route with the taxi driver before getting on the boat. I did all the right things! Even so, he took me via an awful zoo and then via a water market. Both locations were out of my way, and I can only assume the driver was making a commission for taking tourists to these destinations. He then dropped me at the wrong location, I was hours late to the restaurant, and he insisted on a large tip before letting me off the boat—despite my having done everything I could to ensure a safe and direct journey to my destination.

Today's tech companies are involved in this same age-old deception: promise one thing and provide something very different. Modern mobile devices like smartphones, tablets, and smartwatches are revolutionary new technologies that have changed our lives. They are amazing and have the potential to make us more productive and more connected. But as Professor Edward Wilson from Harvard University stated, "The real problem of humanity is the following: We have Palaeolithic emotions, medieval institutions and godlike technology."[1] Unfortunately, as we have discussed, due to the way our devices are designed and the way many of us use them, modern technology is doing way more harm than good. We can put protections in place, but in the end we are giving up control to the tech companies. The algorithms the companies use are designed to capture our attention and hold us on the devices for extended periods. We are less productive, yet we work longer hours; we are less intelligent, yet we have access to more information; and we are less connected, despite being in contact with many more people. Apps are deliberately designed to play on the way our brains work, manipulating our behavior. Tech companies like Google and Facebook give us access for free in exchange for our time, our attention, and our freedom. For them to make money, we need to be on our devices—distracted by our devices. We are less effective at work and disrupted in our interactions with the real people in our lives. To really benefit from these devices, we need to reconfigure and start using them in a way that increases our productivity, intelligence, and connection to the real world.

Let's start with notifications. The beeps, buzzes, and bouncing icons that appear on your device are designed to attract your attention. Notifications pull us away from what we are currently doing and toward our devices. Is it a text, a "like," an email from the boss, or an update from our favorite influencer? And in some circumstances these beeps can kill us. Professor David Strayer and his colleagues have been studying the negative effects of having a phone in your car while driving.[2] They suggest that 25 percent of car accidents in the United States are due to screen distraction and that the effects on our attention could be worse than driving drunk. Many major cities around the world are now installing traffic lights in the pavement at crosswalks at busy intersections because of the increase in pedestrian accidents: people don't look up from their phones when crossing the road. We are literally killing ourselves to check our notifications.

Notifications, whether they indicate something important or not, interrupt our current thoughts and intentions. Or they interrupt the conversation we are having with a real person that could lead to an important insight or a feeling of connection. Or they interrupt our moments of peace, or clarity, or calm, or mindfulness, or deep thought. Notifications distract us from what is important, the here and now, and constantly disrupt our lives.

The remarkable thing is that we are captured by these notifications despite (most of the time) there being no good reason for the urgency. A positive aspect of devices is they have quite a good memory capacity! They can hold and retain that email, or that text, or that "like," or any other notification we receive. And they can hold and retain multiple emails and texts and other notifications for not only minutes but hours and even days. So, we don't have to be notified immediately. If we don't read the notification immediately, it will be saved for later! Although we know this, how often do we allow our devices to do this for us? The ability to store information is one of the huge advantages of this new tech, yet how many of us use it? Instead, we let the urgency of a notification derail us and move us back to our phones.

Professor Nicholas Fitz and his colleagues from Duke University experimented with batching smartphone notifications.[3] They looked at the impact of receiving notifications only three times a day. Participants in the batch group reported improved attention, productivity, and mental health. A great outcome overall from simply programming our devices to hold on to any notifications until we are available to attend to them.

As soon as I get a new phone or download an app, I turn off *all* the notification settings. I choose when I'm going to check my texts, or my emails, or my social media. I check them at a time that is convenient for me, when I am not interacting with people in the real world or busy thinking. This means I am not distracted when I am talking to friends, family, colleagues, or just random strangers, and I can give them my full attention. I can concentrate on what I'm doing, and I can think deeply. By turning off the notifications, I get back my attention, my time, and my freedom. Give it a try!

We have all heard the fairy tale of Hansel and Gretel by the Brothers Grimm. Siblings are left in the woods by their stepmother and can't find their way home. They follow a beautiful white bird to a clearing, where they find a house made of gingerbread and candy. When they start eating the sweets, a witch appears and invites them inside, offering food and shelter. She then traps them and starts fattening them up, as she intends to eat them. Gretel realizes what is happening, shoves the witch into the oven, and frees her brother. Fairy tales were written to warn children of potential dangers in the world. Don't follow or be led by things you don't understand, don't accept free stuff from strangers as there is always a cost, and don't trust strangers as they may have ulterior motives!

Another aspect of this new technology that is tricking us and distracting us from really connecting is social media. There has been a lot written about social media and the impact it has on our lives. *The Social Dilemma*, a documentary-drama hybrid on Netflix, explores many of the issues of social media and how the current situation evolved. Like modern devices, social media has the potential to influence our lives in many positive ways. But we must always remember that if something is free—like social media platforms (or gingerbread houses in the woods)—then the companies that own them are making money by selling us! If there is no product you are buying, then *you are the product*! Advertisers are not going to pay for advertising unless they know they will be getting your attention. Tech companies want you looking at the app for as many minutes or hours a day as possible so they can sell more advertising. Hence new terms such as *likes*, which were not part of our vocabulary ten years ago. They are some of the manipulative tactics used to keep our attention on the platform instead of in the real world.

Social media platforms hold our attention by running algorithms to ensure that we are fed the right information (yep, just like Hansel and Gretel). They collect as much of our data as they possibly can. They use information from our virtual friends, our searches, our "likes," our posts, our "follows," and so on. They then feed us advertisements, posts, and search results in line with what the algorithm determines we are likely to be interested in. Now, this might seem like a great idea, but think about it in the context of the confirmation bias and group membership effects we discussed earlier. The result is that we see posts and discussions that support our views, which strengthens our group membership. They take the in-group/out-group game to a new level we haven't seen before. This then divides us and makes us more embedded in groups. Why? Because we are constantly receiving information that reinforces our in-group mentality. It is a form of external or online confirmation bias run by tech companies to keep our attention. The algorithms feed us the right information to activate our in-group mentality and drive us to attend.

I conducted a little ad hoc social experiment the other day. I asked a group of students if they would mind showing me their social media feeds. It was quite an ethnically diverse group, and guess what I found? Most faces that appeared on their feeds were from their race. It is well documented that the algorithms bias our content to topics and stories that we will like and support. Often not considered is that this means the faces we see will also be biased to groups that we are most connected to. The range of faces we see affects our face templates. Viewing a homogenous stream of faces is going to narrow our range and increase the own-race effect, discussed in chapter 3. Social media is biasing our face templates to be narrower and more exclusive.

Another issue with social media is that groups can be set up and run by anyone. In itself, this is not a big issue. In fact, it is important as it allows someone who has a social conscience and wants to get a message out to do so. Or it enables a local group, business, or charity to set up a group and communicate with members. The issue arises when the agenda is not innocent. There are a lot of people who are now trying to become "influencers" simply for the sake of making money. Because anyone can set up a group, some spread harmful misinformation and hate. Professor Jonah Berger and his colleagues have shown that the more arousing or emotive online content is, the more likely it is to go viral.[4] Online groups try to attract members by being divisive and by attacking members of the out-group. Just look at what InfoWars has done. The information they spread is often false or misrepresented, and the members become isolated. This creates extreme views within the groups, and situations spill over to the real world. Anyone can set up and run a group, and this results in some very harmful situations.

When we become members of a group that is spreading misinformation, we are likely to accept this information much more readily than if we were not a member of the group. As covered earlier, we hear and listen to members of our in-group differently than we do members of an out-group. Combine this with the algorithms running on these platforms that then reinforce these views, and you start to see the scale of the problem. These algorithms feed us information from other sources that are consistent with, and therefore confirm, our bias. And we rely on our own automatic confirmation. Listening to real friends and family with different views then can become very difficult, causing isolation. We are willing to accept the information we receive online because our in-group mentality is in overdrive.

How do we stop this isolation of individuals by influencers on social media? There needs to be a lot more control over the algorithms that tech giants use to manipulate our feeds. Some, such as Jaron Lanier, author of *Who Owns the Future?*, have argued that we need to start paying for access to these platforms so that they are not reliant on advertising revenue, and maybe this is a way forward.[5] Although many issues with paid services, such as equity, need to be overcome, the idea is interesting and might alleviate some of the issues. Tech companies could also take more responsibility to ensure the news on the sites is factual and based in truth and could institute greater control over groups operating on the sites to ensure the agendas and information are appropriate. Some tech companies are starting to label information if it is deemed false or misleading, but the information is still available. And if you don't feel like you are part of the tech company's in-group, then you may not believe the label anyway.

The removal of incentives such as "likes" would decrease the desire to influence and the addictive nature of these platforms. We know that the "likes" create a competition, a need for more "likes," and the more "likes," the more popular you feel. Among the general population, this creates an addictive feedback loop in which we are constantly working to accumulate "likes"—so we get the little hits of dopamine! For the professional influencer, the "likes" are a form of currency that can be used as evidence of popularity. They then use this popularity to receive money or gifts to promote and advertise for companies. If we removed the "likes," we would remove this competition, and the platforms would be less addictive and less manipulative. (Of course, tech companies and influencers don't want this to happen—if their platform is less addictive, people will spend less time on it, and they will make less money.)

Let's turn now to the claim that social media helps people stay connected with friends and make new ones. As anyone can set up a fake account online, making new friends online is a risky business. We can use a fake picture and pretend to be anyone online. Unless you know the person in real life, you don't know whom you are "friending" or talking to. According to the *New York Times*, social media companies remove a billion fake accounts every few months.[6] In extreme cases, accounts are set up to manipulate, abuse, or deceive others. Pedophiles use fake accounts to groom children by pretending to be much younger than they are. Criminals use fake accounts to sell stolen and illicit goods or to deceive and defraud. Internet trolls set up fake accounts to harass and abuse others. Bullies set up fake accounts to terrorize their victims. And the list goes on.

Teenagers and children get warned of the issues online and told not to befriend or chat with anyone they don't know, yet there are still many instances of grooming and predatory behavior. Professor Arun Vishwanath has shown that people are far more susceptible to phishing (i.e., deception in an attempt to get personal information) if the fake account is connected to people they know.[7] We should all be very careful of whom we make contact with and consider whether that "connection" is necessary. And we need to assume that the person we are talking or, most importantly, listening to may not be who they say they are.

Fake accounts are a major issue and make tracking and stopping offenders very difficult. A recent Australian federal government report into family, domestic, and sexual violence recommended that when opening a social media account, the user should be required to supply identification, just as when opening a bank account or staying at a hotel.[8] Although the specifics need to be sorted out, I think it is a great idea that would not hamper those using these platforms legally and could perhaps limit harmful and illegal activities. Some form of regulation is needed to thwart those wanting to set up fake accounts for inappropriate reasons.

Depression and anxiety, especially among teenagers, is increasing at an alarming rate. This significant increase in poor mental health in teenagers has occurred in the last ten years—and correlates strongly with the increase and widespread use of social media and mobile devices.[9] Unrealistic (or completely fake) depictions of other people's lives are creating FOMO (fear of missing out) and mental health issues in teens. We see images of all our friends having exciting lives and always looking amazing on social media sites. This is driving unrealistic expectations and making us all depressed.

Body image issues among teens are also increasing at alarming rates. In Todd Sampson's documentary *Mirror Mirror: Love and Hate*, the obsession with the perfect body for the perfect post is highlighted in all its awful glory. Sampson explores the beauty industry's role in this obsession and suggests that the effect of social media is like pouring petrol on an already out-of-control bush fire. Recent work by Professor Veya Seekis from Griffith University has shown that watching just seven minutes of beauty content on TikTok or Instagram can result in significant feelings of shame and anxiety.[10] We need to realize and acknowledge that these are edited and carefully curated representations of people's lives. These people don't always look that good (in fact, they probably never do), and they only post when something cool is happening. We need to stop looking and get out and start doing.

Even if the account is not fake and belongs to someone you knew once, it is not realistic—we show a version of ourselves online that is not real. Do you post your best self or your "real" self? I'm definitely not saying we should put everything online (the opposite, actually), but by thinking about what you choose to put online, you can also reflect on what others might be doing. If we are constantly comparing our own lives to the edited online lives of others, we'll become very unhappy with what we have.

Now let's talk about sex. That got your attention, didn't it? Sex in one form or another has been happening since well before the internet and even before we were the connected species. Even before the dinosaurs, back when life first emerged, sex in some form was necessary to enable reproduction and mixing of genes. But that discussion is not important here. What is important is the distorted and unrealistic versions of sex we see on the internet today. Using sex to attract our attention has been a marketing tool for years. And unrealistic versions of the human form and what it is capable of have always been part of that industry. But until recently, pornography was pretty limited. We had access to static images in magazines and perhaps a DVD, but that was about it. And most of it was very tame. Not anymore. Sex is everywhere and extreme on the internet.

I work with school psychologists and counselors, and some of the stories I have heard are shocking. A colleague who is a child and teen psychologist recently spoke about the fact that his clients are now 90 percent porn-addicted male teenagers. He spoke of how many of the boys are confused about sex and what is appropriate, of how they are shocked when a young woman accuses them of rape when they thought they were "doing the right thing." They tell of instances when a female partner was screaming, but a boy continued because he thought she wanted him to, when in fact she was in pain and distress. They talk of the number of teenage girls who have had surgical procedures for anal tears, willing to have anal sex only because "all boys expect it now." There is a huge misunderstanding among this generation about sex and relationships because of what they view online.

With the huge popularity of sites like Pornhub, XVideos, and the like, access to hardcore pornography is free and easy. This means these sites need to attract your attention to sell advertising. Although they are supposed to be restricted, the safeguards are usually minimal. Studies have shown that those accessing these sites are getting younger and younger. A recent study by Professor Elisabeth Andrie and her colleagues showed that 24 percent of teens between fourteen and seventeen viewed pornography weekly.[11] It is natural for children and teenagers to be curious about sex and their sexuality, and access to age-appropriate information is important. However, easy access to adult-only hardcore pornography during these formative years has been shown to cause serious issues.

Sexual aggression is now recognized as a public health crisis by the World Health Organization.[12] One of the most harmful aspects of hardcore pornography is that it reinforces fallacious stereotypes about males and females. These stereotypes then impact teenagers'—especially boys'—views of sex. Professor Whitney Rostad and her colleagues studied over fifteen hundred grade-ten high school students and showed links between frequent viewing of online pornography and sexual coercion and violence toward women.[13] The easy access to violent and degrading pornography on the internet is mirrored by increasing violence toward women in society.

One of the major issues with access to internet porn, as with other aspects of the internet, is that these sites run algorithms to present content that will keep you watching. These algorithms use data based on your previous searches and what you previously clicked on, shared, or liked. These companies also know from psychological research that we get bored easily, and so each video needs to be a little bit more extreme. A person may start by watching a perfectly innocent video of a consenting couple having sex in the missionary position. The next videos recommended (or autoplayed) might be a little rougher or show other sexual positions. And then, based on the viewer's selection, the next recommended videos will get more explicit and more extreme. An innocent teenager who simply wanted to know more about sex may quickly end up in a place they never intended (locked in a gingerbread house) based on these algorithms that are designed to keep us watching.

Teenagers (and often even younger children) are turning to these sites to learn what is normal and expected.[14] And even if the child does not search for themselves, friends or others, who might be trying to shame or bully them, might send them this content. There is now a lot of expectation for teenagers to know about pornography and to share it with friends. These formative teen years are extremely important for them to gain a foundation for what sort of adult they will become. The images and content they are seeing as "normal" are anything but. And the expectation for teenage girls to live up to and perform like the content they see is completely unrealistic and often degrading and harmful both physically and emotionally. These years are when we establish many of our personality traits and start experimenting with our gender and sexuality, and having appropriate, respectful information is crucial.

Adding to this confusion is now the complexity of sexting, dick pics, and sextortion. As discussed earlier, we never know whom we are connected to over the internet, and the frequency of people sending sexual content, including pictures of genitalia and extreme videos, is on the rise, especially in these teenage groups. They are also using fake accounts to get people to send them explicit images that they then use to manipulate or extort the individual at a later date. Professor Janis Wolak and her colleagues at the University of New Hampshire have shown that 40 percent of minors who have been pressured into providing sexually explicit material online don't know the perpetrator.[15] And two-thirds of the victims of sextortion said they only provided the original material because they felt pressured, tricked, threatened, or forced to do so. We discussed earlier the schoolboys on the bus who had created female online versions of themselves to use for manipulation. And when we consider that often explicit images are of a person under the age of consent, the legal ramifications could destroy a young person's life.

The information teenagers are getting about sex on the internet is giving them completely false impressions about what real sexual relationships should be like. The explicit, unrealistic, and extreme nature of the images and videos that they see on the internet are designed to capture their attention. They also reinforce unhealthy stereotypes about women and men and the roles they play in relationships. Implicit and confirmation biases reinforce these stereotypes and result in a distorted view of the opposite sex and of gender and sexuality. We need to restrict access to these sites, and we need the companies that run and profit from them to be held responsible for who has access. There are restrictions on who can buy alcohol or gamble, and organizations face serious fines for not ensuring customers are of the appropriate age. Why don't governments regulate porn sites the same way? Serious ramifications for breaches could help protect the next generation. We also need to teach the next generation that porn is not realistic, that the acts are staged, the people are acting, and the videos are edited.

Did you know that you can now specifically target someone you know for manipulation? A company called The Spinner (which has deleted its website) claimed to provide a service that enabled you to influence a specific person subconsciously by controlling the content on the websites he or she usually visits.[16] The targeted person would get repetitively exposed to hundreds of items, which were placed and disguised as editorial content. This company targeted whomever you nominated with fake ads to influence their beliefs or decisions. The previously available campaigns included "ride your bike to work," "buy a dog," "get back with your ex," and "breast augmentation," to name a few. They claimed that their best-selling service was the "initiate sex" campaign, which was sold to men who want their wives or girlfriends to—yes, you guessed it—initiate sex more often. And because we process a huge amount of information automatically, this type of manipulation has merit (but not morals). Why would advertisers spend so much on getting their ads in front of you if they didn't work? Makes you wonder if someone is targeting you, doesn't it? Maybe it is time to take this type of advertising more seriously and require governments to protect us all from targeted manipulation before another similar company appears.

And finally, we all need to take responsibility. When we are with others, hanging out in the real world, we need to put the phone away. Maybe leave it at home occasionally. It will forgive you, and any messages, texts, likes, and emails you receive will still be there waiting for you when you return. Conversations are less personal when we have a smartphone visible. People are less likely to confide in us and are less likely to bring up important issues because they assume they will be interrupted. Isn't that sad? Is your smartphone or that "like" really that important to you? Is it more important than the real person sitting in front of you? You could even help your friend by suggesting the two of you both put away your phones!

It surprises me that many parents don't seem to realize that what children and teenagers are potentially accessing on the internet is far more dangerous than real life. Many parents are more than happy to allow their kids to sit alone in their rooms embedded in this potentially lethal environment. Schools allow students to bring these worlds onto the playground and into the classroom and even require accessing them as part of their homework assignments. The negative consequences are potentially addiction, depression, anxiety, and loneliness. Kids may be interacting with extreme pornography, drug use, violence, grooming, extreme political and religious beliefs, and people who will manipulate, coerce, bribe, and extort, people who will hide their identities so they can bully, harass, abuse, and much worse. Like Hansel and Gretel, youths are following a beautiful white bird to potential disaster. We need to get ourselves and our children out into the real world where we can all learn to read each other's facial expressions, body language, and voice cues. We need to ensure kids get the experiences they need to learn to connect, to play, to negotiate, to collaborate, to innovate, to empathize, to love, and to laugh.

I am often asked by parents what is reasonable when it comes to screen time and if there is a way to know if a child has a problem. I think the easiest way to know if your child is becoming addicted to an app or video game is to perform a simple test. Ask them to choose between spending time with friends doing something fun (not on a device) or sitting at home on their device. If they choose the device, then there is an issue. We should all value spending time with friends and family above time on a machine.

Leading by example is also important, and we should be aware of our own dependence on devices. It is especially important to put the phone away when we are with children. Children learn what different facial expressions mean by seeing us respond to their behavior. If care-givers are using smartphones, then they are not responding to children when they fall or jump or cry. These children are missing out on very important social lessons about emotions and empathy. Even worse is when a child is on a device and not having the opportunity to play and learn. We'll talk more about this in the next chapter. For now, turn your phone off and put it away for everyone's sake.

And finally, I will leave you with a quote from the tech entrepreneur and author Paul Graham: "The world is more addictive than it was 40 years ago. And unless the forms of technological progress that produced these things are subject to different laws than technological progress in general, the world will get more addictive in the next 40 years than it did in the last 40."[17]

In summary:

- Notifications are a way to distract you from the real world and get you back on your device. Turn them all off.
- Algorithms running in the background bias what we see and hear. They are extremely powerful and tend to feed separation and divide groups.

- Boys and men who frequently view internet porn are more likely to be aggressive and violent toward girls and women.
- Criminals, pedophiles, and trolls use fake accounts to conduct illicit activity, and this needs to be controlled by better regulation.

TIP OF THE CHAPTER

Tell the important people in your life, if they need you urgently, to call rather than text. Then turn off all your notifications on your phone and other devices. Schedule some time each day to check your emails, texts, and social media and spend the rest of the day connecting with people face-to-face and being productive. Try setting expectations that you won't have your phone with you and leave it at home while you go for a walk or a coffee—you might find it liberating!

• *14* •

Connected Development

$\mathcal{T}$he amount of DNA or genetic material passed on to us from each parent is equivalent to about 750 megabytes of data.[1] That is about the same as held by one of those old USB thumb drives we used to buy and fill up quickly. Not much at all when you consider this information is used to create you! Everything from the color of your eyes, to the size of your brain, to the number of fingers and toes, to the creation of your heart, lungs, spleen, spinal cord, vasculature system . . . well, you get the point. But, in fact, all of this doesn't simply develop from your DNA. It couldn't because there just isn't enough information. Instead, your DNA sets up the foundations or scaffolding; it creates the potential, and your environment and behavior then impact how you develop.

By now, I hope you're convinced that through generations of evolution, we humans have developed an amazing capacity for connection. We can read facial expressions and body language automatically. We can communicate implicitly through subtle gestures, tone, intonation, and prosody. We have the potential to collaborate through understanding the ideas and direction of others. We have the potential to negotiate through perceiving the feelings and wishes of others. But these abilities are only *potentials* unless we develop them through learning. And to learn these amazing abilities and enable our species to continue to thrive, we need to practice them from an early age and throughout our lives.

As we have discussed, "use it or lose it" is a phrase often applied to our brains, but unlike many such statements (e.g., the "we only use 10 percent of our brains" myth), this one is actually true. Our brains are "plastic," malleable; abilities we use regularly become stronger and more resilient, and abilities we don't use become weaker and atrophy. But a nuance of this idea is often missed. The brain is made up of many parts, which support many different processes that enable a range of abilities. We need to be using *all* these parts and processes to ensure each of them does not atrophy. Simply sitting on the couch and playing a word game for hours at a time won't ensure that areas of your brain involved in social skills or movement don't atrophy. It is a little like doing hundreds of bicep curls with weights. You might get very large biceps, but the rest of your muscles will wither. And when you go to pick up a heavy box, you will hurt yourself despite those strong biceps. We need to use all our abilities.

Let's take this body muscle analogy a bit further. When it comes to kids, we know that they need to learn to crawl before they can walk. They need to walk before they can run. And they need to run before they can play for Leeds, Liverpool, or Arsenal! Similarly, they need to learn how someone responds when they do something good, what a happy face looks like and feels like to portray. Then subtler cues can be learned: how it feels when you are understood or misunderstood, then how to negotiate, how to interact with others, and so on. These abilities need to be practiced and maintained throughout our lives through constant exercise. If they are not developed in the early years, they will not be refined during the teenage years, and they will not exist during the older years. Obviously, there are a few more steps and potential limitations in between, but the essence of the idea is that we need to learn to crawl before we can play for Liverpool, and we need to learn to look someone in the eye before we can become the next CEO of Google.

Children need the opportunity to learn to read faces and body language. These skills, especially identifying facial expressions, are often now taught explicitly in primary schools. Issues with understanding facial expressions are often implicated in poor behavior in class, conflict with peers and teachers, and poor academic outcomes. Unfortunately, you can't teach all the intricacies of facial expression perception. There are many subtle aspects to perceiving someone's expression, including microexpressions, which occur very quickly and are then overridden to hide the real feelings of the person. There are also occasions when someone will smile sarcastically, or frown jokingly, or show disgust mockingly. The good news is that, for most people, learning to pick up on these more complex meanings simply requires experience in the real world.

Many years ago, I used to work with children and teenagers who had autism spectrum disorder. One of the programs I was involved in was teaching teenagers to understand social cues such as facial expressions. And while we could often successfully teach the different cues that differentiate categories of facial expressions, it was using this knowledge in real life that was the issue. Social communication is very complex, and we use multiple sources of information, some explicit and some implicit. It takes many experiences and trials to get it right. In some cases, these subtle cues and strange traits cannot be taught because they are essentially unconscious—both in the person making them and in the person perceiving them; for most people, they just take time and experience to learn.

What's pretty scary is that many children today are not getting the time and experience they need to learn the social skills necessary to survive. Socializing among children and teens in developed countries is at an all-time low. Professor Yalda Uhls and her colleagues looked at a cohort of sixth-grade children from 2012 compared to 2017.[2] They observed marked differences in their social perception abilities, which correlated with their access to devices: kids who spent more time on devices had poorer social perception abilities than those who spent less time on devices. Without these skills, they are going to struggle at school, at university, at work, and in life.

Technologies like smartphones, tablets, and laptops are designed for solo activity and impact learning social skills. Tech companies, educational leaders, and parents often argue that it is vital for children to learn technological skills for work prospects. Many schools and education systems around the world are focusing more and more on technology, with learning from each other diminishing. However, if you look at any list of the most important skills necessary for work in the twenty-first century, you will inevitably find collaboration, communication, negotiation, leadership, and empathy. Using technology negatively impacts all of these skills—so this push for "technology-ready students" is doing our children a massive disservice. How can we prepare our kids to best succeed in an uncertain future? Through face-to-face interaction and real-life socializing.

The skills we need to succeed now and in the future evolved millions of years ago! They are the focus of this book—they allowed humans to get to where we are now. Yet I fear that the next generation will lack these skills because they are spending too much time on devices both at home and at school. According to the American Academy of Child and Adolescent Psychiatry, children aged eight to twelve spend four to six hours a day in front of a screen.[3] That number grows quickly to nine hours a day for teenagers. These crucial abilities, perfected over millions of years, are not developing in the same way.

Our children are not socializing appropriately or nearly enough during critical developmental periods. Remember the study I mentioned earlier? Simply removing all devices from a child's life for five days and having them play and interact improves their facial expression perception and their ability to be empathic.[4] Only five days! How impaired must these crucial abilities be for such a short time to show a significant improvement? It also shows how easy it is for an average child to develop these skills in the correct environment. They need to play with real kids without a screen to distract them. If not, the important skills that we have evolved will not develop.

I've often heard educators suggest that children learn collaboration by working on devices; this is one argument for tech in schools. Unfortunately, in collaborating on a device compared to working on paper, there is less eye contact and less time looking at each other's faces.[5] As a result, children working "together" on devices are not reading each other's facial expressions and body language, which leads to less effective communication and more misunderstandings. The amount of verbal communication also decreases, and the number of disputes increases. To collaborate, we need good communication to understand how each person is feeling and what their thoughts are. When we are on devices, issues arise and collaboration is stifled.

Maybe you're thinking, "Hang on, the next generation needs to learn how to use these devices so they can get a job in the future." But think about that for a moment: actually, they don't have to *learn* how to use these devices. Have you ever met a six-year-old who cannot use a tablet if given ten minutes to play with it? Or a ten-year-old who is unable to use a smartphone or laptop when given the opportunity? These devices are so successful, so endemic in our society, because they are intuitive—super easy to use. My mother learned how to use a laptop at the age of seventy with about sixty minutes of tuition. These kids don't need to be spending hours each day at school, five days a week, for thirteen plus years to learn how to use these devices. And let's face it, these devices will probably be superseded by the next new fancy device before many of them finish school anyway.

Apart from the fact that kids don't need to learn how to use the devices because they are easy to use (especially if you've had a childhood with experiences off a device that allow you to develop your brain to its full potential!) and that the skills most important to future jobs aren't those taught by being on a device, "futureproofing" our kids isn't about giving them tech skills. The available jobs will *not* be in tech. The biggest growth industry, and the most likely one in which the children of this generation will be working, is the health industry, as doctors, nurses, psychologists, physiotherapists, caregivers, therapists, and so on.[6] And what do we need for success in these professions? That's right, good communication, collaboration, negotiation, leadership, and empathy. How do we learn and develop these skills? Not on a screen but with face-to-face communication and play. If we are really interested in equipping the next generation for work in the future, they need to learn how to connect in the real world.

I hear what you are thinking: if the evidence tells us that technology is doing more harm than good in schools today, why is the trend for more rather than less screen time? Well, at the moment the fox is in charge of the hen house—and we keep wondering why grades continue to fall and behavioral issues continue to rise. Edutech is a multi-billion-dollar industry, and the big multinational tech companies are in control. With Google Classroom, Microsoft Education, and the many other education-targeted platforms available, the tech industry is grabbing our students, teachers, and administrators and holding them tight with free programs, courses, videos, and presentations. Covid and homeschooling exacerbated this problem, and the push for the latest fads and shiny new things is pushing us further down a path that is negatively affecting the learning and mental health of our students.

It makes me reflect on the 1970s when we had smoking areas at school. Everyone was smoking, and the real health consequences were only just coming to light. Schools took the stance that smoking was everywhere in society, so students should learn to live with it. It seems crazy now to think about it, but it was quite common back then. Things changed when governments started taking the health issues seriously, and school administrators had to respond. Isn't it time for similar changes in the area of technology in schools?

In our zest for the latest modern technologies and ensuring that our kids have every opportunity to develop skills by making sure they are "taught" all the time, we are unintentionally doing them a great disservice. They are missing out on time to develop their crucial social skills. They need time to come up with new ideas—develop creativity and innovate. They need time to learn to be independent, resilient, and empathetic and how to negotiate and collaborate with other kids. They need to learn to be productive and positive members of the connected species. To do this, they need the opportunities to learn and discover in the real world.

In summary:

- Children and teens need to learn social abilities, including facial expression and body language perception, to enable them to socialize, collaborate, negotiate, empathize, and thrive.
- The most important twenty-first-century work skills are collaboration, communication, negotiation, leadership, and empathy.
- Devices negate learning these crucial skills and impact social development.
- Children and teens need to spend more time in unsupervised play to learn social skills.

TIP OF THE CHAPTER

If you have kids, then restrict the time they are on devices and give them time to be bored. Boredom is the catalyst for creativity. When we are bored, we use our imaginations. And try it for yourself too! Test out what happens and how you feel if you start the day with half an hour of reflection before checking your device, or plan a device-free weekend.

The Future for the Connected Species

*T*here are billions of planets and stars in a perpetual dance of attraction. Groups of planets rotate around stars, creating solar systems. Solar systems rotate around each other, creating galaxies. And galaxies rotate around each other in the unfathomable vastness of space.[1] This perpetual dance occurs because all matter is attracted to other matter by gravity. Gravity is pulling planets and stars in multiple different directions because there are bodies all around them. It is a spectacular phenomenon in an intricate balance. When the balance is upset by a star imploding into a black hole, for example, planets are destroyed, and even systems far away can be destabilized.

Similarly, here on earth, the entire connected species is in a dance of attraction that creates small groups, within larger groups, and so on. And, as in space, the balance can be easily disrupted when something goes awry. Think back to 2021, when the *Ever Given* tanker got stuck in the Suez Canal—a very important international shipping channel. It took less than a week to free the ship and resume operations in the canal, but the effect on markets throughout the world was significant. Supply issues in numerous industries caused prices to skyrocket. A simple thing like a ship being grounded in Egypt upset the intricate balance and resulted in shockwaves around the world.

You have probably heard the saying "Think globally, act locally," but many of us perhaps don't realize that what we do in our communities really can have a big impact. A disruption or shift in one place can affect the entire system. So many huge alterations in society have occurred because a single person, having decided that it was time for a change or that they just couldn't stand the status quo any longer, inspired others to stand up. You can be that person.

We used to connect across generations. Older generations would spend time with the younger generation regularly and teach them right and wrong. Morals, ethics, and history were passed down through these interactions, and the youth had someone to turn to when they were confused or scared. It has now become normal for the peer group to be the primary source of information and support in many societies today, with both parents forced to work and grandparents in retirement villages many miles away.[2] A fantastic TV program now running in many countries, *Old People's Home for 4 Year Olds*, brings a childcare center into a nursing home. The positive interactions between the kids and older residents are not only heartwarming but important learning experiences for both generations. The idea is catching on, with new intergenerational programs popping up regularly, and the results have been positive for everyone involved.[3] Reconnecting across generations is an important shift that could revitalize our species.

In the past, stories like "Hansel and Gretel" warned younger generations of potential dangers. And like Gretel, who realized the witch had ulterior motives, we need to realize that tech companies are not improving our lives or teaching and guiding our kids to better futures. They are capturing our attention to make money. We need to shove them into the oven. We, as individuals and governments around the world, need to act to curb their current insidious practices and hold them accountable. We need to reconnect on a real level across generations and stop relying on the tech industry to teach and entertain our kids or to improve our own lives. We need to connect and teach face-to-face in the real world so we can all thrive.

To allow us all to thrive, equal rights and fair treatment of all need to be realized. The feminist movement rightly aims to dismantle the patriarchal system, but unfortunately some of the unintended consequences have reinforced the very system it opposes. Feminism started with a few women agitating for equal rights and has resulted in major positive changes in many societies. One of those changes was to give women the right to an education, to own property, and to pursue job opportunities. The unintended consequences came from the lack of change to what men were doing. The right to work, which should be universal, meant that the number of workers increased significantly because men didn't stop working to look after the children. The patriarchal system took full advantage of this increased workforce by decreasing real wages. Companies then started making much larger profits, and a small minority of men who were company owners or executives took larger and larger slices of the pie. The world's richest 1 percent now own 45 percent of the wealth, while the poorest 50 percent own less than 1.3 percent of the wealth.[4] Women joining the workforce without a corresponding increase in men taking on childcare and home duties has effectively reinforced patriarchy, which means we all suffer (except for that 1 percent).

Feminism has come a long way in giving women equal rights, but we still have a long way to go. What needed to happen when women gained the opportunity to work was for men to get the opportunity to stay home. But because of the drop in real wages across the board with the expanded workforce, for families to survive, both parents now need to work—which means children are put into after-school programs rather than having the opportunity to be "free-range" kids. What needs to happen? Real wages need to be increased so that, if they choose, either parent can afford to stay at home with their kids.

Where does this money come from? Currently we have the situation where multinational companies like Amazon and Uber take advantage of the larger workforce and pay a pittance to people who do the real work, while individuals like Jeff Bezos and Elon Musk sit on billions of dollars. During the Covid pandemic, the opulence of the top ten wealthiest people tripled, and the wealth of the bottom 50 percent halved.[5] We need a seismic shift. No one needs $1 billion. No one deserves $1 billion!

Look at the top ten wealthiest people in the world. First, and not surprisingly, they are all male. Second, none of them is outstanding enough to deserve the exorbitant amount of money that they are worth. How many people in our communities are finding cures for cancer, looking after the elderly or the sick, teaching our children how to read, fighting against injustice, or saving lives while living on wages that require both parents to work? These people deserve a fairer slice of the pie. No individual is really "worth" billions—we all deserve the opportunity to thrive.

Let's take Elon Musk as an example, simply because *Forbes* rated him as the wealthiest individual in 2022. Is this person really so extraordinary as to merit being "worth" $240 billion? He was born into a wealthy family who sent him to expensive schools in Canada and the United States. He was fortunate to be interested in computers at the start of the tech boom and with his brother designed an online payment system that eBay bought for a large sum of money. He then invested in Tesla and more recently invested in SpaceX and other companies. None of these ideas were that innovative! Banking was around before Musk, electric cars were around before Musk, and rocket ships were around before Musk. Compare what he does to the nurses who work with the sick and injured. Or the teachers who are educating the next generation. I'm not saying Musk doesn't work hard, but apart from being born into the "right" family and having some luck along the way, why is he worth billions when the vast majority of people are struggling to make ends meet?

I'm going to just come right out and say it: we need a major redistribution of resources in society. A small percentage of individuals, families, and companies should not be permitted to have nauseating amounts of wealth. All humanity's innovations and technological advances have occurred because we, as the connected species, collaborate and support each other. Nothing has occurred in isolation, so all new discoveries and innovations are the result of us all working together over many, many years. We need to recognize the contribution of everyone and reward everyone fairly.

You are probably thinking I'm crazy! As if these billionaires would give up their wealth for the betterment of everyone! But there are examples of people who, putting communities and fairness at the heart of what they do, have done exactly this. Patagonia founder Yvon Chouinard and his family gave away the entire company.[6] They decided to set up a trust whereby all the profits now go to saving the planet. Instead of going public and making vast amounts of money, they gave the company away. Patagonia was built on sustainable practices that ensure that the communities it sources resources and products from are looked after, so this positive ethos was entrenched in the organization from the start. Patagonia shows that it can be done.

Unfortunately, not all successful entrepreneurs are like the Chouinard family, who set out to establish a company driven by high ethical and moral standards. Professor Douglas Rushkoff at the City University of New York wrote a piece for *Medium* that is now the topic of his book

Survival of the Richest.[7] The piece explores his interaction with billionaires who either had built or were building doomsday bunkers. Convinced that the world as we know will end, they are spending big on ensuring their own survival (think Musk and his desire to fly to Mars). These individuals, with all their incredible wealth, are not concerned about society or improving the world for everyone. They are concerned about themselves and controlling their security forces after the apocalypse. What a sad group of individuals. And this is the type of people that our governments are protecting and supporting. We need a serious change.

Governments should be working to improve the lives of everyone. These public institutions were set up to represent and protect us all. This is not about the Left versus the Right or one political ideology over another. Governments, regardless of their affiliation, should be about enabling everyone to flourish. They should not be dictated to by big business and the wealthy. Multinational companies and billionaires should be contributing to the countries in which they are making money, and they should be held accountable for their actions. The amazing technological advances that have occurred were not the making of the wealthiest 1 percent. They occurred because we, as the connected species, collaborated and specialized across billions of people and many, many generations. All people need to be rewarded for their efforts.

The United Nations Sustainable Development Goals, established in 2015, were intended to be achieved globally by 2030. These goals include no poverty, zero hunger, good health and well-being, quality education, gender equality, and so on. Tackling many of these goals will require a redistribution of some of this wealth and increased minimum wages. Goal number ten is to reduce income inequality within and among countries. This could be achieved by using a formula to restrict the salary of CEOs and executives to a maximum based on the wages a company pays *all* its staff. For example, if no one on the board of directors can be paid more than five times the average wage of the company's employees, the wealthier the company, the better off everyone would be. And really, do executives contribute over five times more than the person on the factory floor?

Now, you are probably thinking that many of these billionaires are also philanthropists and set up foundations or donate large amounts of money to worthwhile social projects. And yes, that is true, but to what end? Anand Giridharadas, in his book *Winners Take All*, asks,

"Why . . . should our gravest problems be solved by the unelected upper crust instead of the public institutions it erodes by lobbying and dodging taxes?"[8] After spending a significant amount of time within this inner circle, he explains how the uberwealthy use their philanthropic efforts to strengthen their own agendas and ensure their wealth and power are maintained. Why should we trust the people who created these issues to now fix them?

Governments worldwide need to work together to ensure that multinational companies are contributing to and supporting the communities in which they operate. Recent reports by the Centre for International Corporate Tax Accountability and Research suggest that Amazon relies heavily on government contracts for its profits while aggressively avoiding taxation. The center calls "for action by governments to restrain Amazon's aggressive global tax dodging."[9] In a second report it claims, "Uber's global tax structure is an example of a much broader problem with multinationals short-changing global governments by shifting their taxable profits offshore. The business model of Uber and other 'platform' or 'gig' corporations also has the potential to drive down wages and working conditions for everyone."[10] In essence, governments need to step up and stop acting on behalf of the insanely wealthy and start redressing the imbalance.

Despite the challenges, I am optimistic for the connected species. The many obstacles we face provide opportunities for us to grow even more connected. As a result of the Covid pandemic, cities around the world that were shrouded in smog and pollution had clean air for the first time in years. Globally, we collaborated to create, test, and approve multiple vaccines in record time. Corporations and wealthier countries supplied vaccines to countries that could not afford them. During the lockdowns, we saw neighbors connect through songs and acts of support and love. Antiracism and antisexism movements are gaining traction around the world. Even Barbie is getting involved and adapting to the new expectations! More people are talking about implicit biases and privilege, and many are becoming more cautious about believing what they hear and see from politicians and influencers. It feels like, after some hard work, there may be bright skies ahead. Let's talk about each of these in a bit more detail.

The degree of air pollution around the world was made starkly obvious when the Covid pandemic dramatically decreased air travel and the number of cars on the road globally. Both were at an all-time high in 2019. Covid brought international air travel to a screeching halt; then lockdowns put the cars into hibernation, and many factories were closed for extended periods. The result: many major cities saw clean skies for the first time in decades. Zander Venter and his colleagues showed that nitrogen dioxide levels decreased by about 60 percent as a result of the response to Covid.[11] Nitrogen dioxide levels affect people's physical health in the shorter term and climate change in the longer term. In megacities like Delhi, beautiful blue skies were seen for the first time in years, and people could breathe easier. I am hopeful that the dramatic changes in pollution levels seen during the pandemic will bring about permanent change. We will collectively see that we *can* make a positive difference to the environment.

The Covid challenge also resulted in cooperation and collaboration on a global scale to find a solution to the virus we were all facing. Multiple vaccines were created, tested, and approved in record time. Compare this to the response to the Ebola virus, which first appeared in 1976 and severely affected much of Africa from 2014 to 2016. A vaccine was not approved until 2020. The development of the Covid vaccines was a fantastic demonstration of what the connected species can do when it works together on a goal—and the inequity of the way we've done this in the past. Illnesses and viruses that affect some parts of the world are left relatively unchecked—we need to learn from what we've achieved with Covid and apply it to infectious diseases in general. Many countries and companies have enabled less wealthy countries to access the vaccines. I know that there were some hiccups and issues along the way, but I think it was a great example of how, when we come together to face a challenge, we can work as one people to find a solution.

The lockdowns that occurred in many countries, although devastating for many, also shone a light on our true nature: we need to really connect. There were so many stories and pictures of neighbors playing instruments and singing along across balconies. Of people delivering food and checking on elderly residents. Of people desperately missing friends and loved ones, pretending to hug them on screens or through closed windows. Of people stuck overseas and desperate to get back to family and home. Inner-city apartment prices in many cities around the world have dropped since 2020, and house prices in outer suburbs or country areas have skyrocketed. People are moving out of dense cities to quieter areas where they can spend more time with family and friends. We are a species that loves to socialize and loves real connection. The lockdowns highlighted for many of us what is really important, and I think real change is occurring as a result of those insights.

I think (maybe hope) real change is also occurring, although much more slowly, regarding racism. We have a long way to go, but the fact that *Sesame Street* and Barbie are tackling the issue (see "Barbie and Nikki Discuss Racism" on YouTube[12]) shows that the issue is being discussed more widely and, importantly, discussed with children. There are also many school programs introducing the issues around racism, and toy companies are incorporating a greater range of ethnicities into their products. Global corporations are changing brand names in response to public pressure, and collaborations like that between Apple Music and Beats by Dre, such as "You Love Me," are challenging, powerful, and importantly mainstream—questioning the contradiction that white people love black music and culture but discriminate against black people. Challenging our stereotypes and biases and incorporating a range of different faces into those that we (and, most importantly, our children) see regularly will shift our automatic processes and make change possible.

Change also seems to be happening in relation to sexism with the #MeToo trend and the next wave of the feminist movement underway, although to be completely honest, I am not as hopeful in this area. Although Mattel has again tried to tackle this issue by incorporating different sizes and shapes into the dolls' figures (i.e., Curvy Barbie with wider hips and larger thighs) and giving them a range of professions, the Barbies are still not realistic, and the emphasis is still on pink, pretty, and plastic. And in the media and advertising world, women are still portrayed as slim and young and often in need of a man's help or companionship. With the continual growth of online porn and the unrealistic and often degrading portrayal of women seen by young men and boys, I worry that things will not improve as quickly as they should. There are positive initiatives underway, which is fantastic, but we all need to work more on the stereotypes that fuel sexism in our communities.

We need a major shift away from a patriarchal society. We talked earlier about how patriarchy is a relatively new phenomenon that deems women inferior to men. In addition to the massive negative consequences for women, actually most men also suffer within patriarchy because it engenders competition rather than cooperation for resources.

Patriarchy grates against our very nature as the connected species. Patriarchy in all forms needs to be dismantled so that everyone is treated equally.

There does seem to be a more open discussion about sexual harassment, assault, and what constitutes appropriate behavior. In many countries, women have come forward to expose the illegal behavior of men in powerful positions, including in the media and politics. As a result, this behavior is being publicly condemned, and the perpetrators are being punished. Men in particular, as members of the powerful in-group, have an important role to play in systemic change. Men need to stand up when they see inappropriate behavior wherever it occurs. Men need to act and to advocate for appropriate behavior at work and at home. We need to make it easier for women to come forward. Walking into a police station full of men and having to sit down in front of a man to explain what happened is going to add to the harm a woman has already suffered. And having male judges making decisions about how a woman would react or feel has been demonstrated to result in more lenient sentences.[13] We need to embrace the current discussion and make systemic changes to ensure that we continue to move forward for everyone's future.

People do seem to be more aware that stereotypes exist and that they impact our implicit biases and the decisions we make. The fact that multinational companies like Mattel are now making a range of dolls that incorporate different ethnicities, jobs, and sports indicates that stereotypes are being challenged. It is important to continue to challenge these stereotypes in children and adults. With new media players like Netflix and Stan, which seem to be more agile and willing to "stir the pot," we are seeing more diverse entertainment and choices than ever before. By being aware and challenging our stereotypes, we can alter our implicit biases and make fairer decisions.

I am very optimistic about our species. We have evolved an amazing set of abilities that allow and enable us to socialize, collaborate, empathize, support, innovate, and thrive. I hope that our current challenges drive us all closer together rather than push us further apart. We need to constantly reflect on our in-groups and their values. We need to be conscious of the influencers we follow and the leaders we admire. We need to monitor and challenge our stereotypes and those of others with an eye on our implicit biases and the decisions we make. But most importantly, we need to connect *in the real world* and be present with all those we encounter. We have become the superspecies through connection, and we will overcome any challenge by embracing our greatest of abilities: connection.

And finally, there is a lot of pain and suffering in the world. If we all loved a little harder, cared a little more, hugged a little stronger, and opened our circles a little wider, fewer people would feel lonely and depressed. Our brains would be awash with happy neurotransmitters, and we would all feel—as we fundamentally are—part of the connected species.

Notes

INTRODUCTION

1. Rebecca Schwarzlose, *Brainscapes: The Warped, Wondrous Maps Written in Your Brain—and How They Guide You* (Boston, MA: Mariner Books, 2021).
2. M. A. Williams and J. B. Mattingley, "Unconscious Perception of Non-threatening Facial Emotion in Parietal Extinction," *Experimental Brain Research* 154, no. 4 (2004): 403–6; M. A. Williams et al., "Look at Me, I'm Smiling: Searching for Threatening and Non-threatening Facial Expressions," *Visual Cognition* 12, no. 1: 29–50.
3. J. M. Wolfe, "Guided Search 6.0: An Updated Model of Visual Search," *Psychonomic Bulletin & Review* 28 (2021): 1060–92.

PART I

1. Paul Bloom, *How Pleasure Works: The New Science of Why We Like What We Like* (New York: W. W. Norton Company, 2010).

CHAPTER 1

1. "What Does It Mean to Be Human?," Smithsonian National Museum of Natural History, https://humanorigins.si.edu.
2. Q. D. Atkinson, "Phonemic Diversity Supports a Serial Founder Effect Model of Language Expansion from Africa," *Science* 332, no. 6027 (2011): 346–49.

3. S. B. Hedges and S. Kumar, eds., *The Timetree of Life* (Oxford: Oxford University Press, 2009).

4. M. A. Williams et al., "Amygdala Responses to Fearful and Happy Facial Expressions under Conditions of Binocular Suppression," *Journal of Neuroscience* 24, no. 12 (2004): 2898–904.

5. Hedges and Kumar, *The Timetree of Life*.

6. C. Darwin, *The Descent of Man, and Selection in Relation to Sex* (London: John Murray, 1871).

7. T. M. Bartol et al., "Nanoconnectomic Upper Bound on the Variability of Synaptic Plasticity," *eLife* 4 (2015).

8. W. Freiwald, B. Duchaine, and G. Yovel, "Face Processing Systems: From Neurons to Real-World Social Perception," *Annual Review of Neuroscience* 39, no. 1 (2016): 325–46.

9. P. Ekman and W. V. Friesen, "Constants across Cultures in the Face and Emotion," *Journal of Personality and Social Psychology* 17, no. 2 (1971): 124–29.

10. L. Charmet-Mougey, A. Rich, and M. A. Williams, "Mud Sticks: How Biographical Knowledge Influences Facial Expression Perception," *Perception* 41 (2012): 1–269.

11. C. Darwin, *The Expression of the Emotions in Man and Animals* (London: John Murray, 1872).

12. J. Prieur et al., "The Origins of Gestures and Language: History, Current Advances and Proposed Theories," *Biological Reviews* 95, no. 3 (2020): 531–54.

13. K. Ravilious, "The Last Human," *New Scientist* 252, no. 3362 (2021): 38–41.

14. M. D. Sockol, D. A. Raichlen, and H. Pontzer, "Chimpanzee Locomotor Energetics and the Origin of Human Bipedalism," *Proceedings of the National Academy of Sciences* 104 (2007): 12265–69.

15. G. W. Hewes, "Food Transport and the Origin of Hominid Bipedalism," *American Anthropologist* 63 (1961): 687–710.

16. C. Posth et al., "Pleistocene Mitochondrial Genomes Suggest a Single Major Dispersal of Non-Africans and a Late Glacial Population Turnover in Europe," *Current Biology* 26 (2016): 827–33.

17. T. Plummer, "Flaked Stones and Old Bones: Biological and Cultural Evolution at the Dawn of Technology," *American Journal of Physical Anthropology* 125, no. S39 (2004): 118–64.

18. M. K. Chen, V. Lakshminaryanan, and L. R. Santos, "The Evolution of Our Preferences: Evidence from Capuchin Monkey Trading Behavior," *Journal of Political Economy* 114, no. 3 (2006): 517–37.

19. J. B. Leca et al., "Acquisition of Object-Robbing and Object/Food-Bartering Behaviours: A Culturally Maintained Token Economy in Free-Ranging Long-Tailed Macaques," *Philosophical Transactions of the Royal Society London B Biological Science* 376, no. 1819 (2021): https://doi.org/10.1098/rstb.2019.0677.

20. H. J. Griffin, P. W. McOwan, and A. Johnston, "Relative Faces: Encoding of Family Resemblance Relative to Gender Means in Face Space," *Journal of Vision* 11, no. 12 (2011): 1–11.

21. M. J. Taylor et al., "Neural Correlates of Personally Familiar Faces: Parents, Partner and Own Faces," *Human Brain Mapping* 30, no. 7 (2009): 2008–20.

22. J. G. Pausas and J. E. Keeley, "A Burning Story: The Role of Fire in the History of Life," *BioScience* 59, no. 7 (2009): 593–601.

23. L. Chen et al., "Identifying and Interpreting Apparent Neanderthal Ancestry in African Individuals," *Cell* 180 (2020): 677–87.

24. J. L. van Zanden et al., *How Was Life? Global Well-Being since 1820* (Paris: Organisation for Economic Cooperation and Development, 2014). https://doi.org/10.1787/9789264214262-1-en.

CHAPTER 2

1. G. A. Miller, "The Magical Number Seven, Plus or Minus Two: Some Limits on Our Capacity for Processing Information," *Psychological Review* 63, no. 2 (1956): 81–97.

2. A. T. Beck, "A 60-Year Evolution of Cognitive Theory and Therapy," *Perspectives on Psychological Science* 14, no. 1 (2019): 16–20.

3. D. Purves, *Neuroscience*, 6th ed. (New York: Oxford University Press, 2018).

4. R. S. Nickerson, "Confirmation Bias: A Ubiquitous Phenomenon in Many Guises," *Review of General Psychology* 2, no. 2 (1998): 175–220.

5. D. Kahneman, T. Gilovich, and D. W. Griffin, *Heuristics and Biases: The Psychology of Intuitive Judgment* (Cambridge: Cambridge University Press, 2002).

CHAPTER 3

1. Marjorie Coulon et al., "Individual Recognition in Domestic Cattle (Bos taurus): Evidence from 2D-Images of Heads from Different Breeds," *PLOS One* 4, no. 2 (2009): e4441.

2. B. Duchaine and G. Yovel, "Face Recognition," in *The Senses: A Comprehensive Reference*, ed. Bernd Fritzsch (Amsterdam: Elsevier, 2007), 329–58.

3. Mark A. Williams, Nadja Berberovic, and Jason B. Mattingley, "Abnormal fMRI Adaptation to Unfamiliar Faces in a Case of Developmental Prosopamnesia," *Current Biology* 17, no. 14 (2007): 1259–64.

4. D. A. Leopold et al., "Prototype-Referenced Shape Encoding Revealed by High-Level Aftereffects," *Nature Neuroscience* 4, no. 1 (2001): 89–94.

5. G. Feingold, "The Influence of Environment on Identification of Persons and Things," *Journal of the American Institute of Criminal Law and Criminology* 5, no. 1 (1914): 39–51.

6. M. A. Williams, S. A. Moss, and J. L. Bradshaw, "A Unique Look at Face Processing: The Impact of Masked Faces on the Processing of Facial Features," *Cognition* 91, no. 2 (2004): 155–72.

7. J. M. Wolfe, "Guided Search 6.0: An Updated Model of Visual Search," *Psychonomic Bulletin & Review* 28 (2021): 1060–92.

8. Williams et al., "Look at Me, I'm Smiling."

9. N. Kanwisher, "The Quest for the FFA and Where It Led," *Journal of Neuroscience* 37, no. 5 (2017): 1056–61.

10. Thomas Hannagan et al., "Origins of the Specialization for Letters and Numbers in Ventral Occipitotemporal Cortex," *Trends in Cognitive Sciences* 19, no. 7 (2015): 374–82.

11. G. Dehaene-Lambertz, K. Monzalvo, and S. Dehaene, "The Emergence of the Visual Word Form: Longitudinal Evolution of Category-Specific Ventral Visual Areas during Reading Acquisition," *PLOS Biology* 16, no. 3 (2018): e2004103.

12. Dehaene-Lambertz, Monzalvo, and Dehaene, "The Emergence of the Visual Word Form."

13. S. Dehaene et al., "How Learning to Read Changes the Cortical Networks for Vision and Language," *Science* 6009 (2010): 1359–64.

14. Daniel T. Levin, "Classifying Faces by Race: The Structure of Face Categories," *Journal of Experimental Psychology: Learning, Memory, and Cognition* 22, no. 6 (1996): 1364–82.

CHAPTER 4

1. Darwin, *The Expression of the Emotions in Man and Animals.*

2. Ekman and Friesen, "Constants across Cultures in the Face and Emotion."

3. M. A. Williams and J. B. Mattingley, "Do Angry Men Get Noticed?," *Current Biology* 16, no. 11 (2006): R402–4.

4. "Anger Management," *The Economist*, June 8, 2006; N. Bakalar, "Men Are Better Than Women at Ferreting Out That Angry Face in a Crowd," *New York Times*, June 26, 2006.

5. Williams and Mattingley, "Do Angry Men Get Noticed?"

6. Williams et al., "Amygdala Responses to Fearful and Happy Facial Expressions."

7. F. Tong, "Primary Visual Cortex and Visual Awareness," *Nature Reviews Neuroscience* 4, no. 3 (2003): 219–29.

8. Williams et al., "Amygdala Responses to Fearful and Happy Facial Expressions."

9. G. Rizzolatti and C. Sinigaglia, "The Mirror Mechanism: A Basic Principle of Brain Function," *Nature Reviews Neuroscience* 17, no. 12 (2016): 757–65.

10. C. Keysers, *The Empathic Brain: How Mirror Neurons Help You Understand Others* (Createspace, 2011).

11. R. M. Skiba and P. Vuilleumier, "Brain Networks Processing Temporal Information in Dynamic Facial Expressions," *Cerebral Cortex* 30, no. 11 (2020): 6021–38.

12. Keysers, *The Empathic Brain.*

13. J. Haberman and D. Whitney, "Seeing the Mean: Ensemble Coding for Sets of Faces," *Journal of Experimental Psychology: Human Perception and Performance* 35, no. 3 (2009): 718–34; D. Whitney and A. Yamanashi Leib, "Ensemble Perception," *Annual Review of Psychology* 69 (2018): 105–29.

14. M. A. Williams et al., "Differential Amygdala Responses to Happy and Fearful Facial Expressions Depend on Selective Attention," *NeuroImage* 24, no. 2 (2005): 417–25.

15. O. J. Robinson et al., "The Translational Neural Circuitry of Anxiety," *Journal of Neurology, Neurosurgery and Psychiatry* 90, no. 12 (2019): 1353–60.

16. J. Navarro and M. Karlins, *What Every Body Is Saying: An Ex-FBI Agent's Guide to Speed-Reading People* (New York: HarperCollins 2008).

17. Aimee Groth, "You're the Average of the Five People You Spend the Most Time With," *Insider*, July 24, 2012, https://www.businessinsider.com/jim-rohn-youre-the-average-of-the-five-people-you-spend-the-most-time-with-2012-7.

18. Keysers, *The Empathic Brain.*

19. T. Koike et al, "What Makes Eye Contact Special? Neural Substrates of On-Line Mutual Eye-Gaze: A Hyperscanning fMRI Study," *eNeuro* 6, no. 1 (2019): https://doi.org/10.1523/ENEURO.0284-18.2019.

20. W. Jones and A. Klin, "Attention to Eyes Is Present but in Decline in 2–6-Month-Old Infants Later Diagnosed with Autism," *Nature* 504, no. 7480 (2013): 427–31.

PART II

1. Dean Ornish, "Can Online Communities Be Healing?," *Huffington Post*, updated November 19, 2013, https://www.huffpost.com/entry/online-communities-health_b_3953766.

CHAPTER 5

1. "Jane Elliott's 'Blue Eyes/Brown Eyes' Anti-Racism Experiment," *The Oprah Winfrey Show*, July 14, 1992, https://www.oprah.com/own-oprahshow/jane-elliotts-blue-eyesbrown-eyes-anti-racism-experiment.

2. C. Haney, W. C. Banks, and P. G. Zimbardo, "A Study of Prisoners and Guards in a Simulated Prison," *Naval Research Review* 30 (1973): 4–17.

3. P. Molenberghs et al., "The Neuroscience of Inspirational Leadership: The Importance of Collective-Oriented Language and Shared Group Membership," *Journal of Management* 43, no. 7 (2017): 2168–94.

4. A. Ishmael, "Sending Smiley Emojis? They Now Mean Different Things to Different People," *Wall Street Journal*, August 9, 2021.

5. J. Grogger, "Speech and Wages," *Journal of Human Resources* 54, no. 4 (2019): 926–52.

6. P. Molenberghs, "The Neuroscience of In-Group Bias," *Neuroscience & Biobehavioural Reviews* 37, no. 8 (2013): 1530–36.

7. H. Tajfel et al., "Social Categorization and Intergroup Behaviour," *European Journal of Social Psychology* 1, no. 2 (1971): 149–78.

8. A. Fuller, "Trophy Hunter Slammed for Posing with Bloody Heart from Giraffe Hubby Paid £1.5k for Her to Shoot as 'Valentine's Gift,'" *The Sun*, February 22, 2021.

9. M. Cikara et al., "Their Pain Gives Us Pleasure: How Intergroup Dynamics Shape Empathic Failures and Counter-empathic Responses," *Journal of Experimental Social Psychology* 55 (2014): 110–25.

10. J. M. Gaynor, *Inspector-General of the Australian Defence Force Afghanistan Inquiry Report*, ed. Australian Defence Force (Canberra: Commonwealth of Australia, 2020).

11. F. M. Edwards, H. Lee, and M. Esposito, "Risk of Being Killed by Police Use of Force in the United States by Age, Race-Ethnicity, and Sex," *Proceedings of the National Academy of Sciences* 116, no. 34 (2019): 16793–98.

12. M. Morash and J. K. Ford, *The Move to Community Policing: Making Change Happen* (Thousand Oaks, CA: Sage Publications, 2002).

CHAPTER 6

1. C. A. Caldwell, E. Renner, and M. Atkinson, "Human Teaching and Cumulative Cultural Evolution," *Review of Philosophy and Psychology* 9, no. 4 (2017): 751–70.

2. M. A. Arbib, "From Monkey-Like Action Recognition to Human Language: An Evolutionary Framework for Neurolinguistics," *Behavioural Brain Science* 28, no. 2 (2005): 105–24.

3. H. O. Box and K. R. Gibson. *Mammalian Social Learning: Comparative and Ecological Perspectives* (Cambridge: Cambridge University Press, 1999).

4. H. Wiseman and O. Tishby, "Client Attachment, Attachment to the Therapist and Client-Therapist Attachment Match: How Do They Relate to Change in Psychodynamic Psychotherapy?," *Psychotherapy Research* 24, no. 3 (2014): 392–406.

5. D. M. Decker, D. P. Dona, and S. L. Christenson, "Behaviorally At-Risk African American Students: The Importance of Student-Teacher Relationships for Student Outcomes," *Journal of School Psychology* 45, no. 1 (2007): 83–109.

6. R. Dreikurs, *Psychology in the Classroom: A Manual for Teachers*, 2nd ed. (New York: Harper & Row, 1968).

7. G. Maté and G. Neufeld, *Hold On to Your Kids: Why Parents Need to Matter More Than Peers* (London: Vermilion, 2019).

CHAPTER 7

1. M. L. Newman and N. A. Roberts, *Health and Social Relationships: The Good, the Bad, and the Complicated*, 1st ed. (Washington, DC: American Psychological Association, 2013).

2. Newman and Roberts, *Health and Social Relationships.*

3. *Social Isolation and Loneliness in Older Adults: Opportunities for the Health Care System* (Washington, DC: National Academies of Sciences, Engineering, and Medicine, 2020).

4. N. Xia and H. Li, "Loneliness, Social Isolation, and Cardiovascular Health," *Antioxidants & Redox Signaling* 28, no. 9 (2018): 837–51.

5. J. Holt-Lunstad, T. B. Smith, and J. B. Layton, "Social Relationships and Mortality Risk: A Meta-analytic Review," *PLOS Medicine* 7, no. 7 (2010): e1000316.

6. J. Salinas et al., "Association of Social Support with Brain Volume and Cognition," *JAMA Network Open* 4, no. 8 (2021): e2121122.

7. Daniel L. Handel, review of *Stress and Health: Research and Clinical Applications*, by D. T. Kenny, J. G. Carlson, F. J. Mcguigan, and J. L. Sheppard, *American Journal of Clinical Hypnosis* 45, no. 3 (2003): 257–60.

8. P. Sturmey, "Behavioral Activation Is an Evidence-Based Treatment for Depression," *Behavior Modification* 33, no. 6 (2009): 818–29.

9. T. Field, *Touch* (Cambridge: MIT Press, 2003).

10. A. G. Marshall et al., "Spinal Signalling of C-Fiber Mediated Pleasant Touch in Humans," *eLife* 8(2019): e51642.

11. H. F. Harlow, R. O. Dodsworth, and M. K. Harlow, "Total Social Isolation in Monkeys," *Proceedings of the National Academy of Sciences* 54, no. 1 (1965): 90–97.

12. J. S. Hardin et al., "Parent-Training with Kangaroo Care Impacts Infant Neurophysiological Development & Mother-Infant Neuroendocrine Activity," *Infant Behavior & Development* 58 (2020): 101416.

13. T. Field, "Touch for Socioemotional and Physical Well-Being: A Review," *Developmental Review* 30, no. 4 (2010): 367–83.

14. A. Gallace and C. Spence, "The Science of Interpersonal Touch: An Overview," *Neuroscience & Biobehavioural Reviews* 34, no. 2 (2010): 246–59.

15. M. Kosfeld et al., "Oxytocin Increases Trust in Humans," *Nature* 435, no. 7042 (2005): 673–76.

PART III

1. N. Kress, "Who's a Stereotype?," *Writer's Digest*, March 11, 2008, https://www.writersdigest.com/writing-articles/whos-a-stereotype.

CHAPTER 8

1. G. L. Schwartz and J. L. Jahn, "Mapping Fatal Police Violence across U.S. Metropolitan Areas: Overall Rates and Racial/Ethnic Inequities, 2013–2017," *PLOS One* 15, no. 6 (2020): e0229686.

2. M. Dodson, "Indigenous Deaths in Custody, 1989–1996," Office of the Aboriginal and Torres Strait Islander Social Justice Commissioner, 1996.

3. N. Afzal, "Black People Dying in Police Custody Should Surprise No One," *The Guardian*, June 11, 2020.

4. G. Sun et al., "Visual Search for Faces by Race: A Cross-Race Study," *Vision Research* 89 (2013): 39–46.

5. J. L. Eberhardt et al., "Seeing Black: Race, Crime, and Visual Processing," *Journal of Personality and Social Psychology* 87, no. 6 (2004): 876–93.

6. "Explore the Representation of Diversity and Inclusion on TV," Nielson, https://www.nielsen.com/insights/2021/explore-the-representation-of-diversity-and-inclusion-on-tv.

7. W. S. Xiao et al., "Individuation Training with Other-Race Faces Reduces Preschoolers' Implicit Racial Bias: A Link between Perceptual and

Social Representation of Faces in Children," *Developmental Science* 18, no. 4 (2015): 655–63.

8. J. W. Tanaka and L. J. Pierce, "The Neural Plasticity of Other-Race Face Recognition," *Cognitive, Affective, & Behavioral Neuroscience* 9, no. 1 (2009): 122–31.

9. R. Dyer, *White: Essays on Race and Culture* (New York: Routledge, 1997).

10. G. Swoboda, *Making Good Men Great: Surfing the New Wave of Masculinity* (Sydney: Swoboda and Associates, 2018).

11. A. Schlegel, "Hopi Gender Ideology of Female Superiority," *Quarterly Journal of Ideology* 8 (1984): 44–52.

12. W. Bright, "The Sociolinguistics of the 'S-Word': Squaw in American Placenames," *Names* 48, no. 3 (2000): 207–16.

13. L. Jones, "The Distinctive Characteristics and Needs of Domestic Violence Victims in a Native American Community," *Journal of Family Violence* 23, no. 2 (2007): 113–18.

14. L. Eliot et al., "Dump the 'Dimorphism': Comprehensive Synthesis of Human Brain Studies Reveals Few Male-Female Differences beyond Size," *Neuroscience & Biobehavioral Reviews* 125 (2021).

15. M. Bönte et al., "Women and Men with Coronary Heart Disease in Three Countries: Are They Treated Differently?," *Women's Health Issues* 18, no. 3 (2008): 191–98; D. Loikas et al., "Does Patient's Sex Influence Treatment in Primary Care? Experiences and Expressed Knowledge among Physicians—A Qualitative Study," *BMC Family Practice* 16, no. 1 (2015): 137.

16. D. Sansone, "Why Does Teacher Gender Matter?," *Economics of Education Review* 61 (December 2017): 9–18.

17. E. A. Plant, J. Goplen, and J. W. Kunstman, "Selective Responses to Threat: The Roles of Race and Gender in Decisions to Shoot," *Personality & Social Psychology Bulletin* 37, no. 9 (2011): 1274–81.

18. B. Lord, J. Cui, and A. Kelly, "The Impact of Patient Sex on Paramedic Pain Management in the Prehospital Setting," *American Journal of Emergency Medicine* 27, no. 5 (2009): 525–29.

19. W. James, *Pragmatism: A New Name for Some Old Ways of Thinking* (Project Gutenberg).

CHAPTER 9

1. R. J. Doyle and N. C. Lee, "Microbes, Warfare, Religion, and Human Institutions," *Canadian Journal of Microbiology* 32, no. 3 (1986): 193–200.

2. M. H. Green, *Pandemic Disease in the Medieval World: Rethinking the Black Death*, The Medieval Globe 1 (Kalamazoo: Arc Medieval Press, 2015). https://doi.org/10.1515/9781942401018.

3. G. Van Wilson, *Viruses* (Cham, Switzerland: Springer International Publishing AG, 2022).

4. E. Sonuga-Barke and P. Fearon, "Editorial: Do Lockdowns Scar? Three Putative Mechanisms through Which Covid-19 Mitigation Policies Could Cause Long-Term Harm to Young People's Mental Health," *Journal of Child Psychology and Psychiatry* 62, no. 12 (2021): 1375–78.

5. D. Fancourt, A. Steptoe, and F. Bu, "Trajectories of Anxiety and Depressive Symptoms during Enforced Isolation Due to Covid-19 in England: A Longitudinal Observational Study," *Lancet* 8, no. 2 (2021): 141–49.

6. H. McGurk and J. MacDonald, "Hearing Lips and Seeing Voices," *Nature* 264, no. 5588 (1976): 746–48.

7. R. Smiljanic et al., "Face Masks and Speaking Style Affect Audio-Visual Word Recognition and Memory of Native and Non-native Speech," *Journal of the Acoustical Society of America* 149, no. 6 (2021): 4013–23.

8. T. Kastendieck, S. Zillmer, and U. Hess, "(Un)Mask Yourself! Effects of Face Masks on Facial Mimicry and Emotion Perception during the Covid-19 Pandemic," *Cognition and Emotion* 36, no. 1 (2022): 59–69.

9. F. Grundmann, K. Epstude, and S. Scheibe, "Face Masks Reduce Emotion-Recognition Accuracy and Perceived Closeness," *PLOS One* 16, no. 4 (2021): e0249792.

CHAPTER 10

1. J. B. Calhoun, "Population Density and Social Pathology," *Scientific American* 206 (1962): 139–48.

2. J. L. Freedman, S. Klevansky, and P. R. Ehrlich, "The Effect of Crowding on Human Task Performance," *Journal of Applied Social Psychology* 1, no. 1 (1971): 7–25.

3. M. MacDonald, "Overcrowding and Its Impact on Prison Conditions and Health," *International Journal of Prisoner Health* 14, no. 2 (2018): 65–68.

4. B. Spehar and R. Taylor, "Fractals in Art and Nature: Why Do We Like Them?," *Proceedings of SPIE, Human Vision and Electronic Imaging* 18, 865118 (March 14, 2013), https://doi.org/10.1117/12.2012076.

5. R. Taylor et al., "Perceptual and Physiological Responses to Jackson Pollock's Fractals," *Frontiers in Human Neuroscience* 5 (June 22, 2011).

6. K. Engemann et al., "Residential Green Space in Childhood Is Associated with Lower Risk of Psychiatric Disorders from Adolescence into Adulthood," *Proceedings of the National Academy of Sciences* 116, no. 11 (2019): 5188–93.

7. "The Monkey Business Illusion," video posted to YouTube by Daniel Simons, https://www.youtube.com/watch?v=IGQmdoK_ZfY.

8. L. Skenazy, "I Let My 9-Year-Old Ride the Subway Alone. I Got Labeled the 'World's Worst Mom,'" *Washington Post*, January 16, 2015, https://www.washingtonpost.com/posteverything/wp/2015/01/16/i-let-my-9-year-old-ride-the-subway-alone-i-got-labeled-the-worlds-worst-mom.

9. G. Lukianoff and J. Haidt, *The Coddling of the American Mind: How Good Intentions and Bad Ideas Are Setting Up a Generation for Failure* (New York: Penguin Press, 2018).

10. S. Pinker, *The Better Angels of Our Nature: Why Violence Has Declined* (New York: Viking, 2011).

CHAPTER 11

1. D. Maras et al., "Screen Time Is Associated with Depression and Anxiety in Canadian Youth," *Preventive Medicine* 73 (2015): 133–38; J. M. Twenge, "More Time on Technology, Less Happiness? Associations between Digital-Media Use and Psychological Well-Being," *Current Directions in Psychological Science: A Journal of the American Psychological Society* 28, no. 4 (2019): 372–79; J. M. Twenge, "Why Increases in Adolescent Depression May Be Linked to the Technological Environment," *Current Opinion in Psychology* 32 (2020): 89–94; J. M. Twenge et al., "Worldwide Increases in Adolescent Loneliness," *Journal of Adolescence* 93, no. 1 (2021): 257–69.

2. T. Horowitz-Kraus et al., "Longer Screen vs. Reading Time Is Related to Greater Functional Connections between the Salience Network and Executive Functions Regions in Children with Reading Difficulties vs. Typical Readers," *Child Psychiatry and Human Development* 52, no. 4 (2020): 681–92; T. Horowitz-Kraus and J. S. Hutton, "Brain Connectivity in Children Is Increased by the Time They Spend Reading Books and Decreased by the Length of Exposure to Screen-Based Media," *Acta Paediatrica* 107, no. 4 (2018): 685–93.

3. S. K. Tamana et al., "Screen-Time Is Associated with Inattention Problems in Preschoolers: Results from the Child Birth Cohort Study," *PLOS One* 14, no. 4 (2019): e0213995.

4. C. Ra et al., "Association of Digital Media Use with Subsequent Symptoms of Attention-Deficit/Hyperactivity Disorder among Adolescents," *Journal of the American Medical Association* 320, no. 3 (2018): 255–63.

5. J. Koetsier, "There Are Now 8.9 Million Mobile Apps, and China Is 40% of Mobile App Spending," *Forbes*, February 28, 2020.

6. Y. T. Uhls et al., "Five Days at Outdoor Education Camp without Screens Improves Preteen Skills with Nonverbal Emotion Cues," *Computers in Human Behavior* 39 (2014): 387–92.

7. J. S. Radesky et al., "Patterns of Mobile Device Use by Caregivers and Children during Meals in Fast Food Restaurants," *Pediatrics* 133, no. 4 (2014): e843–9.

8. B. Brown, *Daring Greatly: How the Courage to Be Vulnerable Transforms the Way We Live, Love, Parent, and Lead* (New York: Avery, 2012).

9. L. Lin et al., "Association between Social Media Use and Depression among U.S. Young Adults," *Depression and Anxiety* 33, no. 4 (2016): 323–31.

10. A. K. Przybylski and N. Weinstein, "Can You Connect with Me Now? How the Presence of Mobile Communication Technology Influences Face-to-Face Conversation Quality," *Journal of Social and Personal Relationships* 30, no. 3 (2013): 237–46.

11. J. Hari, *Stolen Focus: Why You Can't Pay Attention—and How to Think Deeply Again* (New York: Crown Publishing Group, 2022).

12. J. Becker, E. Porter, and D. Centola, "The Wisdom of Partisan Crowds," *Proceedings of the National Academy of Sciences* 116, no. 22 (2019): 10717–22.

13. "Alex Jones Ordered to Pay Nearly $US1 Billion in Damages to Sandy Hook Massacre Families," *ABC News*, updated October 13, 2022.

14. D. Centola, "Why Social Media Makes Us More Polarized and How to Fix It," *New Scientist*, 2020, https://www.scientificamerican.com/article/why-social-media-makes-us-more-polarized-and-how-to-fix-it.

PART IV

1. E. Fogden and D. Redmond, *Bob's Big Story Collection* (London: Penguin Random House Children's UK, 2001).

CHAPTER 12

1. P. Murray, "An American Credo," *Common Ground* 5, no. 2 (1945): 24.

2. N. Mandela, *Long Walk to Freedom* (New York: Abacus, 1996).

3. M. L. King Jr., *Autobiography of Martin Luther King*, ed. Clayborne Carson (New York: Grand Central Publishing, 2001).

4. B. Naylor, "Read Trump's Jan. 6 Speech, a Key Part of Impeachment Trial," *NPR*, February 10, 2021.

5. J. Rottenberg and S. Perman, "Who Really Gives Out the Golden Globes? A Tiny Group Full of Quirky Characters—and No Black Members," *Los Angeles Times*, February 21, 2021.

CHAPTER 13

1. T. Harris, "Our Brains Are No Match for Our Technology," *New York Times*, December 5, 2019.

2. P. Atchley and D. L. Strayer, "Small Screen Use and Driving Safety," *Pediatrics* 140, Suppl. 2 (2017): S107–11.

3. N. Fitz et al., "Batching Smartphone Notifications Can Improve Well-Being," *Computers in Human Behavior* 101 (2019): 84–94.

4. J. Berger and K. L. Milkman, "What Makes Online Content Viral?," *Journal of Marketing Research* 49, no. 2 (2012): 192–205.

5. J. Lanier, *Who Owns the Future?*, 1st hardcover ed. (New York: Simon & Schuster, 2013).

6. J. Nicas, "Why Can't the Social Networks Stop Fake Accounts?," *New York Times*, December 8, 2020.

7. A. Vishwanath, "Diffusion of Deception in Social Media: Social Contagion Effects and Its Antecedents," *Information Systems Frontiers* 17, no. 6 (2014): 1353–67.

8. A. Wallace, "Inquiry into Family, Domestic and Sexual Violence," ed. House of Representatives Standing Committee on Social Policy and Legal Affairs (Canberra: Commonwealth of Australia, 2021).

9. Twenge, "More Time on Technology, Less Happiness?"

10. K. Bernard, "Young People at 'Significant' Risk of Poor Body Image after Just Minutes on TikTok, Instagram, Researchers Say," *ABC News*, September 28, 2022.

11. E. K. Andrie et al., "Adolescents' Online Pornography Exposure and Its Relationship to Sociodemographic and Psychopathological Correlates: A Cross-Sectional Study in Six European Countries," *Children* (Basel) 8, no. 10 (2021): 925.

12. "Violence against Women," World Health Organization, https://www.who.int/news-room/fact-sheets/detail/violence-against-women.

13. W. L. Rostad et al., "The Association between Exposure to Violent Pornography and Teen Dating Violence in Grade 10 High School Students," *Archives of Sexual Behavior* 48, no. 7 (2019): 2137–47.

14. C. Sun et al., "Pornography and the Male Sexual Script: An Analysis of Consumption and Sexual Relations," *Archives of Sexual Behavior* 45, no. 4 (2014): 983–94.

15. J. Wolak et al., "Sextortion of Minors: Characteristics and Dynamics," *Journal of Adolescent Health* 62, no. 1 (2018): 72–79, https://doi.org/10.1016/j.jadohealth.2017.08.014.

16. P. Olson, "For $29, This Man Will Help Manipulate Your Loved Ones with Targeted Facebook and Browser Links," *Forbes*, January 15, 2019.

17. P. Graham, "The Acceleration of Addictiveness," PaulGraham.com, 2010, http://www.paulgraham.com/index.html.

CHAPTER 14

1. Y. Grigoryev, "How Much Information Is Stored in the Human Genome?," BitesizeBio, 2012, https://www.google.com/url?sa=t&rct=j&q=&esrc=s&source=web&cd=&ved=2ahUKEwj-ia-Y5__8AhW1RXwKHbG0CakQFnoECA0QAQ&url=https%3A%2F%2Funlimitedcomputing.no%2Fwp-content%2Fuploads%2F2015%2F04%2FHow-Much-Information-is-Stored-in-the-Human-Genome_-_-Bitesize-Bio-Copy.pdf&usg=AOvVaw2cpkurMCAxuS2oTe1QNJBZ.

2. Y. T. Uhls et al., "Mobile Technologies and Their Relationship to Children's Ability to Read Nonverbal Emotional Cues: A Cross-Temporal Comparison," *Cyberpsychology, Behavior and Social Networking* 23, no. 7 (2020): 465–70.

3. "Screen Time and Children," American Academy of Child and Adolescent Psychiatry, https://www.aacap.org/AACAP/Families_and_Youth/Facts_for_Families/FFF-Guide/Children-And-Watching-TV-054.aspx.

4. Uhls et al., "Five Days at Outdoor Education Camp without Screens."

5. S. Dau and A. B. Rask, "Connecting Eye to Eye: The Challenge of Computer Supported Contact," *Proceedings of the European Conference on e-Learning* (2017): 124–31.

6. Bureau of Labor Statistics, "5 out of 20 Fastest-Growing Industries from 2019 to 2029 Are in Healthcare and Social Assistance," TED: The Economics Daily, US Department of Labor, 2020.

CHAPTER 15

1. J. Scudder, "How Fast Do Galaxies Circle Each Other?," *Forbes*, December 23, 2017, https://www.forbes.com/sites/jillianscudder/2017/12/23/astroquizzical-galaxy-orbits/?sh=2073a92f2ef4.

2. G. Maté and G. Neufeld, *Hold on to Your Kids: Why Parents Need to Matter More Than Peers* (London: Vermilion, 2019).

3. A. Cole, "Children in Care Homes: 'It Makes Residents Feel More Human,'" *The Guardian*, November 12, 2018.

4. "Global Wealth Report," Credit Suisse Research Institute, 2021; E. McCormick, "Patagonia's Billionaire Owner Gives Away Company to Fight Climate Crisis," *The Guardian*, September 15, 2022.

5. N. Ahmed et al., "Inequality Kills" (Nairobi: Oxfam International, 2022).

6. McCormick, "Patagonia's Billionaire Owner Gives Away Company."

7. D. Rushkoff, "Survival of the Richest: The Wealthy Are Plotting to Leave Us Behind," *Medium*, July 5, 2018, https://onezero.medium.com/survival-of-the-richest-9ef6cddd0cc1.

8. A. Giridharadas, *Winners Take All: The Elite Charade of Changing the World* (New York: Vintage, 2019).

9. "Amazon: The World's Largest Company Is Subsidised by You," Centre for International Corporate Tax Accountability and Research, 2022.

10. "Estimating Uber's Tax Gap in Aotearoa," Centre for International Corporate Tax Accountability and Research, 2021.

11. Z. S. Venter et al., "Air Pollution Declines during Covid-19 Lockdowns Mitigate the Global Health Burden," *Environmental Research* 192 (2021): 110403.

12. Video posted to YouTube, https://www.youtube.com/watch?v=RCzwoMDgF.

13. K. L. King and M. Greening, "Gender Justice or Just Gender? The Role of Gender in Sexual Assault Decisions at the International Criminal Tribunal for the Former Yugoslavia," *Social Science Quarterly* 88, no. 5 (2007): 1049–71.

Bibliography

Afzal, N. "Black People Dying in Police Custody Should Surprise No One." *The Guardian*, June 11, 2020.

Ahmed, N., A. Marriott, N. Dabi, M. Lowthers, M. Lawson, and L. Mugehera. "Inequality Kills." Nairobi: Oxfam International, 2022.

"Alex Jones Ordered to Pay Nearly $US1 Billion in Damages to Sandy Hook Massacre Families." *ABC News*, updated October 13, 2022.

"Amazon: The World's Largest Company Is Subsidised by You." Sydney: Centre for International Corporate Tax Accountability and Research, 2022.

Andrie, E. K., I. Ikbale Sakou, E. C. Tzavela, C. Richardson, and A. K. Tsitsika. "Adolescents' Online Pornography Exposure and Its Relationship to Sociodemographic and Psychopathological Correlates: A Cross-Sectional Study in Six European Countries." *Children* (Basel) 8, no. 10 (2021): 925.

"Anger Management." *The Economist*, June 8, 2006.

Arbib, M. A. "From Monkey-Like Action Recognition to Human Language: An Evolutionary Framework for Neurolinguistics." *Behavioural Brain Science* 28, no. 2 (2005): 105–24.

Atchley, P., and D. L. Strayer. "Small Screen Use and Driving Safety." *Pediatrics* 140, Suppl. 2 (2017): S107–11.

Atkinson, Q. D. "Phonemic Diversity Supports a Serial Founder Effect Model of Language Expansion from Africa." *Science* 332, no. 6027 (2011): 346–49.

Bakalar, N. "Men Are Better Than Women at Ferreting Out That Angry Face in a Crowd." *New York Times*, June 26, 2006.

Bartol, T. M., C. Bromer, J. Kinney, M. A. Chirillo, J. N. Bourne, K. M. Harris, and T. J. Sejnowski. "Nanoconnectomic Upper Bound on the Variability of Synaptic Plasticity." *eLife* 4 (2015).

Beck, A. T. "A 60-Year Evolution of Cognitive Theory and Therapy." *Perspectives on Psychological Science* 14, no. 1 (2019): 16–20.

Becker, J., E. Porter, and D. Centola. "The Wisdom of Partisan Crowds." *Proceedings of the National Academy of Sciences* 116, no. 22 (2019): 10717–22.

Berger, J., and K. L. Milkman. "What Makes Online Content Viral?" *Journal of Marketing Research* 49, no. 2 (2012): 192–205.

Bernard, K. "Young People at 'Significant' Risk of Poor Body Image after Just Minutes on TikTok, Instagram, Researchers Say." *ABC News*, September 28, 2022.

Bloom, P. *How Pleasure Works: The New Science of Why We Like What We Like.* New York: W. W. Norton Company, 2010.

Bönte, M., O. von dem Knesebeck, J. Siegrist, L. M. Marceau, C. Link, S. Arber, A. Adams, and J. B. McKinlay. "Women and Men with Coronary Heart Disease in Three Countries: Are They Treated Differently?" *Women's Health Issues* 18, no. 3 (2008): 191–98.

Box, H. O., and K. R. Gibson. *Mammalian Social Learning: Comparative and Ecological Perspectives.* Cambridge: Cambridge University Press, 1999.

Bright, W. "The Sociolinguistics of the 'S-Word': Squaw in American Place-names." *Names* 48, no. 3 (2000): 207–16.

Brown, B. *Daring Greatly: How the Courage to Be Vulnerable Transforms the Way We Live, Love, Parent, and Lead.* New York: Avery, 2012.

Bureau of Labor Statistics. "5 out of 20 Fastest-Growing Industries from 2019 to 2029 Are in Healthcare and Social Assistance." TED: The Economics Daily, US Department of Labor, 2020.

Caldwell, C. A., E. Renner, and M. Atkinson. "Human Teaching and Cumulative Cultural Evolution." *Review of Philosophy and Psychology* 9, no. 4 (2017): 751–70.

Calhoun, J. B. "Population Density and Social Pathology." *Scientific American* 206 (1962): 139–48.

Centola, D. "Why Social Media Makes Us More Polarized and How to Fix It." *New Scientist*, 2020. https://www.scientificamerican.com/article/why-social-media-makes-us-more-polarized-and-how-to-fix-it.

Charmet-Mougey, L., A. Rich, and M. A. Williams. "Mud Sticks: How Biographical Knowledge Influences Facial Expression Perception." *Perception* 41 (2012): 1–269.

Chen, L., A. B. Wolf, W. Fu, L. Li, and J. M. Akey. "Identifying and Interpreting Apparent Neanderthal Ancestry in African Individuals." *Cell* 180 (2020): 677–87.

Chen, M. K., V. Lakshminaryanan, and L. R. Santos. "The Evolution of Our Preferences: Evidence from Capuchin Monkey Trading Behavior." *Journal of Political Economy* 114, no. 3 (2006): 517–37.

Cikara, M., E. Bruneau, J. J. Van Bavel, and R. Saxe. "Their Pain Gives Us Pleasure: How Intergroup Dynamics Shape Empathic Failures and Counter-empathic Responses." *Journal of Experimental Social Psychology* 55 (2014): 110–25.

Cole, A. "Children in Care Homes: 'It Makes Residents Feel More Human.'" *The Guardian*, November 12, 2018.

Coulon, M., B. L. Deputte, Y. Heyman, and C. Baudoin. "Individual Recognition in Domestic Cattle (Bos taurus): Evidence from 2D-Images of Heads from Different Breeds." *PLOS One* 4, no. 2 (2009): e4441.

Darwin, C. *The Descent of Man, and Selection in Relation to Sex*. London: John Murray, 1871.

———. *The Expression of the Emotions in Man and Animals*. London: John Murray, 1872.

Dau, S., and A. B. Rask. "Connecting Eye to Eye: The Challenge of Computer Supported Contact." *Proceedings of the European Conference on e-Learning* 2010 (October 2017): 124–31.

Decker, D. M., D. P. Dona, and S. L. Christenson. "Behaviorally At-Risk African American Students: The Importance of Student-Teacher Relationships for Student Outcomes." *Journal of School Psychology* 45, no. 1 (2007): 83–109.

Dehaene, S., F. Pegado, L. W. Braga, P. Ventura, G. Nunes Filho, A. Jobert, G. Dehaene-Lambertz, R. Kolinsky, J. Morais, and L. Cohen. "How Learning to Read Changes the Cortical Networks for Vision and Language." *Science* 6009 (2010): 1359–64.

Dehaene-Lambertz, G., K. Monzalvo, and S. Dehaene. "The Emergence of the Visual Word Form: Longitudinal Evolution of Category-Specific Ventral Visual Areas during Reading Acquisition." *PLOS Biology* 16, no. 3 (2018): e2004103.

Dodson, M. "Indigenous Deaths in Custody, 1989–1996." Office of the Aboriginal and Torres Strait Islander Social Justice Commissioner, 1996.

Doyle, R. J., and Nancy C. Lee. "Microbes, Warfare, Religion, and Human Institutions." *Canadian Journal of Microbiology* 32, no. 3 (1986): 193–200.

Dreikurs, R. *Psychology in the Classroom: A Manual for Teachers*. 2nd ed. New York: Harper & Row, 1968.

Duchaine, B., and G. Yovel. "Face Recognition." In *The Senses: A Comprehensive Reference*, edited by Bernd Fritzsch, 329–58. Amsterdam: Elsevier, 2007.

Dyer, R. *White: Essays on Race and Culture*. New York: Routledge, 1997.

Eberhardt, J. L., P. A. Goff, V. J. Purdie, and P. G. Davies. "Seeing Black: Race, Crime, and Visual Processing." *Journal of Personality and Social Psychology* 87, no. 6 (2004): 876–93.

Edwards, F. M., H. Lee, and M. Esposito. "Risk of Being Killed by Police Use of Force in the United States by Age, Race-Ethnicity, and Sex." *Proceedings of the National Academy of Sciences* 116, no. 34 (2019): 16793–98.

Ekman, P., and W. V. Friesen. "Constants across Cultures in the Face and Emotion." *Journal of Personality and Social Psychology* 17, no. 2 (1971): 124–29.

Eliot, L., A. Ahmed, H. Khan, and J. Patel. "Dump the 'Dimorphism': Comprehensive Synthesis of Human Brain Studies Reveals Few Male-Female Differences beyond Size." *Neuroscience & Biobehavioral Reviews* 125 (2021).

Engemann, K., C. Bøcker Pedersen, L. Arge, C. Tsirogiannis, P. Bo Mortensen, and J. Svenning. "Residential Green Space in Childhood Is Associated with Lower Risk of Psychiatric Disorders from Adolescence into Adulthood." *Proceedings of the National Academy of Sciences* 116, no. 11 (2019): 5188–93.

"Estimating Uber's Tax Gap in Aotearoa." Centre for International Corporate Tax Accountability and Research, 2021.

"Explore the Representation of Diversity and Inclusion on TV." Nielson. https://www.nielsen.com/insights/2021/explore-the-representation-of -diversity-and-inclusion-on-tv.

Fancourt, D., A. Steptoe, and F. Bu. "Trajectories of Anxiety and Depressive Symptoms during Enforced Isolation Due to Covid-19 in England: A Longitudinal Observational Study." *Lancet* 8, no. 2 (2021): 141–49.

Feingold, G. "The Influence of Environment on Identification of Persons and Things." *Journal of the American Institute of Criminal Law and Criminology* 5, no. 1 (1914): 39–51.

Field, T. *Touch.* Cambridge: MIT Press, 2003.

———. "Touch for Socioemotional and Physical Well-Being: A Review." *Developmental Review* 30, no. 4 (2010): 367–83.

Fitz, N., K. Kushlev, R. Jagannathan, T. Lewis, D. Paliwal, and D. Ariely. "Batching Smartphone Notifications Can Improve Well-Being." *Computers in Human Behavior* 101 (2019): 84–94.

Fox, C. *Stop Fixing Women: Why Building Fairer Workplaces Is Everybody's Business.* Sydney: NewSouth Books, 2017.

Freedman, J. L., S. Klevansky, and P. R. Ehrlich. "The Effect of Crowding on Human Task Performance." *Journal of Applied Social Psychology* 1, no. 1 (1971): 7–25.

Freiwald, W., B. Duchaine, and G. Yovel. "Face Processing Systems: From Neurons to Real-World Social Perception." *Annual Review of Neuroscience* 39, no. 1 (2016): 325–46.

Fuller, A. "Trophy Hunter Slammed for Posing with Bloody Heart from Giraffe Hubby Paid £1.5k for Her to Shoot as 'Valentine's Gift.'" *The Sun*, February 22, 2021.

Gallace, A., and C. Spence. "The Science of Interpersonal Touch: An Overview." *Neuroscience & Biobehavioural Reviews* 34, no. 2 (2010): 246–59.

Gaynor, J. M. *Inspector-General of the Australian Defence Force Afghanistan Inquiry Report.* Edited by Australian Defence Force. Commonwealth of Australia, 2020.

Giridharadas, A. *Winners Take All: The Elite Charade of Changing the World.* New York: Vintage, 2019.

"Global Wealth Report." Credit Suisse Research Institute, 2021.

Graham, P. "The Acceleration of Addictiveness." PaulGraham.com, 2010. http://www.paulgraham.com/index.html.

Green, M. H. *Pandemic Disease in the Medieval World: Rethinking the Black Death.* The Medieval Globe 1. Kalamazoo, MI: Arc Medieval Press, 2015. doi:10.1515/9781942401018.

Griffin, H. J., P. W. McOwan, and A. Johnston. "Relative Faces: Encoding of Family Resemblance Relative to Gender Means in Face Space." *Journal of Vision* 11, no. 12 (2011): 1–11.

Grogger, J. "Speech and Wages." *Journal of Human Resources* 54, no. 4 (2019): 926–52.

Grundmann, F., K. Epstude, and S. Scheibe. "Face Masks Reduce Emotion-Recognition Accuracy and Perceived Closeness." *PLOS One* 16, no. 4 (2021): e0249792.

Haberman, J., and D. Whitney. "Seeing the Mean: Ensemble Coding for Sets of Faces." *Journal of Experimental Psychology: Human Perception and Performance* 35, no. 3 (2009): 718–34.

Handel, D. L. Review of *Stress and Health: Research and Clinical Applications,* by D. T. Kenny, J. G. Carlson, F. J. Mcguigan, and J. L. Sheppard. *American Journal of Clinical Hypnosis* 45, no. 3 (2003): 257–60.

Haney, C., W. C. Banks, and P. G. Zimbardo. "A Study of Prisoners and Guards in a Simulated Prison." *Naval Research Review* 30 (1973): 4–17.

Hannagan, T., A. Amedi, L. Cohen, G. Dehaene-Lambertz, and S. Dehaene. "Origins of the Specialization for Letters and Numbers in Ventral Occipito-temporal Cortex." *Trends in Cognitive Sciences* 19, no. 7 (2015): 374–82.

Hardin, J. S., N. Aaron Jones, K. D. Mize, and M. Platt. "Parent-Training with Kangaroo Care Impacts Infant Neurophysiological Development and Mother-Infant Neuroendocrine Activity." *Infant Behavior & Development* 58 (2020): 101416.

Hari, J. *Stolen Focus: Why You Can't Pay Attention—and How to Think Deeply Again.* New York: Crown Publishing Group, 2022.

Harlow, H. F., R. O. Dodsworth, and M. K. Harlow. "Total Social Isolation in Monkeys." *Proceedings of the National Academy of Sciences* 54, no. 1 (1965): 90–97.

Harris, T. "Our Brains Are No Match for Our Technology." *New York Times,* December 5, 2019.

Hedges, S. B., and S. Kumar, eds. *The Timetree of Life.* Oxford: Oxford University Press, 2009.

Hewes, G. W. "Food Transport and the Origin of Hominid Bipedalism." *American Anthropologist* 63 (1961): 687–710.

Holt-Lunstad, J., T. B. Smith, and J. B. Layton. "Social Relationships and Mortality Risk: A Meta-analytic Review." *PLOS Medicine* 7, no. 7 (2010): e1000316.

Horowitz-Kraus, T., M. DiFrancesco, P. Greenwood, E. Scott, J. Vannest, J. Hutton, J. Dudley, M. Altaye, and R. Farah. "Longer Screen vs. Reading Time Is Related to Greater Functional Connections between the Salience Network and Executive Functions Regions in Children with Reading Difficulties vs. Typical Readers." *Child Psychiatry and Human Development* 52, no. 4 (2020): 681–92.

Horowitz-Kraus, T., and J. S. Hutton. "Brain Connectivity in Children Is Increased by the Time They Spend Reading Books and Decreased by the Length of Exposure to Screen-Based Media." *Acta Paediatrica* 107, no. 4 (2018): 685–93.

Ishmael, A. "Sending Smiley Emojis? They Now Mean Different Things to Different People." *Wall Street Journal*, August 9, 2021.

James, W. *Pragmatism: A New Name for Some Old Ways of Thinking*. Project Gutenberg.

Jones, L. "The Distinctive Characteristics and Needs of Domestic Violence Victims in a Native American Community." *Journal of Family Violence* 23, no. 2 (2007): 113–18.

Jones, W., and A. Klin. "Attention to Eyes Is Present but in Decline in 2–6-Month-Old Infants Later Diagnosed with Autism." *Nature* 504, no. 7480 (2013): 427–31.

Kahneman, D., T. Gilovich, and D. W. Griffin. *Heuristics and Biases: The Psychology of Intuitive Judgment*. Cambridge: Cambridge University Press, 2002.

Kanwisher, N. "The Quest for the FFA and Where It Led." *Journal of Neuroscience* 37, no. 5 (2017): 1056–61.

Kastendieck, T., S. Zillmer, and U. Hess. "(Un)Mask Yourself! Effects of Face Masks on Facial Mimicry and Emotion Perception during the Covid-19 Pandemic." *Cognition and Emotion* 36, no. 1 (2022): 59–69.

Keysers, C. *The Empathic Brain: How Mirror Neurons Help You Understand Others*. Createspace, 2011.

King, K. L., and M. Greening. "Gender Justice or Just Gender? The Role of Gender in Sexual Assault Decisions at the International Criminal Tribunal for the Former Yugoslavia." *Social Science Quarterly* 88, no. 5 (2007): 1049–71.

King, M. L., Jr. *The Autobiography of Martin Luther King, Jr.* Edited by Clayborne Carson. New York: Grand Central Publishing, 2001.

Koetsier, J. "There Are Now 8.9 Million Mobile Apps, and China Is 40% of Mobile App Spending." *Forbes*, February 28, 2020.

Koike, T., M. Sumiya, E. Nakagawa, S. Okazaki, and N. Sadato. "What Makes Eye Contact Special? Neural Substrates of On-Line Mutual Eye-Gaze: A Hyperscanning fMRI Study." *eNeuro* 6, no. 1 (2019). https://doi.org/10.1523/ENEURO.0284-18.2019.

Kosfeld, M., M. Heinrichs, P. J. Zak, U. Fischbacher, and E. Fehr. "Oxytocin Increases Trust in Humans." *Nature* 435, no. 7042 (2005): 673–76.

Kress, N. "Who's a Stereotype?" *Writer's Digest*, March 11, 2008. https://www
.writersdigest.com/writing-articles/whos-a-stereotype.

Lanier, J. *Who Owns the Future?* 1st hardcover ed. New York: Simon & Schuster, 2013.

Leca, J. B., N. Gunst, M. Gardiner, and I. N. Wandia. "Acquisition of Object-Robbing and Object/Food-Bartering Behaviours: A Culturally Maintained Token Economy in Free-Ranging Long-Tailed Macaques." *Philosophical Transactions of the Royal Society London B Biological Science* 376, no. 1819 (2021). https://doi.org/10.1098/rstb.2019.0677.

Leopold, D. A., A. J. O'Toole, T. Vetter, and V. Blanz. "Prototype-Referenced Shape Encoding Revealed by High-Level Aftereffects." *Nature Neuroscience* 4, no. 1 (2001): 89–94.

Levin, D. T. "Classifying Faces by Race: The Structure of Face Categories." *Journal of Experimental Psychology: Learning, Memory, and Cognition* 22, no. 6 (1996): 1364–82.

Lin, L., J. E. Sidani, A. Shensa, A. Radovic, E. Miller, J. B. Colditz, B. L. Hoffman, L. M. Giles, and B. A. Primack. "Association between Social Media Use and Depression among U.S. Young Adults." *Depression and Anxiety* 33, no. 4 (2016): 323–31.

Loikas, D., L. Karlsson, M. von Euler, K. Hallgren, K. Schenck-Gustafsson, and P. Bastholm Rahmner. "Does Patient's Sex Influence Treatment in Primary Care? Experiences and Expressed Knowledge among Physicians—A Qualitative Study." *BMC Family Practice* 16, no. 1 (2015): 137–37.

Lord, B., J. Cui, and A. Kelly. "The Impact of Patient Sex on Paramedic Pain Management in the Prehospital Setting." *American Journal of Emergency Medicine* 27, no. 5 (2009): 525–29.

Lukianoff, G., and J. Haidt. *The Coddling of the American Mind: How Good Intentions and Bad Ideas Are Setting Up a Generation for Failure.* New York: Penguin Press, 2018.

MacDonald, M. "Overcrowding and Its Impact on Prison Conditions and Health." *International Journal of Prisoner Health* 14, no. 2 (2018): 65–68.

Mandela, N. *Long Walk to Freedom.* New York: Abacus, 1996.

Maras, D., M. F. Flament, M. Murray, A. Buchholz, K. A. Henderson, N. Obeid, and G. S. Goldfield. "Screen Time Is Associated with Depression and Anxiety in Canadian Youth." *Preventive Medicine* 73 (2015): 133–38.

Maté, G., and G. Neufeld. *Hold On to Your Kids: Why Parents Need to Matter More Than Peers.* London: Vermilion, 2019.

McCormick, E. "Patagonia's Billionaire Owner Gives Away Company to Fight Climate Crisis." *The Guardian*, September 15, 2022.

McGurk, H., and J. MacDonald. "Hearing Lips and Seeing Voices." *Nature* 264, no. 5588 (1976): 746–48.

Miller, G. A. "The Magical Number Seven, Plus or Minus Two: Some Limits on Our Capacity for Processing Information." *Psychological Review* 63, no. 2 (1956): 81–97.

Molenberghs, P. "The Neuroscience of In-Group Bias." *Neuroscience & Biobehavioural Reviews* 37, no. 8 (2013): 1530–36.

Molenberghs, P., G. Prochilo, N. K. Steffens, H. Zacher, and S. A. Haslam. "The Neuroscience of Inspirational Leadership: The Importance of Collective-Oriented Language and Shared Group Membership." *Journal of Management* 43, no. 7 (2017): 2168–94.

Morash, M., and J. K. Ford. *The Move to Community Policing: Making Change Happen.* Thousand Oaks, CA: Sage Publications, 2002.

Murray, P. "An American Credo." *Common Ground* 5, no. 2 (1945): 24.

Navarro, J., and M. Karlins. *What Every Body Is Saying: An Ex-FBI Agent's Guide to Speed-Reading People.* New York: HarperCollins 2008.

Naylor, B. "Read Trump's Jan. 6 Speech, a Key Part of Impeachment Trial." *NPR*, February 10, 2021.

Newman, M. L., and N. A. Roberts. *Health and Social Relationships: The Good, the Bad, and the Complicated.* 1st ed. Washington, DC: American Psychological Association, 2013.

Nicas, J. "Why Can't the Social Networks Stop Fake Accounts?" *New York Times*, December 8, 2020.

Nickerson, R. S. "Confirmation Bias: A Ubiquitous Phenomenon in Many Guises." *Review of General Psychology* 2, no. 2 (1998): 175–220.

Olson, P. "For $29, This Man Will Help Manipulate Your Loved Ones with Targeted Facebook and Browser Links." *Forbes*, January 15, 2019.

Ornish, D. "Can Online Communities Be Healing?" *Huffington Post*, updated November 19, 2013. https://www.huffpost.com/entry/online-communities-health_b_3953766.

Pausas, J. G., and J. E. Keeley. "A Burning Story: The Role of Fire in the History of Life." *BioScience* 59, no. 7 (2009): 593–601.

Pinker, S. *The Better Angels of Our Nature: Why Violence Has Declined.* New York: Viking, 2011.

Plant, E. A., J. Goplen, and J. W. Kunstman. "Selective Responses to Threat: The Roles of Race and Gender in Decisions to Shoot." *Personality & Social Psychology Bulletin* 37, no. 9 (2011): 1274–81.

Plummer, T. "Flaked Stones and Old Bones: Biological and Cultural Evolution at the Dawn of Technology." *American Journal of Physical Anthropology* 125, no. S39 (2004): 118–64.

Posth, C., G. Renaud, A. Mittnik, D. G. Drucker, H. Rougier, C. Cupillard, F. Valentin, et al. "Pleistocene Mitochondrial Genomes Suggest a Single Major Dispersal of Non-Africans and a Late Glacial Population Turnover in Europe." *Current Biology* 26 (2016): 827–33.

Prieur, J., S. Barbu, C. Blois-Heulin, and A. Lemasson. "The Origins of Gestures and Language: History, Current Advances and Proposed Theories." *Biological Reviews* 95, no. 3 (2020): 531–54.

Przybylski, A. K., and N. Weinstein. "Can You Connect with Me Now? How the Presence of Mobile Communication Technology Influences Face-to-Face Conversation Quality." *Journal of Social and Personal Relationships* 30, no. 3 (2013): 237–46.

Purves, D. *Neuroscience.* 6th ed. New York: Oxford University Press, 2018.

Ra, C., J. Cho, M. Stone, J. De La Cerda, N. Goldenson, E. Moroney, and A. Leventhal. "Association of Digital Media Use with Subsequent Symptoms of Attention-Deficit/Hyperactivity Disorder among Adolescents." *Journal of the American Medical Association* 320, no. 3 (2018): 255–63.

Radesky, J. S., C. J. Kistin, B. Zuckerman, K. Nitzberg, J. Gross, M. Kaplan-Sanoff, M. Augustyn, and M. Silverstein. "Patterns of Mobile Device Use by Caregivers and Children during Meals in Fast Food Restaurants." *Pediatrics* 133, no. 4 (2014): e843–49.

Ravilious, K. "The Last Human." *New Scientist* 252, no. 3362 (2021): 38–41.

Rizzolatti, G., and C. Sinigaglia. "The Mirror Mechanism: A Basic Principle of Brain Function." *Nature Reviews Neuroscience* 17, no. 12 (2016): 757–65.

Robinson, O. J., A. C. Pike, B. Cornwell, and C. Grillon. "The Translational Neural Circuitry of Anxiety." *Journal of Neurology, Neurosurgery and Psychiatry* 90, no. 12 (2019): 1353–60.

Rostad, W. L., D. Gittins-Stone, C. Huntington, C. J. Rizzo, D. Pearlman, and L. Orchowski. "The Association between Exposure to Violent Pornography and Teen Dating Violence in Grade 10 High School Students." *Archives of Sexual Behavior* 48, no. 7 (2019): 2137–47.

Rottenberg, J., and S. Perman. "Who Really Gives Out the Golden Globes? A Tiny Group Full of Quirky Characters—and No Black Members." *Los Angeles Times*, February 21, 2021.

Rushkoff, D. "Survival of the Richest: The Wealthy Are Plotting to Leave Us Behind." Medium, July 5, 2018. https://onezero.medium.com/survival-of-the-richest-9ef6cddd0cc1.

Salinas, J., A. O'Donnell, D. J. Kojis, M. P. Pase, C. Decarli, D. M. Rentz, L. F. Berkman, A. Beiser, and S. Seshadri. "Association of Social Support with Brain Volume and Cognition." *JAMA Network Open* 4, no. 8 (2021): e2121122.

Sansone, D. "Why Does Teacher Gender Matter?" *Economics of Education Review* 61 (December 2017): 9–18.

Schlegel, A. "Hopi Gender Ideology of Female Superiority." *Quarterly Journal of Ideology* 8 (1984): 44–52.

Schwartz, G. L., and J. L. Jahn. "Mapping Fatal Police Violence across U.S. Metropolitan Areas: Overall Rates and Racial/Ethnic Inequities, 2013–2017." *PLOS One* 15, no. 6 (2020): e0229686.

Schwarzlose, R. *Brainscapes: The Warped, Wondrous Maps Written in Your Brain—and How They Guide You.* Boston, MA: Mariner Books, 2021.

"Screen Time and Children." American Academy of Child and Adolescent Psychiatry, updated February 2020. https://www.aacap.org/AACAP/Families_and_Youth/Facts_for_Families/FFF-Guide/Children-And-Watching-TV-054.aspx.

Skenazy, L. "I Let My 9-Year-Old Ride the Subway Alone. I Got Labeled the 'World's Worst Mom.'" *Washington Post,* January 16, 2015. https://www.washingtonpost.com/posteverything/wp/2015/01/16/i-let-my-9-year-old-ride-the-subway-alone-i-got-labeled-the-worlds-worst-mom.

Skiba, R. M., and P. Vuilleumier. "Brain Networks Processing Temporal Information in Dynamic Facial Expressions." *Cerebral Cortex* 30, no. 11 (2020): 6021–38.

Smiljanic, R., S. Keerstock, K. Meemann, and S. M. Ransom. "Face Masks and Speaking Style Affect Audio-Visual Word Recognition and Memory of Native and Non-native Speech." *Journal of the Acoustical Society of America* 149, no. 6 (2021): 4013–23.

Social Isolation and Loneliness in Older Adults: Opportunities for the Health Care System. Washington, DC: National Academies of Sciences, Engineering, and Medicine, 2020.

Sockol, M. D., D. A. Raichlen, and H. Pontzer. "Chimpanzee Locomotor Energetics and the Origin of Human Bipedalism." *Proceedings of the National Academy of Sciences* 104 (2007): 12265–69.

Sonuga-Barke, E., and P. Fearon. "Editorial: Do Lockdowns Scar? Three Putative Mechanisms through Which Covid-19 Mitigation Policies Could Cause Long-Term Harm to Young People's Mental Health." *Journal of Child Psychology and Psychiatry* 62, no. 12 (2021): 1375–78.

Spehar, B., and R. Taylor. "Fractals in Art and Nature: Why Do We Like Them?" *Proceedings of SPIE, Human Vision and Electronic Imaging* 18, 865118 (March 14, 2013), https://doi.org/10.1117/12.2012076.

Sturmey, P. "Behavioral Activation Is an Evidence-Based Treatment for Depression." *Behavior Modification* 33, no. 6 (2009): 818–29.

Sun, C., A. Bridges, J. A. Johnson, and M. B. Ezzell. "Pornography and the Male Sexual Script: An Analysis of Consumption and Sexual Relations." *Archives of Sexual Behavior* 45, no. 4 (2014): 983–94.

Sun, G., L. Song, S. Bentin, Y. Yang, and L. Zhao. "Visual Search for Faces by Race: A Cross-Race Study." *Vision Research* 89 (2013): 39–46.

Swoboda, G. *Making Good Men Great: Surfing the New Wave of Masculinity.* Sydney: Swoboda and Associates, 2018.

Tajfel, H., M. G. Billig, R. P. Bundy, and C. Flament. "Social Categorization and Intergroup Behaviour." *European Journal of Social Psychology* 1, no. 2 (1971): 149–78.

Tamana, S. K., V. Ezeugwu, J. Chikuma, D. L. Lefebvre, M. B. Azad, T. J. Moraes, Padmaja Subbarao, et al. "Screen-Time Is Associated with Inattention Problems in Preschoolers: Results from the Child Birth Cohort Study." *PLOS One* 14, no. 4 (2019): e0213995.

Tanaka, J. W., and L. J. Pierce. "The Neural Plasticity of Other-Race Face Recognition." *Cognitive, Affective, & Behavioral Neuroscience* 9, no. 1 (2009): 122–31.

Taylor, M. J., M. Arsalidou, S. J. Bayless, D. Morris, J. W. Evans, and E. J. Barbeau. "Neural Correlates of Personally Familiar Faces: Parents, Partner and Own Faces." *Human Brain Mapping* 30, no. 7 (2009): 2008–20.

Taylor, R., B. Spehar, C. Hagerhall, and P. Van Donkelaar. "Perceptual and Physiological Responses to Jackson Pollock's Fractals." *Frontiers in Human Neuroscience* 5 (June 22, 2011).

Tong, F. "Primary Visual Cortex and Visual Awareness." *Nature Reviews Neuroscience* 4, no. 3 (2003): 219–29.

Twenge, J. M. "More Time on Technology, Less Happiness? Associations between Digital-Media Use and Psychological Well-Being." *Current Directions in Psychological Science: A Journal of the American Psychological Society* 28, no. 4 (2019): 372–79.

———. "Why Increases in Adolescent Depression May Be Linked to the Technological Environment." *Current Opinion in Psychology* 32 (2020): 89–94.

Twenge, J. M., J. Haidt, A. B. Blake, C. McAllister, H. Lemon, and A. Le Roy. "Worldwide Increases in Adolescent Loneliness." *Journal of Adolescence* 93, no. 1 (2021): 257–69.

Uhls, Y. T., J. Broome, S. Levi, J. Szczepanski-Beavers, and P. Greenfield. "Mobile Technologies and Their Relationship to Children's Ability to Read Nonverbal Emotional Cues: A Cross-Temporal Comparison." *Cyberpsychology, Behavior and Social Networking* 23, no. 7 (2020): 465–70.

Uhls, Y. T., M. Michikyan, J. Morris, D. Garcia, G. W. Small, E. Zgourou, and P. M. Greenfield. "Five Days at Outdoor Education Camp without Screens Improves Preteen Skills with Nonverbal Emotion Cues." *Computers in Human Behavior* 39 (2014): 387–92.

Van Wilson, G. *Viruses.* Cham: Springer International Publishing AG, 2022.

van Zanden, J. L., J. Baten, M. M. d'Ercole, A. Rijpma, C. Smith, and M. Timmer. *How Was Life? Global Well-Being since 1820.* Paris: Organisation for Economic Cooperation and Development, 2014. https://doi.org/10.1787/9789264214262-1-en.

Venter, Z. S., K. Aunan, S. Chowdhury, and J. Lelieveld. "Air Pollution Declines during Covid-19 Lockdowns Mitigate the Global Health Burden." *Environmental Research* 192 (2021): 110403.

"Violence against Women." World Health Organization. https://www.who .int/news-room/fact-sheets/detail/violence-against-women.

Vishwanath, A. "Diffusion of Deception in Social Media: Social Contagion Effects and Its Antecedents." *Information Systems Frontiers* 17, no. 6 (2014): 1353–67.

Wallace, A. *Inquiry into Family, Domestic and Sexual Violence.* Edited by House of Representatives Standing Committee on Social Policy and Legal Affairs. Canberra: Commonwealth of Australia, 2021.

"What Does It Mean to Be Human?" Smithsonian National Museum of Natural History. https://humanorigins.si.edu.

Whitney, D., and A. Yamanashi Leib. "Ensemble Perception." *Annual Review of Psychology* 69 (2018): 105–29.

Williams, M. A., N. Berberovic, and J. B. Mattingley. "Abnormal fMRI Adaptation to Unfamiliar Faces in a Case of Developmental Prosopamnesia." *Current Biology* 17, no. 14 (2007): 1259–64.

Williams, M. A., and J. B. Mattingley. "Do Angry Men Get Noticed?" *Current Biology* 16, no. 11 (2006): R402–4.

———. "Unconscious Perception of Non-threatening Facial Emotion in Parietal Extinction." *Experimental Brain Research* 154, no. 4 (2004): 403–6.

Williams, M. A., F. McGlone, D. F. Abbott, and J. B. Mattingley. "Differential Amygdala Responses to Happy and Fearful Facial Expressions Depend on Selective Attention." *NeuroImage* 24, no. 2 (2005): 417–25.

Williams, M. A., A. P. Morris, F. McGlone, D. F. Abbott, and J. B. Mattingley. "Amygdala Responses to Fearful and Happy Facial Expressions under Conditions of Binocular Suppression." *Journal of Neuroscience* 24, no. 12 (2004): 2898–904.

Williams, M. A., S. A. Moss, and J. L. Bradshaw. "A Unique Look at Face Processing: The Impact of Masked Faces on the Processing of Facial Features." *Cognition* 91, no. 2 (2004): 155–72.

Williams, M. A., S. A. Moss, J. L. Bradshaw, and J. B. Mattingley. "Look at Me, I'm Smiling: Searching for Threatening and Non-threatening Facial Expressions." *Visual Cognition* 12, no. 1 (2005): 29–50.

Wiseman, H., and O. Tishby. "Client Attachment, Attachment to the Therapist and Client-Therapist Attachment Match: How Do They Relate to Change in Psychodynamic Psychotherapy?" *Psychotherapy Research* 24, no. 3 (2014): 392–406.

Wolak, J., D. Finkelhor, W. Walsh, and L. Treitman. "Sextortion of Minors: Characteristics and Dynamics." *Journal of Adolescent Health* 62, no 1 (2018): 72–79. https://doi.org/10.1016/j.jadohealth.2017.08.014.

Wolfe, J. M. "Guided Search 6.0: An Updated Model of Visual Search." *Psychonomic Bulletin & Review* 28 (2021): 1060–92.

Xia, N., and H. Li. "Loneliness, Social Isolation, and Cardiovascular Health." *Antioxidants & Redox Signaling* 28, no. 9 (2018): 837–51.

Xiao, W. S., G. Fu, P. C. Quinn, J. Qin, J. W. Tanaka, O. Pascalis, and K. Lee. "Individuation Training with Other-Race Faces Reduces Preschoolers' Implicit Racial Bias: A Link between Perceptual and Social Representation of Faces in Children." *Developmental Science* 18, no. 4 (2015): 655–63.

Index

Page references for figures are italicized.

accents, 50–51
accidents, car/pedestrian, 138
accounts, fake, 142–43
actors, recalling, 16, 18
addictive technology, 111–12, 117
ADHD, 110–11
Adler, Alfred, 62–63
ads, fake, 147
Afghanistan, 53
African Americans, 41–42, 53–54,
    81–82
air pollution, 162–63
algorithms, 140, 141, 145
Amazon, 162
American Academy of Child and
    Adolescent Psychiatry, 154
amygdala, 5, 37–39, 41–42, 104
Andrie, Elisabeth, 144
angry faces, 37–38
animals
  breeding, 11
  crowding and, 100, 101
  grooming, 71
  group living, 4, 6
  learning, 59–60, 61
  loneliness, 68
  mirror neurons, 39

touch, 71
  trading for goods and services, 10
anti-fragility, 106
anxiety, 143
apps, 111–12
Arbib, Michael, 61
Arcimboldo, Giuseppe, 30, 32
Ardern, Jacinda, 125, 130
armies, 53
art, nature in, 103
arthritis/rain connection, perceived, 23
Atkinson, Quentin, 3
Attenborough, David, 60
attention, 36–37, 103–4
Australia
  accent, 50–51
  Islamophobic retaliation, concern
    about, 130
  outlaw motorcycle gangs, 127–28
  racism, 81
  Special Forces in Afghanistan, 53
  suicide prevention, 69
autism spectrum disorder (ASD),
    43–44, 153
automatic processes, xvii, 4–5, 15–16,
    19, 28. *See also* face perception
Aztec Empire, 90

babies, 43, 72
Barbie dolls, 162, 164
behavioral sink, 100
Berger, Jonah, 141
The Better Angels of Our Nature
    (Pinker), 107
biases
    confirmation, 22–23, 84, 86
    implicit, 22–23, 132–33
    other-race, 27–28, 37, 81–82, 83
Biden, Joe, 78, 79
billionaires, 159–62
binocular rivalry, 38
Black Death, 90
Blackheath Park, 90
Black Lives Matter movement, 79–80
black men, 53–54, 79–80, 84
Bloom, Paul, 1
Bob the Builder, 123
body image, 143
body language, 42–43, 93–94, 105
body muscle analogy, 152
brain
    amygdala, 5, 37–39, 41–42, 104
    face perception and, 29–30
    fusiform face area, 29, 30
    in-group/out-group mentality and,
        48
    male/female, 86–87
    neuroplasticity, 110
    prefrontal cortex, 101, 111
    reuse theory, 30
    "use it or lose it," 151–52
    visual word form area, 30
    white matter tracts, 109–10
Brazil, 30
British royal family and "the firm,"
    127
Brown, Brené, 114
bubonic plague, 90
Buddhism, 129
bullying, xiv, 7

Calhoun, John B., 100, 101
campaigns, political, 73
Capitol riot, US, 77–78
caregivers, 113–14
catfishing, 118
Centola, Damon, 118–19, 120
Centre for International Corporate
    Tax Accountability and
    Research, 162
change, effects of, 157–58
Chauvin, Derek, 79
child rearing, 9–10
children
    devices, impact of, 109–10
    facial expression perception, 152–53
    fear culture and, 105–6
    nature and, 103
    socializing needs, 153–54
    supervision of, 105–7
    technology, impact of modern,
        109–10, 110–11, 113–15,
        147–48
chimpanzees, 4
Chouinard, Yvon, 160
Christenson, Sandra, 62
Cikara, Mina, 52
Cobain, Kurt, 101
The Coddling of the American Mind
    (Haidt and Lukianoff), 105–6
cognitive behavioral therapy, 19
collaborating on devices, 154
Common Sense Media, 112
communication, 3–4, 112, 114, 153
community policing, 54
companies, tax dodging by, 162
confidence, lack of, 55
confinement, solitary, xviii, 68
confirmation bias, 22–23, 84, 86
conversation, 19, 21, 115
Covid-19 pandemic
    about, 89–90
    air pollution and, 162–63

campaigning during, 73
connection, need for, 163–64
devices, connecting over, 92–95
fear during, 107
groups emerging during, 57
health and well-being, effects on, 91–96
impact of, 73
income inequality during, 73
incubation period, 91
infection rate, 91
mental health issues, 68, 92
schools, 67
social/physical distancing, 92
vaccine development, 89–90, 96, 162, 163
virulence, 91
virus characteristics, 89, 91, 96
criminal justice system, 27–28, 37, 53–54, 73, 79–80, 101
cross-race effect, 27–28, 37, 81–82, 83
crowding, 99–108
amygdala and, 104
animals and, 100, 101
attention and, 103–4
concert example, 101
density *versus*, 101–2
face and facial expression perception, 104–5
fear and, 105–7
individuals, effect on, 99–100, 101–2
prison, 101
relaxing and, 99, 102
society, effect on, 100, 101
visual system and, 102–3
c-tactile afferents, 71
cues, lack of, 112

Darwin, Charles, 6, 36
decision-making, 72–73

Dehaene, Stanislas, 30
density *versus* crowding, 101–2
depression, 143
The Descent of Man (Darwin), 6
devices
actions of other people and, 94–95
body language and, 93–94
children, impact on, 109–10
collaborating on, 154
connecting over, 92–95
face masks and, 95–96
fast food metaphor, 67–68, 93
learning and, 154–55
school instruction in, 154–55
smartphones, 109, 112, 113–14, 115–16
social perception abilities and, 153
touch, lack of, 93
turn-taking information, loss of, 94
dinner party conversation, 16, 19, 21
discrimination, xiv–xv
disgust, 36
disruption, effects of, 157–58
division of labor, xv–xvi, xvii, 9–10, 64–66
DNA, 151
dopamine, 70, 117
Dreikurs, Rudolf, 63
dress, 126, 127–28
driving, on autopilot, 18–19
Dyer, Richard, 84

Eberhardt, Jennifer, 82
Ebola virus, 163
economic inequality, 159–62
edutech, 155
Edwards, Frank, 53–54
Ekman, Paul, 36
elephant riding metaphor, 19, 23
Elliott, Jane, 47
emojis, 50
emotional awareness training, 135

emotional contagion, 35, 39–41
empathy, 51
engagement party story, 35, 40
Engemann, Kristine, 103
ethnic group representation in media, 132–33
Ever Given tanker, 157
exchange of goods, 10
exchange of people, 10–11
explicit processes, 16
The Expression of the Emotions in Man and Animals (Darwin), 36
eye color groups, 47, 48
eye gaze perception, 43–44, 94

face blindness, 26
Facebook, 64. *See also* social media
face masks, 95–96
face perception
    amygdala and, 5, 41
    as ancient skill, 29–30
    as automatic and quick, xvii, 28
    brain regions involved in, 29–30
    in complex scenes, 28–29
    cross-race effect, 27–28, 37, 81–82, 83
    crowding and, 104–5
    exposure, broadening, 132–33
    human evolution and, 6–7
    importance of, 25–26
    in-group/out-group mentality and, 32–33, 51
    pareidolia, 30, *31*, 32
    priming experiments, 28, 82
    racism and, 27–28, 32–33, 81–82, 83
    social media and, 140
    technology, modern, and, 140
    as template-matching process, 26–27, 140
    visual search experiments, 28–29, 32

face-to-face *versus* online connection, 67–68, 93–95
facial expression perception
    amygdala and, 5, 37–39, 41
    autism spectrum disorder and, 153
    children, 152–53
    crowding and, 104–5
    face masks and, 95–96
    smartphones and, 113–14
    technology, modern, and, 113–14
    See also facial expressions
facial expressions
    angry, 37–38
    attentional capture of, 36–37
    as contagious, 39–40, 60–61, 70, 96
    disgusted, 36
    evolution of, 36
    group, average of, 40
    happy, 38–39
    human history and, 7–8
    mirror neurons and, 39–40
    smiling, 39–40, 60–61, 70, 96
    universal/basic, 36
    See also facial expression perception
fake accounts, 142–43
Fancourt, Daisy, 92
fast food metaphor, 67–68, 93
fear culture, 105–6, 107
Feingold, Gustave, 27
females. *See* women
feminist movement, 158–59
FFA (fusiform face area), 29, 30
Field, Tiffany, 71
fight-or-flight response, 37, 38, 39, 41–42, 104
films, Hollywood, 84
fire, 3, 11–12
Fitz, Nicholas, 138
Floyd, George, 79
football team fanaticism, xviii
Forbes, 111

Fouda, Gamal, 130
Freedman, Jonathan, 101
"Free-Range Kids" movement, 105
friendships at work, 115–16
Friesen, Wallace, 36
fusiform face area (FFA), 29, 30
future, 157–66
    air pollution, 162–63
    change, effects of, 157–58
    feminism, 158–59
    government policy, 161, 162
    income inequality, 159–62
    optimism about, 165–66
    racism, 164
    sexism, 164–65
    vaccine development, 162, 163

Gallace, Alberto, 72
gangs, outlaw motorcycle, 127–28
generations, reconnecting across, 158
genetics, 151
Gen Z, 50
Germany, 55, 128
Giridharadas, Anand, 161–62
Golden Globes, 133
Goodes, Adam, 81
governments, 161–62
Graham, Paul, 148
greeting rituals, 71, 93
grooming (in-group), 71
grooming (predatory behavior), 142
grouping things and people, 22
group mentality. *See* in-group/out-
    group mentality
groups
    about, xvii–xviii
    Covid-19 pandemic and, 57
    evolution over time, 56–57
    extreme, 118–20
    eye color, 47, 48
    facial expressions, average, 40
    formation of, 141

harmless/beneficial, 128, 133–34
history of, xvii
human history and, 4, 8
influencers and, 130–31, 134–35
in-group, expanding, 129–32
members, xviii, xix
membership, signaling, 126–28
outlaw motorcycle gangs, 127–28
peer, 63–64
radical, 64, 126
religious, 125, 128, 129–30
right-wing male chauvinist, 55–56
similarities within, 42–43
violent, 127–28, 129
worldview and, xviii–xix
groupthink, 53, 135
Grundman, Felix, 96
Grylls, Bear, 65

Haidt, Jonathan, 105–6
hairstyle, 126–27
"Hansel and Gretel," 139, 158
happy faces, 38–39
Hari, Johann, 116
Harris, Tristan, 116
health, 68, 92, 109–10, 143
health industry jobs, 155
hearing, 49–50
Hedges, Blair, 4
heroes in film, 84
High Line Park (New York City), 30
Hitler, Adolf, 128
Hold On to Your Kids (Neufield and
    Maté), 64
Hollywood Foreign Press
    Association, 133
Horowitz-Kraus, Tzipi, 109–10
hospices, 70–71
human history, 3–13
    automatic processes, 4–5
    child rearing, 9–10
    communication methods, 3–4

exchange of goods, 10
exchange of people, 10–11
extinction, early danger of, 9
face perception, 6–7
facial expressions, 7–8
fire and, 3, 11–12
group living, evolution of, 4, 8
labor, division of, xv–xvi, xvii,
    9–10, 64–66
phylogenic tree, 5–6
reading and writing, 3
spoken language, 3, 12
survival of the fittest, 6
toolmaking, 3, 9, 10
trade, 10
walking upright, 3, 8–9
hunting, 52, 64–65
Hutton, John, 109–10

"I Have a Dream" speech (King),
    131
illiteracy, 30
#IllRideWithYou movement, 130
illusions, 20, *21*, 103–4
implicit biases, 22–23, 132–33
implicit processes, 16
income inequality, 73, 159–62
incubation period, 91
inequality, economic, 73, 159–62
infection rate, 91
influencers, 56, 118–20, 130–31,
    134–35
InfoWars, 119, 141
in-group/out-group mentality
    about, xvii–xviii
    accents and, 50–51
    brain and, 48
    bullying, xiv, 7
    emoji interpretation and, 50
    empathy and, 51
    evolution of, 49
    face perception and, 32–33, 51

group evolution, 56–57
groupthink, 53, 135
hearing and, 49–50
in-group, expanding, 129–32
law enforcement and, 53–54
learning and, 61–64
military and, 53
The Oprah Winfrey Show
    experiment, 47, 48
politics and, 77–79
schadenfreude and, 52–53
social media and, 52, 140
speaking and, 50
Stanford Prison Experiment, 48
susceptibility to, 54–56
threat detection and, 51–52
violence and, 52–53
innovation, 59
intergenerational programs, 158
International Men's Shed
    Organization, 69, 134
internet, 92–95, 107, 144–46, 147–
    48. *See also* technology, modern
Islamophobia, 130

Jackson, Joe, 84
James, William, 88
Japan, 82
Jews, 55, 128
jobs, future, 155
John, bullied student story, xiv, 7
Jones, Alex, 119
justice system, 27–28, 37, 53–54, 73,
    79–80, 101

Kahneman, Daniel, 23
Kanwisher, Nancy, 29
Kastendieck, Till, 96
Kershner, Ali, 87
killing, mass, 125
King, Martin Luther, Jr., 131
Kosfeld, Michael, 72

Kress, Nancy, 75
Ku Klux Klan (KKK), 127, 128

labor, division of, xv–xvi, xvii, 9–10,
    64–66
language
    body, 42–43, 93–94, 105
    learning, 61
    spoken, 3, 12, 50
    written, 3
Lanier, Jaron, 141
law enforcement, 53–54
learning, 59–66
    animals, 59–60, 61
    connection as key to, 59, 61–64
    devices and, 154–55
    humans as good at, 63
    in-groups and, 61–64
    innovation and, 59
    language, 61
    mirror neuron system and, 60–61
    peer group dominance and, 63–64
    radicalization and, 64
    specialization and, 64–66
Leca, Jean-Baptiste, 10
Leopold, David, 26
Levin, Daniel, 32
light contrast illusion, 20, *21*
"like" button, 117, 120, 142
lions, 11
lip reading, 95–96
listening, 49–50
literacy, 30
LOL, as term, 50
loneliness, xviii, 68–69
long-term memory, 17–19
Los Angeles Times, 133
Lukianoff, Greg, 105–6

MacDonald, Morag, 101
Macquarie University Widening
    Participation Unit, 62

magicians, 20
magic number seven, 17–18
Make America Great Again (MAGA)
    movement, xix, 77–79
male chauvinist groups, right-wing,
    55–56
males. *See* men
mammals, 59–60, 61
Mandela, Nelson, 130–31
manipulation, 146–47
March Madness college basketball, 87
Markle, Meghan, 127
masks, face, 95–96
massage, hand/foot, 70–71
Maté, Gabor, 64
Mattel, 164, 165
Mattingly, Jason, 36–37
media, 82–84, 107, 132–33
Medium, 160–61
Melbourne, Australia, 35, 40
memory
    long-term, 17–19
    working, 16–18
men
    angry faces, 37
    black, 53–54, 79–80, 84
    brain, 86–87
    right-wing male chauvinist groups,
        55–56
    sexism, changes related to, 165
    stereotypes, 86–87, 145
    suicide prevention among, 69, 134
    white, 53–54, 79–80, 84
Men's Shed, 69, 134
mental health, 68, 92, 109–10, 143
military, 53
millennials, 50
Miller, George, 17
Mirror Mirror: Love and Hate, 110, 143
mirror neuron system
    body language perception and, 43
    crowding and, 104–5

eye gaze perception and, 43
facial expressions and, 39–40
learning and, 60–61
smiling and, 39–40, 60–61, 70, 96
technology, modern, and, 113
misrepresentation on social media,
    117–18
modern technology. *See* technology,
    modern
Molenberghs, Pascal, 49
"The Monkey Business Illusion,"
    103–4
monkeys, 10, 39, 68, 71
mosque attacks (New Zealand), 125
motorcycle gangs, outlaw, 127–28
movie stars, recalling, 16, 18
Murley, Brendan, 71
Murray, Anna Pauline "Pauli," 129
Musk, Elon, 159–60
Muslims, 125, 128, 130

National Academies of Sciences,
    Engineering, and Medicine, 68
Native American traditional societies,
    85
natural selection, 6
nature, 102–3
Nazi movement, 55, 127, 128
Neanderthals, 11–12
Neufield, Gordon, 64
neurons, xvi. *See also* mirror neuron
    system
neuroplasticity, 110
neurotransmitters, 69, 70, 72, 117
New Scientist, 120
New York City, 30, 99, 102, 105
New York Sun, 105
New York Times, 142
New Zealand, 125, 130
Nirvana concert, 101
nitrogen dioxide levels, 163
notifications, 138–39

online *versus* face-to-face connection,
    67–68, 93–95
The Oprah Winfrey Show, 47, 48
Ornish, Dean, 45
other-race bias, 27–28, 37, 81–82,
    83
out-groups. *See* in-group/out-group
    mentality
outlaw motorcycle gangs, 127–28
overcrowding. *See* crowding
oxytocin, 69, 72

pareidolia, 30, *31*, 32
parents at soccer matches, 22–23
Patagonia (company), 160
patriarchy, 85–86, 158–59, 164–65
peer group, 63–64
people
    exchange of, 10–11
    grouping, 22
    identifying (*See* face perception)
perception. *See also* face perception;
    facial expression perception
    eye gaze, 43–44, 94
    social, 153
petting zoo story, 117
phishing, 142
phylogenic tree, 5–6
physical distancing, 92
physical health, 68
Pinker, Steven, 107
police, 53–54, 79. *See also* criminal
    justice system
politics, 49–50, 73, 77–79
pornography, 144–46
positive emotional contagion, 35, 40
predatory behavior, 142
prefrontal cortex, 101, 111
priming experiments, 28, 82
prison crowding, 101
prosopagnosia (face blindness), 26
Proud Boys, 134

Przybylski, Andrew, 115
psychotherapy, 62–63

racial/ethnic group representation in media, 132–33
racism
  Australia, 81
  Black Lives Matter movement, 79–80
  changes related to, 164
  confirmation bias and, 23, 84
  cross-race effect and, 27–28, 37, 81–82, 83
  evolution and, 80–81
  face perception and, 27–28, 32–33, 81–82, 83
  law enforcement and, 53–54
  media portrayals and, 82–84
  United States, 81–84
Radesky, Jenny, 114
radical groups, 64, 126
rain/arthritis connection, perceived, 23
rats, 100
reading, 3, 30
"Real Men" (song), 84
relationships, modern technology and, 109–10
relaxing, 99, 102
religion, 86, 125, 128, 129–30
resources, scarcity of, 55
responsibility, taking, 141–42, 147–48
reuse theory of the brain, 30
Rich, Rob, *31*
right-wing male chauvinist groups, 55–56
Rizzolatti, Giacomo, 39
Rohn, John, 43
Rostad, Whitney, 145
royal family, British, 127
Rushkoff, Douglas, 160–61

Sampson, Todd, 110, 143
Sandy Hook massacre, 119
Santos, Laurie, 10
schadenfreude, 52
Schlegel, Alice, 85
school, 154–55
school workshops, 15–16
Scientific American, 100
Seekis, Veya, 143
self, sense of, 55–56
"Sending Smiley Emojis?", 50
serotonin, 69
seven as magical number, 17–18
sexism, 84–87, 164–65
sex on the internet, 144–46
sexual harassment and assault, 145, 165
signs and symbols, 127
Simons, Dan, 103–4
Skenazy, Lenore, 105
skinheads, 126–27
smallpox, 90
smartphones, 109, 112, 113–14, 115–16. *See also* devices
smile emoji, 50
smiling, 39–40, 60–61, 70, 96
Smiljanic, Rajka, 95
Smithsonian, 3
smoking areas at school, 155
soccer, 22–23
social communication, 114, 153
The Social Dilemma, 116, 139–40
social distancing, 92
socializing, xvii, 114–15, 116–17, 153–54
social media
  addictive features of, 117
  algorithms, 140, 141
  body image and, 143
  catfishing, 118
  face perception and, 140
  fake accounts, 142–43

grooming/predatory behavior,
142
groups, dangerous, 118–20
groups, formation of, 141
harmful nature of, 139–44
influencers, 118–20
in-group/out-group mentality and,
52, 140
"like" button, 117, 120, 142
mental health and, 143
as misnomer, 116
misrepresentation on, 117–18
phishing, 142
radicalization and, 64
remedies, proposed, 141–42
socializing *versus*, 116–17
unrealistic nature of, 143–44
social perception abilities, 153
solitary confinement, xviii, 68
sound, 20
spatial-frequency information,
102–3
speaking, 3, 12, 50
specialization, xv–xvi, xvii, 9–10,
64–66
Spehar, Branka, 103
Spence, Charles, 72
The Spinner (company), 146–47
spoken language, 3, 12, 50
squaw, as term, 85
Stanford Prison Experiment, 48
stereotypes
awareness of, 165
changing, 84
confirmation bias and, 23, 84, 86
male/female, 86–87, 145
problems with, 75
as short-hand heuristic, 21–22
Stolen Focus (Hari), 116
Strayer, David, 138
stress reduction, 69–70
Suez Canal, 157

suicide prevention, 69, 134
Sun, Gang, 81
Sun UK, 52
support, need for, 55
survival, 6, 65
Survival of the Richest (Rushkoff),
160–61
Swoboda, Gunter, 85
sympathetic nervous system, 68

Tajfel, Henri, 51
Tanaka, James, 83
Tarrio, Enrique, 134
tax dodging by companies, 162
team fanaticism, xviii
technological advances, xvi
technology, modern
abilities lost by, 110–11
about, 137–38
addictive nature of, 111–12, 117
adults, impact on, 115–16
algorithms, 140, 141, 145
apps, 111–12
children, impact on, 109–10, 110–
11, 113–15, 147–48
communication and, 112, 114
face perception and, 140
facial expression perception and,
113–14
fake accounts, 142–43
harmed caused by, 137–49
in-group/out-group mentality and,
140
"like" button, 117, 120, 142
manipulation and, 146–47
mental health and, 109–10, 143
mirror neurons and, 113
notifications, 138–39
responsibility, taking, 141–42,
147–48
sex on the internet, 144–46
socializing and, 114–15

teenagers and, 143, 145–46,
147–48
touch, lack of, 112–13
work friendships, impact on,
115–16
See also social media
teenagers, 112, 143, 145–46, 147–48
template-matching process, face
perception as, 26–27, 140
Thailand water taxi story, 137
things, grouping, 22
threat detection, 37, 38, 39, 41–42,
104
A Time to Kill (film), 133
Tishby, Orya, 62
tool creation and use, xv, 3, 9, 10
touch, 70–73, 93, 112–13
trade, 10
travel, 131–32
tree, seeing face in, 30, *31*
tribalism. *See* in-group/out-group
mentality
Trump, Donald, 56, 73, 77–79, 131
turn-taking information, 94
Tversky, Amos, 23
TV shows, racial representation on,
82–83
Twenge, Jean, 109

Uber, 162
Uhls, Yalda, 113, 153
United Kingdom, 92, 127
United Nations Sustainable
Development Goals, 161
United States
accent, 50–51
Capitol riot, 77–78
films, 84
racism, 81–84
TV shows, 82–83

vaccine development, 89–90, 96,
162, 163
Valentine's gifts, 52
Venter, Zander, 163
violence, 37, 52–53, 107, 125
Violent Femmes concert, 101
violent groups, 127–28, 129
virulence, 91
viruses. *See also* Covid-19 pandemic
bubonic plague, 90
connection and, 90–91
incubation period, 91
infection rate, 91
smallpox, 90
virulence, 91
Vishwanath, Arun, 142
visual search experiments, 28–29, 32,
81–82
visual system, 102–3
visual word form area (VWFA), 30
vulnerabilities, personal, 55–56

walking, 3, 8–9, 19
Wall Street Journal, 50
war crimes, 53
water taxi story, 137
wealth, 159–62
Weinstein, Netta, 115
well-being, 91–96
Where's Wally?/Where's Waldo?
books, 28–29
White (Dyer), 84
White Australia policy, xiv
white men, 53–54, 79–80, 84
white supremacism, 125
Whitney, David, 40
Wilson, Edward, 137
Winners Take All (Giridharadas),
161–62
Wiseman, Hadas, 62
Wolak, Janis, 146
wolves, 61

women
  brain, 86–87
  feminist movement, 158–59
  stereotypes, 86–87, 145
work friendships, 115–16
working memory, 16–18
World Health Organization, 145

worldview, xviii–xix
writing, evolution of, 3

Yerkes-Dodson law, 70

Zimbardo, Philip, 48
Zimmerman, George, 79

About the Author

Mark A. Williams, PhD, has worked with thousands of students, teachers, health professionals, and company directors keen to understand how their brain works, how to perform optimally, and how to maintain a healthy brain. He regularly runs programs on the neuroscience of learning, the neuroscience of emotions, how to hack your habits, how our brains create our reality, and the impact of modern technologies on our brains.

Mark draws on his extensive scientific background to work with schools, companies, and the public to develop evidence-based practices using neuroscience to enhance our education, work, and personal lives. His work has been highlighted in the media internationally, including in the *Guardian*, the *New York Times*, and the *Economist*, and he has been involved with several popular science documentaries.

Mark is a professor of cognitive neuroscience with over twenty-five years' experience conducting behavioral and brain-imaging research, focusing on our social skills. He has taught neuroscience to a wide range of students, published dozens of scientific articles, been awarded numerous high-profile fellowships and grants, and worked at both the Massachusetts Institute of Technology in the United States and at universities in Australia. He has lately focused on making the many recent discoveries in cognitive neuroscience more accessible to the public. His academic background allows him to write with authority on science, and his passion for education makes his work accessible to a wide audience.

Mark currently resides in Sydney, Australia. To learn more, please visit www.drmarkwilliams.com.